PARTY AND STATE IN POST-MAO CHINA

China Today series

Greg Austin, *Cyber Policy in China*
David S. G. Goodman, *Class in Contemporary China*
Stuart Harris, *China's Foreign Policy*
Elaine Jeffreys with Haiqing Yu, *Sex in China*
Michael Keane, *Creative Industries in China*
Joe C. B. Leung and Yuebin B. Xu, *China's Social Welfare*
Pitman B. Potter, *China's Legal System*
Xuefei Ren, *Urban China*
Judith Shapiro, *China's Environmental Challenges*
LiAnne Yu, *Consumption in China*
Xiaowei Zang, *Ethnicity in China*

PARTY AND STATE IN POST-MAO CHINA

Teresa Wright

polity

The right of Teresa Wright to be identified as Author of this Work has been asserted in accordance with the UK Copyright, Designs and Patents Act 1988.

First published in 2015 by Polity Press

Polity Press
65 Bridge Street
Cambridge CB2 1UR, UK

Polity Press
350 Main Street
Malden, MA 02148, USA

ISBN-13: 978-0-7456-6384-5 (hardback)
ISBN-13: 978-0-7456-6385-2 (paperback)

A catalogue record for this book is available from the British Library.

Library of Congress Cataloging-In-Publication Data

Wright, Teresa.
  Party and state in post-Mao China / Teresa Wright.
    pages cm.
  Includes bibliographical references and index.
  ISBN 978-0-7456-6384-5 (hardback) – ISBN 0-7456-6384-2 (hardcover) – ISBN 978-0-7456-6385-2 (paperback)   1. Zhongguo gong chan dang–History.   2. China–Politics and government–1976-2002.   3. China–Politics and government–2002-
4. China–Economic conditions–1976-2000.   5. China–Economic conditions–2000-
I. Title.
  JQ1519.A4W75 2015
  324.251'075–dc23
                              2014038111

Typeset in 11.5 on 15pt Adobe Jenson Pro
by Toppan Best-set Premedia Limited
Printed and bound in the UK by Clays Ltd, St Ives PLC

The publisher has used its best endeavors to ensure that the URLs for external websites referred to in this book are correct and active at the time of going to press. However, the publisher has no responsibility for the websites and can make no guarantee that a site will remain live or that the content is or will remain appropriate.

Every effort has been made to trace all copyright holders, but if any have been inadvertently overlooked the publisher will be pleased to include any necessary credits in any subsequent reprint or edition.

For further information on Polity, visit our website:
politybooks.com

Need to do history/chronology before doing this book.

Contents

Map	vi
Chronology	vii
Acknowledgments	xiv
Acronyms	xvi
1 Sources of Stable Governance in China	1
2 Party and State, or Party-State?	18
3 Who Serves in the Party-State?	41
4 Maintaining Public Relations	76
5 Managing the Economy	113
6 Providing Goods and Services	145
7 Stable Authoritarianism?	180
Notes	196
Index	210

Last part on Xi Jinping
After this - cover ② Xi Jinping period and go on to ① Minxin + The Party

1. Intro stuff
2. History 1911-1992
3. 1992-2012 - key developments
*   Rise Xi Jinping and people*
4. This book - Party and State
*   w/ other readings*
5. Development + Environment
6. Conclusion

Read Minxin Pei after this + The Party

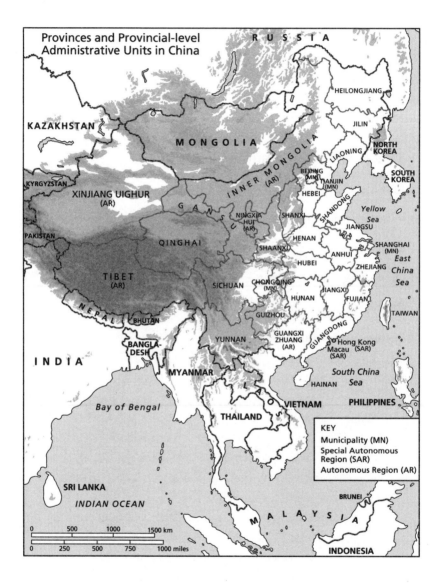

Provinces and Provincial-level Administrative Units in China

Chronology

1911	Fall of the Qing dynasty
1937–45	Japan invades China
1945–9	Civil War between Nationalists (KMT) and Communists (CCP)
1949	Mao Zedong founds People's Republic of China (PRC); KMT retreats to Taiwan
1950	Land Reform Law
1950–3	Korean War
1953–7	First Five-Year Plan: PRC adopts Soviet-style economic planning
1954	Constitution of the PRC implemented; first meeting of the National People's Congress
1957	Hundred Flowers Movement
1958–60	Great Leap Forward
1959	Ministry of Justice eradicated from PRC state apparatus; Tibetan uprising and departure of the Dalai Lama for India
1959–61	Widespread famine, tens of millions of deaths
1960	Sino–Soviet split
1966–76	Great Proletarian Cultural Revolution
1968	Liu Shaoqi, President of PRC, publicly branded China's "number one capitalist-roader," stripped of all Party and state posts, and jailed
1969	Liu Shaoqi dies in prison; Deng Xiaoping publicly branded China's "number two capitalist-roader," sent to countryside to engage in manual labor
1971	PRC regains UN seat and Security Council membership

1972	"Shanghai Communiqué," issued during Richard Nixon's visit to China, pledges to normalize US–China relations (February)
1974	Zhou Enlai, Vice-Chair of CCP and Premier of PRC, convinces Mao to "re-habilitate" Deng Xiaoping; Deng becomes Vice-Premier of PRC
1976	Death of Zhou Enlai (January)
1976	CCP Central Committee criticizes Deng; Deng removed from high-level Party and state posts (February)
1976	Mass public outpouring of grief over Zhou Enlai's death, support for Deng Xiaoping, at Beijing's Tian'anmen Square (April)
1976	The Great Tangshan Earthquake: Largest earthquake of the 20th century by death toll (July)
1976	Death of Mao Zedong (September)
1976	Hua Guofeng becomes Chair of CCP and CMC; Maoist "Gang of Four" arrested (October)
1977	Deng restored to high-level CCP and state posts, including Vice-Chair of CCP Central Committee
1978–80	Democracy Wall Movement
1978	Deng Xiaoping consolidates power as top CCP leader; 3rd Plenum of 11th CCP Central Committee repudiates Great Proletarian Cultural Revolution, endorses economic reform (November)
1979	US and PRC establish formal diplomatic ties; PRC invades Vietnam; introduction of one-child policy, restricting married, urban couples to one child; Ministry of Justice restored as part of PRC state

1980   Special Economic Zones endorsed; PRC joins
International Monetary Fund and World Bank

1981   Hu Yaobang replaces Hua Guofeng as Chair
of CCP

1982   Locally elected community mediation committees
encouraged; title of CCP "Chair" changed to
"General Secretary"; small-scale private businesses
officially allowed

1983   Rural "household responsibility system" endorsed
nationwide

1984   New state-sector workers hired without guarantees of
lifetime employment or "iron rice bowl" benefits;
Sino-British Joint Declaration agreeing to return Hong
Kong to the PRC in 1997

1986–7   Student protests at University of Science and
Technology and other universities; Hu Yao-bang,
General Secretary of the CCP, forced to resign;
Zhao Ziyang becomes General Secretary of
the CCP (Winter)

1987   New law establishes the right to hold elections
for rural village councils; Deng Xiaoping steps
down as chair of CCP Central Advisory
Commission

1988   PRC Constitution "encourages" and "supports" the
development of China's private sector; Ministry of
Civil Affairs establishes province-level guidelines for
implementing 1987 village council law

March
1989   University students attempt to submit petition to
National People's Congress, asking for amnesty for
political prisoners

April
1989   Hu Yao-bang dies, mass mourning turns into student-
led Tian'anmen Square movement

1989   Chinese military uses force to end Tian'anmen Square movement; up to 2,000 killed (June 3–4)

1989   Zhao Ziyang, General Secretary of the CCP and President of PRC, forced to resign, placed under house arrest; Jiang Zemin becomes General Secretary of the CCP (June)

1989   Jiang Zemin replaces Deng Xiaoping as chair of Central Military Commission (CMC) (November)

1990   New law calls for the election of urban residents' committees

1992   Deng Xiaoping's Southern Tour re-energizes economic reform; 14th meeting of National Party Congress calls for the establishment of a "socialist market economy" and declares that economic growth is the country's highest priority; migration restrictions eased; Chinese universities begin to charge tuition

1994   PRC's first Company Law passed; uniform national tax code instituted; citizens granted legal right to sue government officials for abuse of authority or malfeasance; "Friends of Nature" becomes China's first officially recognized environmental NGO

1995   Central Party-state leaders announce intention to "keep the large" state-owned enterprises (SOEs) and "let the small go"

1997   Death of Deng Xiaoping (Feb.); Hong Kong returned to PRC (July); 15th National Party Congress describes private enterprise as an "important" element of China's economy, introduces plan to privatize SOEs; all CCP Politburo and SC members over the age of 70 (aside from Jiang Zemin) step down (September)

1998	Large-scale SOE privatization begins; National People's Congress expands 1987 law on rural village council elections, grants deliberative rights to village assemblies
1999	National People's Congress approves Jiang Zemin as President of PRC, amends Constitution to describe private enterprise as "important" element of China's economy; CPPCC adds special "economic" constituency that includes roughly 100 private entrepreneurs (March); students engage in street protests in response to US bombing of Chinese embassy in Belgrade (May)
2000	Central leaders stipulate that urban residents' committee leaders should be directly nominated and elected by local residents
2001	PRC joins World Trade Organization; all new lawyers required to pass a "bar" exam
2002	16th Plenum of the National Party Congress, Hu Jintao replaces Jiang Zemin as General Secretary of the CCP; NPC endorses Jiang's "Three Represents," effectively embracing the entry of private entrepreneurs into the CCP; large-scale protests in NE China by laid-off state-owned enterprise workers; local rural taxes and fees banned
2003	Hu Jintao replaces Jiang Zemin as President of PRC; Jiang Zemin remains chair of CMC; remaining SOEs placed under control of State-owned Assets Supervision and Administration Commission (SASAC)

2004   Constitution amended to include right to protection of private property; Hu Jintao replaces Jiang Zemin as chair of CMC

2005   Student anti-Japan street protests; Zhao Ziyang dies, still under house arrest; PRC begins to allow value of the Chinese yuan to drop relative to the US dollar

2006   "New Socialist Countryside" initiative announced

2007   Two non-CCP members of CPPCC appointed to State Council; CCP Constitution amended to give public and private sectors equal economic standing; PRC overtakes the USA as the world's biggest emitter of CO_2

2008   Violent clashes in Tibet, foreign criticism and protests, domestic counter-protests; Sichuan earthquake; Beijing Summer Olympic Games; dissident Liu Xiaobo arrested for "Charter 08"; central government passes US$585 billion economic stimulus package

2009   Violent clashes between ethnic Uighurs and local Han Chinese in Xinjiang; national pension program enacted to cover all elderly rural residents

2010   Liu Xiaobo awarded Nobel Peace Prize, while in prison; Shanghai World Expo

2011   Citizens given legal right to sue government for release of information; major crash on China's new bullet train

2012   18th National Party Congress approves Xi Jinping as General Secretary of the CCP and chair of CMC; official media report "rigorous rule" that Politburo SC members must retire by age 68

2013   12th National People's Congress approves Xi Jinping as President of PRC; 3rd Plenum of 18th CCP CC states that market plays a "decisive" role in the economy; Xi Jinping launches anti-corruption campaign and calls for more comprehensive cadre evaluation criteria, including the "people's livelihood," the "development of local society," and the "quality of the environment" in the area under an official's purview; CCP issues "Document 9," warning of the threat of "false ideological trends, positions and activities;" SUV in front of Tian'anmen Square bursts into flames and runs into a group of bystanders; Shanghai Pilot Free Trade Zone announced

2014   CCP Central Committee announces stricter scrutiny of and higher standards for new and existing members; individuals of Uighur ethnicity wielding knives and axes attack passengers at a train station in Kunming; train station bombed and car crashes into bystanders at public market in Xinjiang; armed clashes between Uighur protestors and government forces in Xinjiang (June)

Acknowledgments

Writing a book is never easy – at least not in my experience. It takes a village to see it through. Several years ago, Louise Knight contacted me with the idea of writing a book for Polity about China's government. I balked at the thought of slogging through the details of CCP and state structures. But with Louise's encouragement, I was able to formulate an outline that I felt inspired to take to fruition. Louise has been a model editor – smart, reasonable, and cheerful. Similarly, my work with Polity's Pascal Porcheron has been an absolute pleasure.

This book has benefited tremendously from the input of colleagues – none of whom, of course, bears any responsibility for my errors or omissions. I am grateful to the members of my department (Political Science) at California State University, Long Beach who read portions of the manuscript and offered helpful suggestions. I feel lucky to have such a wonderful group of colleagues. The book also was improved by the opportunity to present parts of it at academic conferences. For this, I thank Sujian Guo and the Fudan Institute for Advanced Study in Social Science; Zhiqun Zhu and Bucknell University; Arthur Ding, Chih-shian Liou, and the Institute of International Relations at National Chengchi University; and Jane Golley and the Australian National University Centre on China in the World. Further, I thank Nancy Lewis and the Research Program at the East–West Center for providing me with a place of refuge where I could think and write.

Beyond help with the content of the manuscript, I could not have persevered without the support of many others. Amelia Marquez, my main administrative assistant, has through her tireless efforts and positive attitude made it possible for me to keep a handle on my duties as Department Chair and still find time to write. My parents, Pete and Nancy Wright, have been a constant source of encouragement, and I will never be able to thank them enough for their love and support. I am particularly grateful to my mom for her research assistance; many of the articles that she mailed to me informed my thinking for the book. My gratitude also is deep for Ty Von Hoetzendorff, whose words and actions kept me focused and happy through one deadline after another. And I thank my amazing children, Nicholas and Anna, for their patience as I sit in front of the computer, and for surrounding me with their kindness, compassion, and joy.

Acronyms

ABC	Agricultural Bank of China
BOC	Bank of China
CAC	Central Advisory Commission
CC	Central Committee
CCB	China Construction Bank
CCDI	Central Commission for Discipline Inspection
CCP	Chinese Communist Party
CDP	China Democracy Party
CLSG	Central Leading Small Group
CMC	Central Military Commission
CMC	community mediation committee
CPPCC	Chinese People's Political Consultative Conference
CPS	Central Party School
EAB	East Asian Barometer
FDI	Foreign Direct Investment
GW	gigawatts
ICBC	Industrial and Commercial Bank of China
KMT	Kuomintang (Nationalist Party)
MOCA	Ministry of Civil Affairs
NDRC	National Development and Reform Commission
NGO	non-governmental organization
NPC	National Party Congress
OD	Organization Department
PLA	People's Liberation Army

PRC	People's Republic of China
RC	residents' committee
SASAC	State-owned Assets Supervision and Administration Commission
SC	Standing Committee
SEZ	Special Economic Zone
SIA	social insurance agency
SOE	state-owned enterprise
TVE	Township and Village Enterprise
UN	United Nations
UST	University of Science and Technology
VC	village committee
WPO	World Public Opinion
WVS	World Values Survey

1 | Sources of Stable Governance in China

For more than a century, the Chinese people have experienced dramatic social, political, and economic changes. In 1911, the upheavals that resulted from the intrusion of industrializing Western powers and Japan on Chinese soil culminated in the fall of the imperial system that had governed China for millennia – a system that in its general form was longer-lasting than any political system in the world, before or since. From 1911–49, political turmoil, foreign invasion, and civil war continually upturned the Chinese people's daily lives. Since the Chinese Communist Party (CCP) took power in 1949, fundamental economic and social transformations have continued. However, over the long course of CCP rule, China's political system has in many ways become more stable.

Since 1949, this political system has been composed of a deeply intertwined, yet in some ways differentiated, ruling Chinese Communist Party (CCP) and governing state. From 1949–76, Mao Zedong led China's political system, fomenting continuous change in the lives of the Chinese people. Though officials within the political system were not infrequently attacked as a result of Mao's determination to avoid ossification within the political system, the CCP-led political system itself remained stable. Since Mao's death in 1976, China's social and economic structures have again been dramatically altered. The totalitarian social and economic controls of the Mao era largely have gone by the wayside, as has the continual inculcation of Maoist ideology. China has moved toward a free-wheeling, convoluted, and sometimes contradictory blend of capitalist and socialist economic features, and great social freedom in some areas, but strict controls in others.

Since the death of Mao in 1976, Chinese citizens at times have engaged in public protests. Especially since the early 1990s, mass demonstrations have been commonplace. However, simultaneously, the Chinese public has demonstrated little interest in systemic political change, including liberal democratic transformation. In fact, from the early 1990s through the present, China's CCP-led regime has enjoyed greater popular support than it did in the earlier part of the post-Mao period (the late 1970s through the 1980s).

The stability of China's political system has been puzzling to many, particularly those who believe that authoritarian regimes are inherently unstable. Those who refuse to accept public opinion polls and other evidence indicating widespread public acceptance of China's post-Mao government typically argue that the CCP has maintained its power mainly through repression, and that the Chinese public is too fearful to challenge its control. Others maintain that it is just a matter of time before the CCP-controlled system falls, as its communist and authoritarian features increasingly will inhibit its ability to effectively govern.

In contrast, many specialists in Chinese politics emphasize that China's post-Mao political system has remained stable because it has been adaptable. This book agrees. At the same time, it makes a more specific argument – that the stability of the CCP-led government in China – particularly since the early 1990s – has derived both from its greater openness and responsiveness to the public, and from some of its still communist and authoritarian features.

To explain how this can be so, this book dives deep into the workings of China's political system, uncovering how the system is set up (including its major institutions and structures); how people come to occupy positions of power within the system; and how these people formulate and implement public policies. In addition, it examines how well the institutions, structures, and processes that comprise China's political system fulfill the functions that are required in order for any governing regime to be stable. Without a doubt, there are many important governmental functions. But among these, this book focuses on three that are particularly essential: (i) ameliorating public grievances and satisfying key demographic groups; (ii) ensuring economic growth and stability; and (iii) enabling access to necessary goods and services.

In Western countries, most citizens believe that only a liberal democratic political system (i.e., one with competitive elections at all levels and with guarantees of civil liberties such as freedom of expression and assembly) can adequately satisfy these requirements. In terms of the first function listed above (ameliorating public grievances and satisfying key demographic groups), governments that lack competitive elections and do not protect civil liberties are seen as uninterested in listening to and acting on the public's input. With regard to the second function (managing the economy), many Westerners argue that economic growth and stability require a free flow of information, and that this can occur only in a liberal democratic political context. When it comes to the third function (ensuring access to necessary goods and services), it is believed that unless a government is subject to popular election, it will have no incentive to guarantee the provision of the goods and services that citizens need. For these reasons, many assume that authoritarian political regimes are inherently unstable. If they do not fulfill the basic functions of government, the public will lose patience with their rule, and will force liberal democratic political change (or at least will attempt to do so). At that point, the leaders of the authoritarian regime will have to choose between democratization and repression.

These Western assumptions are challenged by the case of China. Despite dramatic economic and social change in the post-Mao period, the political system has in many basic ways remained authoritarian: opposition parties are not permitted, the public has no right to vote for top political leaders, the media is censored, and political dissent is repressed. But at the same time, Chinese citizens have evidenced remarkable toleration of – and even support for – China's CCP-controlled political system.

The political attitudes of China's citizens – however shocking and disconcerting they may be to Westerners – have been documented in a range of studies. These include numerous surveys conducted by highly respected international organizations that are led by accomplished scholars. One such organization is the World Values Survey Association, which since 1981 has conducted once-a-decade surveys in nearly 100 countries. The population samples are rigorously chosen so as to be nationally representative of the various demographic groups found among citizens aged eighteen and older, and respondents are surveyed via face-to-face interviews overseen by trained social scientists working in academic institutions.[1] In the 2012 World Values Survey (WVS), nearly 85 percent of Chinese respondents expressed "quite a lot" or "a great deal" of confidence in the national government. In addition, approximately 78 percent expressed "a great deal" (29 percent) or "quite a lot" (49 percent) of confidence in China's national legislative body, the National People's Congress.[2] Another well-known international survey organization, World Public Opinion (WPO) [run by the Program on International Policy Attitudes (PIPA) at the University of Maryland], has conducted public opinion surveys via polls, focus groups, and face-to-face interviews in most countries since 1992. In the most recent WPO survey of China, in 2008, respondents were supportive of the political system, with 83 percent reporting that they could trust the national government to do the right thing "most of the time" (60 percent) or "just about always" (23 percent). Even stronger results were found in a nationally representative study conducted in 2008 by the East Asia Barometer (EAB), another internationally recognized survey organization that queries respondents via face-to-face interviews.[3] In the EAB poll, more than 93 percent of Chinese respondents expressed "a great deal" (69 percent) or "quite a lot" (24 percent) of trust in the national government.[4]

Further, in surveys such as these, Chinese respondents' stated trust in and support for their political system is higher than is the case in almost every other country in the world, including liberal democracies such as the US, Great Britain, France, South Korea, and India. In the 2012 WPO survey, these countries were among the nineteen that were polled. Among all nineteen, Chinese citizens reported the highest levels of trust in their government. In response to a question asking for whom one's government is run, 65 of percent of Chinese selected "for the benefit of the people." In Britain and France, in contrast, roughly 60 percent selected "by a few big interests looking out for themselves," and in the US a whopping 80 percent chose this answer. Perhaps even more surprising, WPO respondents from China evidenced less dissatisfaction with their government's level of "democratic responsiveness" than did respondents from the US, Britain, France, and South Korea.[5]

In addition, surveys indicate that the Chinese public believes that the existing political system is fairly democratic. In the 2012 WVS, respondents were asked to evaluate "how democratically" China is "being governed today," with a score of 1 indicating "not at all democratic" and 10 signifying "completely democratic." The vast majority of respondents (61 percent) chose a positive score of 6–10. Only about 24 percent chose a negative score of 1–5, and most of these selected a ranking of 5. [14.6 percent did not respond or selected "I don't know".] Similarly, in the 2008 EAB, more than 87 percent of Chinese respondents reported being "fairly satisfied" (70 percent) or "very satisfied" (17 percent) with the "way democracy works" in China. Relatedly, in the 2012 WVS nearly 70 percent of respondents stated that there is a "great deal of" or "fairly much" respect for individual rights at present in China. Overall, in the 2008 EAB, over 89 of respondents rated China's "present political situation" as "very good" (30 percent) or "good"

(59 percent). Among the remainder of respondents, about 8 percent rated it as "average," while less than 3 percent considered it to be "bad" or "very bad."[6]

Survey results such as these must be taken with a grain of salt. As critics point out, respondents may not have been entirely honest in their answers, due to their concern that a negative response might have dangerous political consequences. Given the Chinese regime's proclivity to arrest and jail those who are deemed subversive – as well as its enormous budget for maintaining domestic "stability" (at the time of this writing this budget exceeds that of China's formal military budget) – this is an important question. To assess this possibility, various scholars have included in their surveys of Chinese citizens questions about respondents' level of fear of political persecution. They have found no correlation between a respondent's stated level of support for China's political system and his or her fear of the governing regime.[7] Relatedly, critics of survey results such as those found in the WVS, WPO, and EAB argue that respondents' views simply reflect the ignorance or brain-washing of Chinese citizens that result from the government's censorship of the media. However, this argument also is problematic. For, researchers have found that Chinese citizens with greater exposure to China's domestic media actually express less confidence in the government.[8] And, Chinese who regularly skirt China's Internet restrictions and access international news media reports are among the population's most vocal critics of Western governments and media outlets.[9]

A more persuasive criticism of WVS, WPO, EAB, and other mass survey results concerns their comparability across countries. For "democracy" can mean different things in different countries, and can be judged by varied standards and comparative reference-points. The veracity of this point is not in doubt. At the same time, however, questions about the comparability of national survey results do not invalidate the findings of individual country surveys; such questions simply remind us to consider each country's survey results within that country's particular context.

Additional evidence of popular acceptance of, and even support for, China's government – particularly at the national level – is found in more focused scholarly studies. These include on-the-ground interviews with and observations of a wide range of demographic groups – including private entrepreneurs, "blue collar" public and private sector workers, farmers, environmental activists, and participants in mass protests. This research consistently has found that although many citizens are deeply disillusioned with local political and economic elites, they do not blame the overall political system; to the contrary, most have a remarkably positive attitude toward China's central government.[10]

The political views expressed by Chinese citizens in the studies and surveys outlined above are puzzling to most Westerners. For such views challenge the prevalent notion that the Chinese government is a backward, repressive and ossified communist dictatorship. Yet if one deeply examines China's political system over the course of the post-Mao period, one finds that this system has in fact changed in significant ways, and in some respects has even democratized.

Indeed, the case of post-Mao China forces us to re-think how we categorize different kinds of governments. Though typically we refer to political regimes as "democratic" or "authoritarian," in reality, "democracy" and "authoritarianism" are concepts (or ideal types, in Max Weber's conceptualization) that can be placed on opposite ends of a spectrum. Real-world regimes lie somewhere in between these endpoints, and are never completely "authoritarian" or "democratic." Moreover, where a particular government sits on this spectrum changes over time. And, political regimes do not always move in the direction of becoming more democratic; they can become more authoritarian as well. Relatedly, different parts of a government may be more or less democratic, and can become more or less so over time.

The US government is a case in point. Most people would categorize the American political system as a democracy, and would say that it has been a democracy since the time of its founding. But virtually all also would agree that in some very basic respects (particularly voting rights) the US government has become much more democratic over time. Further, some aspects of the American political system are more democratic than others. For example, members of the US House of Representatives are directly elected by their constituents, but the President is chosen by the Electoral College, which only indirectly follows the popular vote of the citizenry, and in some cases has chosen a president who received fewer popular votes than his opponent.

Similarly, the Chinese government has in some ways become more democratic over time, and has some areas that are more democratic than others. The most important democratic change in the post-Mao era is the initiation of local elections, particularly in rural villages. As will be discussed in more detail in Chapter 3, residents of rural villages regularly hold direct elections for village committees (VCs). According to the policy, voting rights are inclusive, as are candidacy requirements: all registered adults in the village are eligible both to vote and to run for office. One does not need to be a member of the CCP. This policy has had a significant impact on China's roughly 650 million rural residents.

Other aspects of the Chinese political system have become more democratic as well. As will be discussed more fully in Chapter 3, residents of urban neighborhoods have the official right to directly nominate and elect local "residents' committees." In addition, some townships and cities have been allowed to experiment with direct elections.[11] Further, local Party leaders have been made subject to popular review. Overall, despite the Chinese political system's still authoritarian nature in many respects, parts of it have become much more democratic over time.

But what do we mean by "democracy"? If one looks at the work of scholars – particularly those from the West – one will find that a focus

democracy

on liberal democracy predominates: democracy is seen as a system with "fully contested elections with full suffrage and the absence of massive fraud, combined with effective guarantees of civil liberties, including freedom of speech, assembly, and association."[12] If we apply this definition to China, we would categorize many rural VCs as being democratic. But higher level entities within China's political system would not be considered so. With regard to civil liberties, the Chinese Party-state is much more democratic than it was during the rule of Mao, but even so, the protection of civil liberties has ebbed and flowed over the course of the post-Mao period. And at the time of this writing, many civil liberties have been curtailed.

Yet this is not the only possible way to define "democracy." A more basic definition can be traced back to the Greek origins of the word: "demos" (the people) and "kratein" (to rule). Under this conceptualization, democracy can be defined as "rule by the people," or as a system wherein the government obeys, or follows, the will of the people. Without a doubt, elections are one method by which a government can obey the will of the people. However, elections are not necessarily the only way in which this can occur. If governmental officials listen and respond to the wishes and demands of the people, then they may be seen as acting democratically regardless of whether or not they attained their position through a popular election. Conversely, if an elected official does not listen and respond to the wishes and demands of the people, that official may be seen as acting undemocratically despite the fact that the procedure by which s/he was chosen was democratic. Further, if civil liberties are protected in a polity, such that people have the freedom of expression, association, and assembly, but politicians do not heed the expressed will of the people, then those politicians are not acting democratically in the basic sense of the word. And, this is true regardless of whether or not those politicians were elected. If one focuses on the more basic definition of democracy, then elections and civil liberties can act as means to achieving a democratic system, but they may not be necessary and sufficient conditions for democratic rule.

This discussion can help us to examine the ways in which "democracy" relates to the three basic requirements of a stable governing regime. With regard to the first requirement, satisfying key demographic groups and responding to public grievances, certainly elections may help ensure that this function is fulfilled. The example of China's local VC elections illustrates how this can be so. But, the case of post-Mao China also indicates that elections are not the only way in which a government can fulfill this requirement. Perhaps most notably, every government agency in China has an office devoted to the collection of, and response to, citizen petitions. Known as the "letters and visits" (*xinfang*) system, it is a way in which the government attempts to follow the will of the people even without elections at all levels. In addition, public protests have been extremely common in post-Mao China, particularly since the early 1990s. And, since the early 1990s, central authorities generally have been very tolerant of these actions, seeing them as a way to find out about public grievances. To the extent that China's central government has responded to such protests in a way that satisfactorily addresses the protestors' grievances, the government has behaved democratically in a basic sense, even without meaningful elections at the national level. Importantly, however, the Chinese government has been able to act democratically in this sense only in as much as civil liberties, such as the freedom of expression and assembly, have been protected. In cases where petitioners or protestors have been subject to repression, the perpetrators of the repression have acted in a profoundly undemocratic manner. To the extent that this has occurred, the Chinese political system has failed to fulfill the first key function of a stable governing regime.

One may also assess the degree to which elections and civil liberty protections are critical to the fulfillment of the second key governmental function addressed in this book – maintaining economic stability and growth. Although China lacks meaningful elections at the national and most sub-national levels, and freedom of expression (for both individual citizens and domestic media outlets) is constricted by the CCP-led regime, China's economy has for the past three decades grown at a rate that has never been matched in world history. Between 1979 and 2010, China averaged nearly 10 percent GDP growth *per year*. Although Western pundits continually warn that the Chinese economy is nothing but a flimsy house of cards on the brink of collapse, even following the economic crisis of the fall of 2008, China's GDP posted a 6 percent *growth* rate, as compared with the US GDP's nearly 7 percent *decline*. In 2013, China's growth rate was 7.7 percent; in America it was 1.9.

Finally, the importance of elections and civil liberties can be examined with regard to the third key government function – ensuring the provision of necessary goods and services. As will be discussed in great detail in Chapter 6, the post-Mao Chinese Party-state has done an only barely satisfactory job in terms of essential goods and services provision. However, it is hard to support a claim that China's lack of competitive elections at the highest levels has been the cause of existing problems. For, as will be further explained in Chapter 6, some key goods – such as health care and pensions for urban residents – were better provided in China's less procedurally democratic periods, including even the Maoist era. It was not a lack of national elections that imperilled the provision of these necessary goods and services, but rather the privatization of many state-owned enterprises in the late 1990s. Meanwhile, infrastructure, though in some cases short on quality, has expanded and improved at a stunning pace, particularly since the mid-1990s. This has occurred despite the lack of national elections. Overall, China's record in terms of the three basic functions of government suggests that although elections and the protection of civil liberties may help to ensure that a government does a satisfactory job, they may not be crucial.

With this discussion in mind, this book undertakes two often entwined, but conceptually separate inquiries: (1) how well does China's Party-state satisfy the basic functions of government? and (2) how have the Chinese government's democratic and authoritarian features influenced its ability to fulfill these functions? Perhaps even more surprising to Westerners than the claim that national-level elections may not be necessary in order for a regime to be legitimate and stable, this book argues that in some respects, the Chinese political system's lack of elections at most levels actually has contributed to the post-Mao Party-state's legitimacy by aiding in the fulfillment of the three fundamental governmental functions. Further this book makes the claim that some of the Chinese government's "communist" features – namely, state direction and a commitment to guaranteeing basic economic security – have made a positive contribution as well.

At the same time, it must be emphasized that this book is not making the argument that it is inherently better for a political system to lack meaningful elections. To the contrary, unelected regimes can be – and historically have been – far more destructive and inept than elected ones. The case of Mao-era China illustrates the extreme harm that can occur to a population when national political leaders are not subject to popular review. Rather, the claim being made here is that, in the same way that it is inaccurate to categorize a government as wholly "democratic" or "authoritarian," governments are never entirely "good" or "bad" in terms of their governance. While some features of a political system may help it to effectively respond to the demands of the populace, manage the economy, and ensure access to necessary goods and services, other features may not. And, all of these typically change over time. This is true of all political regimes. The point is that the "authoritarian" or "communist" characteristics of a government do not *necessarily* cause bad governance, and in some cases can facilitate good governance. The keys in a non-liberal democratic context are the attitude and ability of the political leadership. If government leaders are pragmatic and competent, and seek to satisfy the demands of the public, their lack of dependence on popular election can in some respects free them to craft policies that are effective and beneficial to the populace as a whole. But if political leaders do not have these qualities, their lack of accountability to the public can be disastrous.

Just as unelected governments have both good and bad potential, elected regimes do as well. One potential problem with liberal democratic rule is that when power alternates between or among political parties with widely varying political goals and ideologies, policy is inconsistent, and is not be carried through in the long term. Further, when politicians are focused primarily on getting elected (and re-elected), they must focus on the short term, and they also must think as much about how to defeat their opponent as about how to best serve the interest of the country. In the American political system in particular, an additional phenomenon has arisen in the context of elections: candidates who wish to have a fighting chance must garner massive campaign contributions from wealthy donors, and as a result, must constantly be concerned with satisfying the demands of those donors. Despite the many potential dangers that may arise when political leaders are not subject to popular election, unelected governments generally are not prone to the problems listed above.

Overall, China's post-Mao political leaders have been pragmatic and competent, and this is why they have been successful at satisfying the basic functions of a stable government. But they have been far from perfect in doing so, and serious problems persist. The regime's most pervasive and fundamental shortcoming is political corruption: governing authorities frequently use their power to benefit themselves or their cronies, at the expense of the general population. This has been the general cause of most of the collective popular contention that has arisen in the post-Mao period: it was the core complaint of the protestors who took to the streets in the spring of 1989; it has been at the heart of rural demonstrations about arbitrary taxes and fees in the early

1990s and unfair land acquisition since the early 2000s; and it has been the key spark of environmental protests (particularly prevalent since the early 1990s). To the extent that political leaders do not satisfactorily address and resolve cases of corruption, they will not be able to satisfactorily respond to public demands and grievances. And to the degree that corruption leads to faulty and unsafe infrastructure (as not infrequently has been the case with schools, roads, bridges, and railways), such corruption diminishes the regime's ability to satisfy this other core function of government.

A second problem is that most political leaders in China are fearful of civil liberties such as the freedom of expression, association, and assembly. As a result, governing elites have been deeply ambivalent about protecting these liberties. This is particularly problematic with regard to the second key governmental function – satisfying important demographic groups and responding to public grievances. As noted earlier, although China's political system includes non-electoral mechanisms by which the public can express its concerns and complaints (most notably, the "letters and visits" system and mass protests), the effective functioning of these communication channels is predicated on the citizenry's freedom to express its views, associate, and assemble. When these freedoms are restrained, either through acts of repression or as a result of people's fear of potential repression, then China's political system is unable to adequately fulfill this key governmental function, and as a consequence may become unstable. Ironically, the CCP's fear of instability often leads it to smother the very features of the political system that have worked to enhance its stability.

LAYOUT OF THE BOOK

The two chapters that immediately follow comprise Part I of the book, which examines the nature of the Chinese Party-state, and how it has changed over the course of the post-Mao era. Chapter 2 lays out the basic institutions and entities that comprise China's ruling Party and state, from the highest central level to the lowest local level. This overview includes the responsibilities and powers of each entity, and how these have changed over time. The chapter argues that while Party and state bodies are nominally separate, the Party ultimately controls the state. This is achieved both by embedding Party leaders in state institutions and positions, and by asserting Party authority over all political decisions. At the same time, the chapter addresses how these features have changed and fluctuated over time.

Chapter 3 examines the changing demographic composition of the people who serve in the Chinese Party-state. This discussion begins with the ruling regime's criteria and processes for CCP membership and ascension within the Party, including leadership succession at the highest levels. The chapter also looks at how various Party elites formulate their policy preferences and perceive their tasks. Next, the chapter turns to the changing selection processes and demographic composition of the various entities that comprise China's state structure. A key focus is the institution and progression of elections for VCs in rural areas, as well as experimentation with elections at other levels of governance. The chapter argues that overall, China's state structure has become more representative of the population and more open to popular input. Concurrently, the power and autonomy of state institutions vis-a-vis the CCP have remained weak. Despite changes, China continues to be ruled by a one-Party dictatorship. The chapter also investigates how state elites at various levels formulate their policy preferences and perceive their tasks.

Chapters 4, 5, and 6 comprise Part II of the text, which assesses how well China's governing regime has fulfilled the necessary functions of stable political rule. Chapter 4 begins with a sector-by-sector analysis of the Party-state's relationship with key groups, focusing on private entrepreneurs, college-educated professionals, rank and file public and private sector workers, and farmers. In various ways, governing authorities have attended to the basic needs of each group. At the same time, though, relations between the Party-state and these different sectors have not always been harmonious, particularly in the case of rank and file workers and farmers. Next, the chapter looks at how governing authorities have responded to public dissatisfaction in the post-Mao period, including popular protests, cyberspace dissent and criticism, and petition efforts. The chapter finds that central authorities generally have been effective in deflecting and ameliorating potential political dissatisfaction with the political system as a whole. This has been achieved through efforts to rein in corrupt local officials. At the same time, however, public dissatisfaction remains real and potentially potent. Finally, Chapter 4 assesses the degree to which the Chinese Party-state has become more democratic over the course of the post-Mao period – an assessment which revisits the discussion of how to define democracy.

Chapter 5 examines the ways in which CCP and state entities have intervened in, regulated, and transformed the Chinese economy over the course of the post-Mao period. While all governments are involved in the economy in some way, this subject is particularly important in China. For, from the 1950s through the early 1990s, the economy was almost entirely state-run. Further, state ownership of all land and many key industries has persisted through the present. Chapter 5 examines the changing role of the Party-state in China's rural and urban economies, as well as the international economy. In so doing, it lays out how, when, and why most state-owned enterprises were privatized. In addition, the chapter discusses the areas of the economy where the Party-state still maintains strict control, and the areas that have been granted greater autonomy. Finally, the chapter assesses the success of the Party-state's economic efforts in the post-Mao period, analyzing the ways in which the authoritarian/communist political structure has aided and hindered economic growth and stability over this period of time.

Chapter 6 looks at how well China's Party-state has assured the provision of necessary goods and services. Although the Chinese government generally has moved away from the Maoist system of government control and delivery of most key goods and services, the chapter shows how the Party-state has maintained a commitment to some basic social safety nets for the population. At the same time, the chapter charts the areas in which the governing regime has retracted its prior provision of social services, leading to deterioration in quality and accessibility. Finally, the chapter assesses the ways in which China's lack of liberal democracy both helps the Party-state to provide social services, and leads it to fall short.

The concluding chapter, Chapter 7, revisits the major points raised in Chapters 1 through 6, and concludes that, on balance, the Chinese Party-state has remained stable because it has been able to adequately fulfill the basic needs and wants of the populace. While it has achieved this goal in part by becoming more open and responsive to popular input, the Party-state's success also has been aided by its retention of some key communist and authoritarian characteristics. Chapter 7 also emphasizes the specific ways in which the Chinese Party-state has fallen short in its governance, pointing to problems that – if left unresolved – may destabilize it in the future.

2   Party and State, or Party-State?

Before further exploring the ways in which the Chinese Party-state fulfills, or fails to fulfill, the basic functions of government, we must closely examine the structure and composition of China's unique ruling regime. And, we must explore how it has changed over time. The basic institutions and entities that comprise China's ruling Party and state extend to the most local level – the village in the countryside, and the neighborhood (*shequ*) in urban areas. On the Party side, key bodies and positions include: the General Secretary, the Standing Committee of the Politburo, the Politburo, the Central Committee, the National Party Congress, Provincial Party Congresses, Township/County Congresses, local Chinese Communist Party branches, the Secretariat, and the Party Central Military Commission. On the state side, key bodies and positions include: the President, the Premier, the Standing Committee of the State Council, the State Council, the National People's Congress, Provincial People's Congresses, Township/County People's Congresses, village councils, the Chinese People's Political Consultative Conference, the State Central Military Commission, and bureaucratic ministries. Though each of these entities has particular powers and responsibilities, in many cases these powers and responsibilities overlap with those of other entities. And, as with all things human and political, the mix of these powers and responsibilities has changed over time, and surely will continue to change in the future. In addition, as is the case in all countries, there are powerful informal institutions that exert a substantial influence within the formal political structure.

The most important thing to understand about the Chinese ruling regime is that even though the Party and state are nominally separate, the Party ultimately controls the state; this is why the regime typically is referred to as a "Party-state." The Party (the CCP) controls the state through a variety of mechanisms. Most importantly, CCP leaders occupy virtually all important positions in state institutions. And, the CCP has final authority over all political decisions. Despite some changes and fluctuations in the relationship between the Party and the state in the post-Mao period, these general features have characterized the Chinese Party-state from the time of Mao through the present, and are unlikely to change in the near future.

In many countries – including those that are liberal democratic in nature – various governmental bodies and positions have powers and responsibilities that overlap. However, in China, governmental powers and responsibilities tend to be even more convoluted and blurred than is the case elsewhere. Further, in many liberal democratic countries, a small number of powerful political parties control the governmental bodies and positions that comprise the "state." In China, the situation is more extreme: only one political party (the CCP) has controlled the state since 1949.

Finally, in all political systems, there are both formal/official and informal/unofficial political institutions. Formal, or official, institutions usually are created by constitutions, and appear on official organizational charts. In China there is both a Party Constitution and a state Constitution. The Party Constitution lays out the powers, responsibilities, and selection mechanisms for all formal Party institutions, from the most central to the most local – including all of the institutions listed above. The state Constitution does the same for all formal state institutions. Yet in China, as in virtually all other countries, there are informal and/or unofficial groups, networks, and practices that are not created by constitutions or other formal rules, and do not appear on official organizational charts, but nonetheless wield substantial amounts of political power. China differs from most other political regimes – particularly liberal democratic ones – in that there are no powerful lobby groups that exist outside of the Party-state. Big business, labor unions, and special interest groups have virtually no power external to the government. Most big businesses and all key industries are state-owned; all legal labor unions are formally affiliated with the Party-state; and special interest groups are either affiliated with the Party-state, or have such miniscule resources that their power is inconsequential.

One informal and unofficial, yet quite powerful, Chinese political institution consists of "functional systems" (*xitong*) that include Party and state officials that sit on various Party and state bodies that have responsibility for a particular issue or area, such as energy or foreign affairs. In addition, the Chinese political system includes informal "Central Leading Small Groups" (CLSGs) that serve as powerful consulting and coordination bodies on important issues as they arise. Further, there are Party groups (known as *dangzu*) that exist within each state body. Informal political entities such as *xitong*, CLSGs and *dangzu* are some of the mechanisms through which the CCP maintains control of the Chinese state.

A major difference between the political systems in China and most Western liberal democracies is that in the latter, political parties *grew out of* a pre-existing state. In the US, for example, there were no political parties in existence when the Constitution was ratified. In fact, at the time no country in the world had political parties in the form that we recognize them today. Political parties were formed in the US only after the first presidential election, as a way to maximize electoral success within the boundaries laid out in the Constitution. Similarly, political parties in other Western liberal democratic countries emerged only in the 1800s, alongside the development of elections and voting rights. In China post-1949, in contrast, the state *was created by the* CCP.[1] It never has had an existence prior to or separate from the CCP.

Rather, the CCP created and has subsequently adapted the state to suit its dual and related goals of maintaining power and encouraging economic development. During the Maoist era (1949–1976), the state also was used by the CCP to promote Mao's commitment to egalitarianism and continual revolution.

THE FORMAL STRUCTURE AND COMPOSITION OF THE CCP

Given this, any discussion of the Chinese government must begin with the Chinese Communist Party (CCP). As noted above, the Chinese government (or "state") was created by the CCP when it assumed national power (in 1949), and the CCP has controlled it ever since. On paper, the basic structure of the Party has remained fairly consistent over time. But the Party's human composition in terms of membership and leadership has changed quite dramatically – particularly when one compares the Maoist and post-Mao periods. These demographic changes within the Party (and state) will be detailed in the subsequent chapter. In this chapter, we will examine the structure of the Party (and state).

If you read the Constitution of the CCP or look at an official organizational chart, it will appear that power flows from the bottom of the Party to the top. In reality, however, power flows from the top to the bottom. At the national level, the bottom of the Party is the National Party Congress. One level up is the Party's Central Committee, followed by the Politburo, and then the Standing Committee of the Politburo.

According to the CCP Constitution, the "highest leading bodies" of the Party are the National Party Congress (NPC) and the Central Committee (CC) that the NPC elects. However, the NPC is not a standing body that meets frequently or for extended periods of time; it typically meets only once every five years, for about one week.

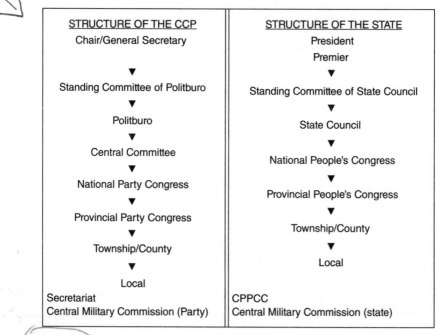

Figure A: Organizational Structure of the Chinese Party-State

Delegates, who number roughly 2,500 in total, are chosen mostly at the provincial level, but also include delegates from nine central Party-state organs and about 60 special delegates (see Chapter 3 for more details on the selection process for and demographic composition of NPC delegates).

The Constitution of the CCP states that the "functions and powers" of the NPC are as follows: to hear and examine the reports of the Party's Central Committee (CC) and the Central Commission for Discipline Inspection (CCDI); to discuss and decide on major questions concerning the Party; to revise the Constitution of the Party; and to elect the Party's Central Committee and Central Commission for Discipline Inspection. Though these sound like powerful responsibilities, in reality the NPC does not make decisions; instead, it ratifies decisions made at higher levels within the Party. Importantly, prior to a new meeting of the NPC, the "candidates" for the new CC and CCDI are agreed upon by high-ranking leaders within the Party Politburo and its Standing Committee. When the NPC meets, it is presented with the pre-selected list of candidates, and then proceeds to "elect" them (for more detail on the selection process for CC and CCDI members, see Chapter 3).

As noted above, the NPC also has the constitutional power to discuss and pass resolutions on Party policies and reports, and on amendments to the Party Constitution. At the NPC's most recent meeting in November 2012, it passed resolutions to approve reports made by various Party bodies (including the prior CC) and unanimously voted to accept the prior CC's proposed amended CCP Constitution. In other words, it put its rubber stamp on proposals and decisions made by other, more powerful, Party bodies, such as the CC. Thus, despite the words in the CCP Constitution, in reality, the NPC does not "decide on major questions" or itself "revise" the Party Constitution; instead, it legitimizes and approves decisions made at higher levels within the Party structure.

One level up from the NPC is the Party's Central Committee (CC) – a much more powerful body. The CC has far fewer members than the NPC, with a total of about 350. Moreover, the CC meets more frequently than the NPC, typically once or twice per year. When the NPC meets every five years, it elects a new CC. Each of these CCs is numbered; the current CC is the 18th, and it was chosen at the NPC meeting of November 2012. Each meeting of a given CC is called a "plenum;" typically, a CC holds one or two plenums a year. Unlike NPC delegates, which include a range of individuals who in their normal daily lives hold non-political positions or are engaged in non-political occupations, CC members generally occupy other high-ranking positions within the CCP. To ensure broad geographic representation on the CC, since 1997 the CC has included at least two members from each of China's provincial-level administrations, usually the provincial Party secretary and governor.[2] CC members are privy to insider Party information that is not made available to NPC delegates, and are given special privileges that NPC delegates do not receive.[3] At some CC meetings, important debates have occurred that have had an impact on policy and leadership selection. The most notable of these occurred in December of 1978, when the 3rd plenum of the 11th CC repudiated the Cultural Revolution, recognized Deng Xiaoping as the most powerful leader of the CCP, and supported the economic, social, and political changes that marked China's transition to its post-Mao "Reform Era."

But the CC is not where the real power lies within the CCP. One level higher than the CC is the CCP's Politburo, and one level higher than the Politburo is the Standing Committee (SC) of the Politburo. The Politburo does not have a set number of members. As of 2014, the Politburo (numbered the 18th, just as with the CC) has twenty-five members, but the total number has been as low as fourteen in earlier Politburos. Because Politburo meetings are not publicized, it is not possible to state for certain how often they are held, but most informed observers agree that such meetings occur roughly once per month. Virtually all Politburo members simultaneously hold other important Party and state posts. They, along with a few other powerful Party leaders who may or may not hold official positions within the Party structure – namely, Party elders – constitute the real "power elite" within the Party, and by extension China's Party-state, or government.

Even one step higher than the Politburo is the Standing Committee (SC) of the Politburo – the true pinnacle of political power in China. There is no set number of positions within the SC, but in recent years the total has hovered around seven (the number of seats in the SC as of 2014). The very top leader among SC members is the Party General Secretary, who as of 2014 is Xi Jinping. As with the Politburo, the meetings of the SC generally are not publicized. However, the group meets very frequently – usually once a week. This is where central policy, as well as future Party leadership, is determined. At the same time, throughout much of the post-Mao period, SC decisions also have been influenced by Party elders who no longer sit on the SC (or even on the Politburo, or may hold no current posts at all). A key example was Deng Xiaoping, who held no significant official Party posts (aside from being a member of the NPC) from late 1989 through his death in 1997, but in fact had ultimate decision-making power regarding Party leadership and policy until his passing. As of the time of this writing, former Party General Secretaries Jiang Zemin and Hu Jintao hold a similar – though markedly less powerful – status as "retired" Party elders.

There are some other important national Party bodies as well. The Secretariat, which is headed by the General Secretary, currently is mainly an administrative entity that prepares documents for the Politburo and SC, and translates decisions made by the Politburo and SC into more specific implementation instructions for relevant parts of the Party and state bureaucracy.[4] The central Organization Department

Secretariat

Org dept

Mao Zedong (1943–1976)
Hua Guofeng (1976–1981)
Hu Yaobang (1981–1987)
Zhao Ziyang (1987–1989)
Jiang Zemin (1989–2002)
Hu Jintao (2002–2012)
Xi Jinping (2012–)

Figure B: CCP Chairs/General Secretaries* in the People's Republic of China
*The title of CCP "Chair" was changed to "General Secretary" in 1982

(OD) oversees personnel appointments. As will be discussed more fully below, this is one of the key mechanisms by which the CCP maintains close control of the Chinese state. The OD's top leader is also a member of the Politburo, and often the Politburo SC as well. The Central Commission for Discipline Inspection (CCDI) is charged with investigating and meting out punishment for CCP cadre corruption; in recent years, it has conducted over 100,000 investigations a year. The Secretary of the CCDI typically is also a member of the SC of the Politburo.

The Party's Central Military Commission controls the Chinese military, which is known as the People's Liberation Army (PLA). In perhaps the perfect illustration of how the CCP controls all elements of the Chinese government, although the Chinese state structure also includes a Central Military Commission (CMC) that on paper is in charge of the PLA, the actual membership of the state CMC is identical to the membership of the Party CMC. That is, although the Party and state CMCs are two separate bodies on paper, in reality they are one and the same. And, all of the members of the Party and state CMC are high-ranking Party leaders. In fact, throughout virtually the entire history of the PRC, the chair of the Party and state CMCs has been the single most powerful person in China. This is because Chinese leaders from Mao through the present have recognized that "political power grows out of the barrel of a gun."

From the start of the PRC (and even before its establishment) through the death of Mao in 1976, Mao Zedong was the chair of the Party and state CMC. From 1981–1989, Deng Xiaoping was the CMC chair – even when (from 1987–1989) he no longer held any other high-level positions in the Party. During the massive student-led demonstrations centered in Beijing's central Tian'anmen Square in the spring of 1989, Deng was not the General Secretary of the Party (the post was then held by Zhao Ziyang), and he also was not a member of the Politburo or the SC of the Politburo. However, Deng remained the chair of the Party/state CMC, and was without question the most powerful political leader in China. Thus, Deng bears ultimate responsibility for the decision to use the Chinese military to clear out the protestors at the Square on June 3–4, 1989, which resulted in the deaths of hundreds, and perhaps thousands, of ordinary citizens, and the serious injury of many more. After the crack-down, and again under Deng's direction, Zhao Ziyang was dismissed from his post as General Secretary, and placed under house arrest, where he remained until his death. Jiang Zemin was appointed the new General Secretary in June of 1989, but did not become the CMC chair until November of 1989, when Deng finally stepped down. When Jiang Zemin finished his term as General Secretary and ceased to be a member of the Politburo (and its SC) in November of 2002, he retained the post of CMC chair until September 2004, when Hu Jintao (who had become General Secretary in November of 2002) took the post of CMC chair. In November of 2012, when Hu's term as General Secretary came to an end, he also stepped down as CMC chair, and the new General Secretary, Xi Jinping, became the CMC chair. This was seen as a sign of a more complete leadership transition.

Below the central level, the Party reaches all the way down to the village (in the countryside) and neighborhood (in the cities). China is divided into twenty-three provinces. It also has other geographic units that have the same status as provinces; in this category are four municipalities (the major cities of Beijing, Shanghai, Tianjin, and Chongqing), five autonomous regions (where most of China's ethnic minorities reside, such as in Tibet and Xinjiang), and two special administrative regions (the former colonies of Hong Kong and Macau, which returned to Chinese rule in the late 1990s) [see map, p. vi]. Below that are cities, counties, and townships. In the two years prior to a meeting of the National Party Congress, Party Congresses are held at each of these lower levels, to select delegates to the National Party Congress. Each of these levels also has a Party committee, or branch, as does every rural village and urban neighborhood. Unlike the Party Congresses, which meet only once every five years, Party committees and branches at these levels meet regularly to discuss policy implementation and affairs.

In sum, despite a Party Constitution that states otherwise, power within the CCP flows from the top to the bottom. Even so, in the post-Mao period top Party leaders increasingly have not made decisions in an insulated bubble or by fiat; rather, there has been a great deal of discussion and consultation within the Party, from the highest level to the lowest, such that decisions made at the top typically have reflected well-considered judgments based on a substantial amount of evidence and input. Indeed, the preferred method of decision-making has been to allow lower levels sufficient autonomy to experiment with new practices, such that the relative success and failure of various practices can be gauged, and the most successful can be endorsed and presented as national models. Thus, although the CCP's structure and distribution of power have not changed much since the time of Mao, in practice the Party has become much more open to discussion and debate based on empirical findings than was the case under Mao, when ideological principle (as defined by Mao) drove policy, and opinions deviating from these principles were castigated and smothered.

THE STRUCTURE AND COMPOSITION OF THE CHINESE STATE

The Party entities described above shadow and ultimately control every level of the Chinese state; thus, the structure of the Chinese state mirrors that of the CCP. As noted earlier, this design is intentional: the state was created by the CCP to serve its ends. The structure of Chinese state is similar to that of the CCP in that, on paper, its organizational hierarchy shows power flowing from the bottom to the top, but in reality power flows from top to bottom. At the same time, as has been the case with the CCP, the Chinese state in the post-Mao period has become more pragmatic in focus and has featured a slightly greater degree of consultation with and input from lower levels within the power hierarchy.

Just as the CCP's National Party Congress is described in the Party Constitution as the Party's highest leading body, China's state Constitution stipulates that the National People's Congress is the Chinese government's highest body. On paper, the National People's Congress is China's legislature. Its nearly 3,000 members meet once a year, usually in early March. National People's Congress representatives serve five-year terms, and are elected by provincial-level people's congresses (people's congresses also are held in China's municipalities, autonomous regions, and special administrative regions – all of which have provincial-level status in the government hierarchy). Provincial-level people's congresses are elected by township and county people's congresses, which are in turn elected by the people of that locality. However, as discussed in Chapter 3, these elections generally have not been free, fair, and competitive. Although the National People's Congress is charged with debating and passing legislation and amendments to the state constitution, and has the constitutional power to elect and approve top state leaders (most importantly, China's President and the Premier of the government's State Council), the annual meetings of the National People's Congress last only two weeks, and generally feature only the "rubber-stamp" passage of legislation, amendments, and leadership choices that have been handed to it by higher level political bodies dominated by the CCP. When a National People's Congress meeting concludes, the delegates are supposed to return to their localities and regular workplaces to convey the current policies and goals of the central political leadership.

Another informal function of the National People's Congress is to allow a venue of political representation and participation for potentially disaffected demographic groups. Perhaps most importantly, in a given session, roughly 30 percent of the National People's Congress delegates are not CCP members. Although this is far short of a majority, it allows some representation of views from outside the Party. Representatives of China's ethnic minorities also are included among National People's Congress delegates. This has received great attention in the CCP-affiliated media, in an apparent attempt to show that China's ethnic minorities (particularly those with a history of struggle against CCP/Chinese rule) are integrated within the political system.

Relative to the Maoist period (1949–1976), when the National People's Congress was completely obedient to the CCP and entirely docile, during the post-Mao period (1976–present) the National People's Congress on occasion has been approached by regular citizens for political support, has drafted its own legislation, and has even questioned central government/Party policies. During the student-led political protests in and near Beijing's Tian'anmen Square in the spring of 1989, students attempted to submit a petition to the National People's Congress during its March session, and intellectuals petitioned the National People's Congress to support an amnesty for political prisoners. Later that spring, roughly one-third of the members of the National People's Congress Standing Committee signed a petition (generated from within) asking central Party authorities to reconsider their decision to invoke Martial Law. In 1992, about one-third of all National People's Congress delegates voted against or abstained in a vote to support the central leadership's proposed Three Gorges Dam project in central China. In 2006, a new property law that was expected to pass the National People's Congress was postponed when leftist groups criticized the law (the law was approved by the National People's Congress the following year).[5] Since 2008, the National People's Congress has posted on its website some draft laws and invited the public to submit comments by post or e-mail. In 2012, for example, about 10,000 people submitted comments on a draft of a new environmental law. The National People's Congress also accepts citizen petitions, which since the start of the new millennium have numbered in the hundreds of thousands. Although virtually every new law that is passed by the National People's Congress is drafted by higher-level Party leaders, National People's Congress delegates regularly draft and submit hundreds of bills for consideration. However, only an infinitesimal portion of these National People's Congress -drafted bills are ever put on the National People's Congress agenda; from 1983–1993, for example, National People's Congress delegates drafted and submitted 3667 bills, but only four were actually placed on the agenda and discussed by the National People's Congress.[6] Overall, although in the post-Mao period the National People's Congress has become somewhat more autonomous and active, it still has no real power.

Much greater power lies in the Standing Committee (SC) of the National People's Congress, which at present has 175 members, each serving five-year terms. Technically, the SC is elected from among the delegates to each meeting of the National People's Congress, but in reality SC candidates are selected by the CCP's top leadership and then presented to the National People's Congress delegates for their vote of approval. Virtually all of the members of the SC are high-ranking CCP leaders, and the chair of the National People's Congress SC is always also on the SC of the CCP Politburo. Thus it was quite noteworthy when in 1989 many National People's Congress SC members signed the petition questioning the imposition of Martial Law. Since the full body of the National People's Congress meets for only two weeks, the SC takes care of the daily business of the National People's Congress. It typically meets once every other month.

Technically, the National People's Congress also chooses China's State Council, which on paper is equivalent to the executive Cabinet. In reality, members of the State Council are selected in the same fashion as are members of the National People's Congress SC, and they are almost always top CCP leaders. The head of the State Council is the Premier, who is chosen by the state President and approved by the National People's Congress. The Premier usually is the second-most-powerful official leader within the CCP, and is always also on the SC of the CCP Politburo. China's present Premier, Li Keqiang, was considered the main rival to current CCP General Secretary and state President Xi Jinping when former CCP General Secretary and state President Hu Jintao's term was coming to an end. During the Maoist period, the State Council was used as a mechanism to execute Party campaigns, such as the Great Leap Forward. In the post-Mao period, even though the State Council has remained firmly under the control of the Party (due in no small part to the fact that its leader – the Premier – and members are also high-ranking Party leaders), it has functioned with much more autonomy in administering the day-to-day affairs of the state, which is its primary charge.

Another central government body – the Chinese People's Political Consultative Conference (CPPCC) – meets once every five years, at the same time as the National People's Congress. The simultaneous meetings of both bodies are known colloquially and officially as the "Two Meetings" (*lianghui*). However, officially, the CPPCC is not a part of the state. The CPPCC originally was created before the CCP officially took control of China; it was designed to bring together the various political parties and groups in existence at the time, and to allow them some input and representation in the new regime. These parties have continued to legally exist in China throughout the period of CCP rule, and the CPPCC has continued to have this representative function. Thus, when CCP leaders claim that China allows multiple political parties to exist, they are making an accurate statement – there are eight legal political parties in China other than the CCP.[7] The CPPCC also includes representatives from China's official labor unions and other trade and professional groups, ethnic minorities, and some specially selected individuals. There are about 2,100 representatives within the CPPCC. The CPPCC also has a Standing Committee with just under 300 members; lower-level CPPCC bodies exist at the provincial level and below as well.

Although the CPPCC is officially described as a consultative body that allows non-CCP parties and groups to "exercise democratic supervision," the chair of the CPPCC and its SC is almost always a high-ranking CCP leader who also sits on the SC of the CCP's Politburo. This is true of the current CPPCC chair, Yu Zhengsheng, who stated at the March 2013 general meeting of the CPPCC that "we need to steadfastly uphold the leadership of the Communist Party of China."[8] In other words, the CPPCC leadership has no intention of challenging CCP rule. Nonetheless, as with the National People's Congress, relative to the Maoist period, the CPPCC in the post-Mao era has played a somewhat more active consultative role. And, this is not by accident; the central CCP leadership has consciously worked to make this happen. In 2005, for example, a CCP Central Committee document explicitly called for greater consultation with and input from the CPPCC. Accordingly, since the early part of the first decade of the new millennium, top CCP leaders (including former Party General Secretary Hu Jintao and members of the CCP Politburo) have held dozens of forums with the CPPCC. Further, in 2007, two non-CCP members of the CPPCC were appointed to top posts in the State Council (the Minister of Health and the Minister of Science and Technology).[9]

At the central level, the Chinese state also has a number of other bodies, including the state Central Military Commission (discussed above), and twenty-two ministries devoted to different topical areas, such as the Ministry of Education and the Ministry of Foreign Affairs. Each Ministry is headed by a Minister chosen by the President (who, recall, is also the General Secretary of the Party). The rank of Minister is equal in hierarchical status to that of a provincial governor. Ministries also have myriad sub-offices (bureaus, administrations, commissions, authorities, etc.) that deal with the many sub-issues under the purview of that Ministry.

In addition, the State Council oversees the official Chinese news agency, Xinhua (pronounced "shin-hwah"; literally, "New China"). Simultaneously, Xinhua is part of the central government's Central Propaganda Department. Like virtually all important government offices, Xinhua is headed by a top CCP leader. As a news service, it produces news stories. These stories appear in the official national newspaper of the CCP – the People's Daily – as well as in many other Chinese media outlets (including Chinese-language media outlets outside of China). Xinhua also has its own news website. Regarding domestic and foreign events and incidents that the CCP deems to be of extremely serious concern, all official Chinese media outlets are required to print or air Xinhua's report on the subject word-for-word.[10] Like the Chinese state as a whole, Xinhua exists to serve the interests of the CCP. Even so, its news coverage in the post-Mao era has been much less political than was the case in the Maoist period.

Below the central level, state institutions exist at the provincial, county/city,[11] township, and village/neighborhood levels. All of the central ministries and other executive bodies have provincial offices, and some have county/city, township, and village/neighborhood offices as well. Depending on the size of a given locality, as well as the importance of a central ministry or other executive body's charge to that locality, a central ministry or other central body may have only one official representative, or may not have an official representative at all. For example, each village typically has a representative of the Health and Family Planning Commission, to oversee and enforce China's "one child" policy. This is because the "one child" policy universally affects all villagers, and has been perceived by central leaders to be of great importance. But other central bodies that are seen as less critical may not have a local representative, and some poor localities lack official representatives of central bodies due to a lack of resources (e.g., they may be unable to pay local officials' salaries, or they may have such a low living standard that there are no takers for the position). For example, some villages do not have a representative of the office of the Ministry of Civil Affairs or a representative of the State Administration for Religious Affairs. Yet in China, all religious groups are required to register with the state through both of these institutions. In such localities, some religious groups simply go about their activities without any governmental knowledge or oversight.

Each province, county/city, and township also has a general government office, which includes a top leader for that level, such as the governor of each province. Positions within general government offices and ministerial offices at the township level and higher are appointed, and the vast majority (though not all) of office-holders are CCP members.

At the village level, the official state body is the village council. As noted in Chapter 1, in 1987, a new law was promulgated stipulating that village councils would be elected by a popular vote, with all adult residents eligible to vote and run for office. Today, in the vast majority of China's villages, this is the case. More details on how these elections have worked, and what kinds of candidates have been elected, is found in Chapter 3.

In cities, the lowest level of state (and Party) administration is the neighborhood, or *shequ*. Prior to the mid-1990s, the primary local urban administrative unit was not the neighborhood but the work unit (*danwei*) in the state-owned enterprise (SOE) in which an urban resident was employed. During this period, the *danwei* provided virtually all social services at the local level. When most of China's SOEs were privatized in the late 1990s, most urban residents no longer had a *danwei* to fulfill this function, and the CCP lost this method of contact with and control over the urban citizenry. Prior to large-scale SOE privatization, some smaller SOEs had been privatized, and the CCP had allowed some localities to experiment with new types of local administration. The merits and demerits of the new experimental types were then debated, both in academia and in Party and state bodies. In

1998, when large-scale SOE privatization took off, the CCP made a concerted national push to establish "residents' committees" (RCs) in all urban neighborhoods. The stated goal was to promote citizen participation in local leadership and public service provision. And, as was the case regarding China's rural village councils, the RCs were to be elected by the local population. In the middle of the first decade of the new millennium, the Chinese government further recommended that the Party Secretary of each neighborhood stand for election as head of the RC, and similarly that a new neighborhood Party Secretary should be appointed only if s/he had first been elected by local residents to be the head of the RC.[12] Thus, as in China's local rural communities, urban residents currently have the legal right to vote for and elect their local "state" leadership. And, this citizen oversight has even extended to local Party leadership. Nonetheless, as will be discussed more fully in Chapter 3, these elections have remained far from legitimate in most cases. Moreover, the goal of these elections has been to solidify and strengthen CCP leadership, not to challenge it.

INFORMAL/UNOFFICIAL POLITICAL ENTITIES

As noted at the start of this chapter, the Chinese political system – as with all political systems – also has powerful informal and unofficial entities that in some cases overshadow and control formal and official bodies. Thus, in order to understand the Chinese political system, we must look beyond the offices and institutions that are explicitly discussed on paper. In China, the most important informal/unofficial political entities are "functional systems" (*xitong*), "central leading small groups," and Party groups (*dangzu*). If you look in the Party or state Constitution, you will find no mention of these entities, and if you search the Party and state's organization charts and publications, you will not see these entities listed. Even the most knowledgeable of China scholars do not know exactly who is a part of these entities. And yet it is within these entities that many important political decisions – regarding both leadership appointments and policies – are made.

Functional systems, or *xitong*, are composed of Party and state units that deal with a broadly similar task, such as Propaganda/Education, Political/Legal Affairs, or Finance/Economics. The precise composition of a *xitong* is not fixed, and can change according to what top CCP leaders deem appropriate. Further, a given Party or state entity can be part of multiple *xitong*. *Xitong* include entities from highest levels of the political system to the lowest that relate to that issue.

One of the most important *xitong* is focused on organizational affairs: its members decide who will be appointed to state and Party positions. In each territorial unit (e.g., province, county) the Party and state entities are charged with overseeing organization and personnel work together, maintaining and updating dossiers on all current and potential appointees. The information in the dossiers is then used to determine who will be appointed to which positions. Another powerful *xitong* deals with Party affairs. It has thousands of major participants, including the CCP General Secretary, the Party Secretary of each province and provincial-level unit, and the Party heads of every lower-level unit. Its main purposes are to ensure that Party policies and priorities are being followed at all levels, to resolve disputes within territorial levels, and to enable Party leaders at lower levels to advocate for the interests of their territorial unit. A third key *xitong* deals with propaganda/education. It includes the Party's Central Propaganda Department, as well as all media outlets, schools, and cultural entities (such as museums).[13] The other three most important *xitong* focus on political/legal affairs (including all courts, police and public security units, prisons, customs units, as well as the Party Central Discipline Inspection Commission); finance/economics (including the banking system, state-owned enterprises, and the Ministry of Finance); and the military (including the People's Liberation Army, the state and Party Military Affairs Commissions, and the Ministry of Defense). Thus, *xitong* are a key mechanism through which the Party is deeply intertwined with the state, and are one reason that it is more accurate to describe China's political system as a "Party-state" than as a system with a separate Party and state.

One step higher in terms of informal/unofficial power are central leading small groups (CLSGs), which typically act as the leadership of each *xitong*. Usually, each member of the CCP Politiburo SC is tasked with a particular subject area, and will serve on the CLSG for that subject.[14] Thus, CLSGs are closely controlled by top CCP leaders. There are also Leading Small Groups for more specific topic areas, such as the Taiwan Work Leading Small Group. As with *xitong*, the precise membership of CLSGs is not revealed publicly. But these leaders have a great deal of power to shape policies and priorities in their respective issue domains. And their behind-closed-doors work ensures that the CCP remains in firm control of all governing bodies.

Finally, each state entity has within it a Party group (*dangzu*). These groups are appointed by the Party's Central Organization Department, and are responsible for overseeing the activities of all officials within that entity – regardless of whether or not the officials in question are all Party members.[15] Thus, Party groups are yet another mechanism through which the CCP maintains oversight and control over all state activities.

CONCLUSION: PARTY-STATE RELATIONS

In sum, although the CCP and the Chinese state have separate constitutions and organizational structures, they are in fact deeply intertwined, and the CCP remains firmly in charge of China's state. This is seen both in the formal and official entities that comprise the Party and state, and in the informal and unofficial entities that are less visible, but in many ways more powerful. On paper, the formal/official structures of the Party and state are mirror images of one another, such that each Party entity has its state counter-part. And in some cases – such as the Military Affairs Commission – the membership of both the state and the Party entity is identical. In virtually all other cases, the people who lead the most important state entities are the same people who lead the most important Party entities; as noted above, for example, the Premier of the State Council is always also a member of the CCP's highest leading body – the Standing Committee of the Politburo.

In addition, there are numerous informal/unofficial mechanisms through which the CCP maintains its dominance. Perhaps most notably, the Organizational Affairs *xitong* keeps close tabs on all sitting and potential political appointees in both the state and the Party, and based on these records decides who will occupy which positions. Thus, if a sitting or potential appointee runs afoul of Party policies – and especially if such a person openly criticizes the Party or engages in political dissent – his or her political career will suffer, or come to an abrupt end. Simultaneously CLSGs maintain central Party control over all *xitong*, with the members of the Party's Politburo SC each tasked with a topic area covered by a CLSG. And in each Party and state entity from the top of the system to the bottom, Party groups appointed by the Party's central leadership oversee all activities.

Yet even so, relative to the Maoist period, in the post-Mao era relations between the Party and state have become slightly more regularized and professionalized, as the Party's focus has been on pragmatism (in the service of both economic growth and continued CCP rule) rather than ideological correctness, which in the Maoist period led to radical political campaigns, such as the Great Leap Forward and the Great Proletarian Cultural Revolution. And because the Party in the post-Mao period has come to recognize that the stability of its rule rests in large part on its ability to respond effectively to social dissatisfaction as economic reform and growth bring continual change to people's lives, the Party has made some effort to become more consultative from within, and to allow state entities a slightly greater ability to participate in political decision-making. As was the case under Mao, the Party sees the Chinese state as a vehicle through which to pursue Party goals, but in the post-Mao period the Party's goals have led it to see its relationship with the people in a fundamentally different way. And as will be seen in Chapter 3, this change has led to a notable transformation in the way in which Party-state officials are selected, in which types of people have become political leaders, and in the basis upon which they have formulated policies.

3 Who Serves in the Party-State?

As discussed in Chapter 2, the structures of the CCP and the Chinese state have not dramatically changed in the post-Mao era, and neither has their relationship; the Chinese state continues to be a creation of the CCP, existing to serve the Party's ends. Yet in the post-Mao period, the CCP's goal has been fundamentally different from that of the Maoist era. Under Mao, the CCP aimed to establish a communist society, characterized by economic prosperity and economic equality, and led by the CCP. The CCP, in turn, based its legitimacy on its claim to be the representative of China's working masses. In the post-Mao era, the CCP has sought to achieve economic prosperity and political stability, underscored by the assertion that only CCP leadership of the political system can achieve this. And, since the early part of the first decade of the new millennium, the CCP explicitly has claimed to represent not only the working masses, but the entire Chinese populace – including capitalists and intellectuals, groups that were castigated and excluded from the Party under Mao.

This change in goal has been manifested in significant changes in the criteria and processes for CCP membership and ascension within the Party, including leadership succession at the highest levels. Overall, the CCP's membership and leadership have become younger and more educated over the course of the post-Mao period. Concurrently, the representation of different socio-economic groups (e.g., college-educated professionals, blue-collar workers, and peasants) within the CCP has shifted. Equally consequential changes have

occurred in the selection processes for and the demographic composition of the various entities that comprise China's state structure. Most
importantly, mechanisms for public input and assessment – including
meaningful elections for some positions – have been implemented.
Concomitant with these changes, Party and state elites at various levels
have come to formulate their policy preferences and perceive their tasks
in different ways.

Overall, during the course of the post-Mao period China's governing institutions have become more representative of the population and
more open to popular input. These changes have made both the Party
and the state far more responsive to public grievances than was the case
during the Mao era. In this sense, China's political system has moved
somewhat closer to the democratic end of the political spectrum in the
post-Mao period. Yet even so, top CCP leaders show no intention of
transforming China into a competitive multi-party democracy with
elections at the highest level. Indeed, the democratic changes that have
transpired in the post-Mao period have been motivated by Party
leaders' desire to *strengthen* CCP rule.

PARTY MEMBERSHIP SELECTION PROCESSES AND CRITERIA

From the time of Mao to the present, membership in the CCP has
been an exclusive privilege offered to select members of the populace
who have gone through an intensive screening process. As noted above,
during the Maoist period, the CCP based its legitimacy on its claim to
represent the working masses. Accordingly, membership within the
Party was open only to those with unquestionable class "credentials"
and communist commitment. In large part, this meant that persons
coming from peasant or blue-collar worker family backgrounds were
privileged in the application process. Persons who themselves had what

in the West could be considered a higher socio-economic status, or whose family had been more privileged in the past (prior to communist rule) generally were not eligible. This included landlords, wealthy peasants, merchants, factory owners and managers, and intellectuals. It also included anyone whose family had collaborated with the CCP's earlier enemy, the Kuomintang (KMT). During the Mao era's Great Proletarian Cultural Revolution (1966–1976) the Party castigated persons belonging to what it referred to as the "Nine Black Categories:" landlords, wealthy peasants, "counter-revolutionaries," "bad influences," "right-wingers," "traitors," "spies," "capitalist roaders," and intellectuals. Falling last in this list, during this period intellectuals commonly were referred to as the "Stinking Old Ninth."

Yet even among those who had a clearly peasant or working-class status, Party membership was far from automatic. In order to join the Party, one was required to submit a formal application (supported by two sponsors) and undergo a probationary period of assessment. The process took years to complete. Those seeking entrance into the Party typically worked from a young age to establish their communist credentials, often first seeking membership in the Party's exclusive Young Pioneers (for children aged six to thirteen) and Communist Youth League (for youths between the ages of fourteen and twenty-eight). During the probationary period, information about the person was collected from the applicant him/herself and also through official channels. This was done to test the trustworthiness of the applicant. The applicant had to declare loyalty to the Party, and attend study sessions organized by Party members and organizations. Throughout, the applicant's behavior and conduct were evaluated, as was that of their family members. Next, members of the local Party branch would vote on whether or not to allow the applicant to move to the next stage. If successful, the candidate would be allowed to begin a one-year probationary period, during which s/he would be able to participate in Party activities, but would not have voting rights. Only after successfully passing scrutiny during this period would s/he be allowed to become a full Party member. Just a select few made it to this stage.[1]

In the post-Mao period, Party membership has remained exclusive, with applicants subject to the same strict application and screening process, and membership in the Young Pioneers and Communist Youth League still viewed as a vehicle to future entrance into the Party. However, the Party's focus changed dramatically in the years following the December 1978 meeting of the 3rd plenum of the 11th CCP Central Committee. At this meeting, CCP elites repudiated the Cultural Revolution, embraced the pragmatist Deng Xiaoping as the CCP's most powerful leader, and endorsed economic reform and modernization. As a result, the Party shifted its focus from cultivating and seeking out "redness" (i.e., communist ideological purity) to cultivating and seeking out "experts" – particularly those with expertise in science, technology and engineering. The "Stinking Old Ninth" category of intellectuals now was viewed as a valuable asset in the CCP's new quest for economic modernization. China's universities, which had been closed during much of the Cultural Revolution (and even when open during the Maoist period generally featured only "communist" education in Party ideology and manual labor) were re-opened. And, a new national college entrance exam was instituted, focusing more on academic knowledge than on communist ideology.

Despite the CCP's new attitude toward higher education and intellectuals, many college students and intellectuals initially remained wary of the Party, and showed little interest in joining it. The memory of their mistreatment during the Maoist period was fresh, resulting in a deep cynicism toward the Party and communism in general. In the 1980s, Party membership among university enrollees hovered around 2–5 percent. In the spring of 1989 college students took to the streets in Beijing and China's other major cities to demand further political reform. The movement culminated in an extended sit-in and hunger strike in central Beijing's Tian'anmen Square that ultimately was ended with violent force by the CCP, resulting in the deaths of hundreds, and perhaps thousands, of citizens.

Yet in the early 1990s, the CCP did not reject college students due to their participation in the protests of 1989. To the contrary, the Party stepped up its efforts to recruit them. And they responded enthusiastically. This was not because college students were ardent communists; rather, their desire to join the Party was based on pragmatism: they viewed Party membership as a means to attain material comfort and high social status. For most of the 1980s, the government assigned jobs to college graduates. But since the early 1990s, those with a secondary education have had to fend for themselves in the job market. In this context, Party membership has come to be seen as an important way to improve one's job prospects. For, Party members are seen by potential employers as reliable, intelligent, and hard-working – and as having helpful political connections. Consequently, the portion of university students who are CCP members has risen exponentially from the early 1990s through the present. In 1990, less than one percent of college attendees had been accepted to the Party; by 2001, this percentage had increased to 8 percent. Surveys conducted in the early 2000s found that 50 percent of new college students expressed interest in joining the Party. Among graduate students, by 2000, nearly 30 percent were Party members. According to *Xinhua*, as of 2013, over 40 percent of all CCP members had a degree from a higher education institution.[2] Further, whereas in 1978 (the beginning of the post-Mao period), less than 13 percent of Party members were high-school graduates, by 2002 nearly 53 percent had attained this level of education.[3] Thus, the Party has become far more educated (in the Western sense of the word) over time. And, in this respect its membership has changed drastically from the Maoist period, when individuals with an academic or intellectual background were looked down upon and excluded from the Party.

In the early years of the new millennium, another momentous change occurred in terms of Party membership: business owners ("capitalists" in communist parlance) were allowed openly to join the Party, and indeed were encouraged to do so. This change was even more monumental than the Party's changed attitude toward intellectuals: a "communist" Party was embracing "capitalists." From the mid-1950s through Mao's death in 1976, private entrepreneurs generally were scorned as "capitalist roaders" and faced substantial restrictions and punishment. On top of that, all major businesses were state-owned. In this atmosphere, there were virtually no private business owners in existence, and certainly none in the Party.

During the first part of the post-Mao period, the Party slowly changed its attitude – first tolerating very small-scale private businesses (such as street-side fruit-stands, shoe-repair services, and improvised taxis). Yet throughout most of the 1980s, private entrepreneurs remained politically suspect and subject to discrimination, as well as periodic punishment and castigation by the authorities. Even so, private businesses proliferated and expanded. And some became quite profitable. Most of the more successful and larger-scale business owners had close connections with Party-state officials, and some were themselves Party members. As of the end of the 1980s, only one percent of private entrepreneurs were Party members, and virtually all of them had joined the Party prior to their entry into business; private entrepreneurs seeking Party membership generally were not admitted.[4]

From the late 1980s through the present, the Party has moved from tolerating to embracing private business. In 1988, the state Constitution was amended to say that the state "encourages" and "supports" (but also "guides") the development of China's private sector. In early 1992, the Party's most powerful leader, Deng Xiaoping, made a much-touted "Southern tour" of "Special Economic Zones" that had been established in a number of southern and eastern cities beginning in the late 1970s, where experiments with foreign investment and free markets had been allowed. Deng declared the experiments a great success, and called for further economic liberalization. At the 14th meeting of the

National Party Congress in late 1992, Deng's appeal was enshrined in official doctrine, which now openly called for the establishment of a "socialist market economy," and stated that economic growth was the country's highest priority. As the clear engine of China's remarkable economic growth at the time, private business gained a much-elevated status. In 1994, China's first Company Law came into effect, allowing for the establishment of limited liability shareholding corporations. At the 15th National Party Congress in 1997, private enterprise was described as an "important" element of China's economy, and in 1999, the state Constitution was modified to reflect this shift in status. Further, Party cadres no longer were restrained from engaging in private enterprise. In 2002, the Party made a final step toward embracing private entrepreneurs. This occurred as part of the Party's adoption of then CCP General Secretary Jiang Zemin's idea of the "Three Represents." This notion states that the CCP represents "advanced culture," the "interests of the majority of citizens," and China's "advanced productive forces." Importantly, "advanced productive forces" include private entrepreneurs. Since the "Three Represents" were endorsed by the 16th Plenum of the CCP National Party Congress in 2002, private entrepreneurs have been not only allowed to join the Party, but encouraged to do so. And, as has been the case with college-educated individuals, private entrepreneurs have responded enthusiastically. By 2011, 40 percent were Party members – comprising 6 percent of the Party's total membership. Moreover, over 90 percent of China's 1,000 wealthiest individuals are government officials and/or Party members.[5] The Chinese Communist Party is clearly no longer the representative of solely the "working masses."

Even so, small-scale family farmers and blue-collar workers continue to comprise a substantial percentage of Party members. As of 2013, roughly 44 percent of all CCP members fell into these categories.[6] However, this marks a dramatic reduction from the Maoist period, when nearly two-thirds of CCP members were peasants or rank-and-file workers. And, the trend over the course of the entire post-Mao period has been a continual and consistent decline in the percentage of CCP members from these demographic groups.

The percentage of female CCP members remains small, at just under 23 percent in 2011. But, this number has been slowly growing over the course of the past decade. Women made up 17 percent of CCP members in 2002, 19 percent in 2005, and 20 percent in 2007.

Overall, the number of CCP members and their proportion of the population has risen over the course of the post-Mao period. In 1982, there were approximately 40 million CCP members among a population of just over 1 billion, or 4 percent of the population. As of 2011, there were roughly 82 million CCP members among a population of over 1.3 billion, or just over 6 percent of the population. In June 2014, the CCP Central Committee announced new rules for recruiting CCP members. These rules were intended to make Party membership somewhat more exclusive, calling for stricter scrutiny and higher standards for new members – including an emphasis on a candidate's belief in "communism and socialism with Chinese characteristics."[7] It is not clear how the latter will be evaluated. However, given the Party's current emphasis on eradicating political corruption, as well as its embrace of many aspects of capitalism, ideological correctness is likely to be seen more in terms of behavioral integrity than as adherence to Mao-era notions of "redness." The 2014 CC document also calls for the dismissal of unqualified and/or corrupt Party members. As a result, growth in CCP membership may slow.

In sum, the criteria by which the Party evaluates and selects members have changed dramatically in the post-Mao period, and the Party's demographic composition has changed accordingly. The Party excluded and castigated many categories of people during the Maoist period, and focused on "redness," or ideological purity as its main membership requirement. In the post-Mao period, the Party has cast a much wider net in terms of the demographic groups that it has admitted to its ranks, such that groups (including college students, intellectuals, and private entrepreneurs) that previously were shunned now comprise a notable and growing portion of CCP members. Although the Party still considers loyalty to the Party a pre-eminent requirement for membership, the Party's selection criteria clearly have changed. Today, the Party seeks out applicants of high "quality," which can include education, wealth, integrity, hard work, and good citizenship.

PARTY LEADERSHIP SELECTION PROCESSES

Similar changes have transpired in terms of CCP leadership. During the Maoist period, ideological correctness – as defined by Mao – was the main determinant of a person's ability to rise through the Party ranks. There was no clear or consistent term of office, or leadership selection or succession processes. At the top level of the Party, Mao remained the dominant CCP leader for decades; only his death in 1976 ended his leadership. During the very long period of Mao's rule, Mao (with the agreement of other top Party leaders) had final say over who would sit on the Standing Committee of the Politburo and other high-level Party and state bodies. When two top CCP leaders – Liu Shaoqi and Lin Biao – successively fell out of Mao's favor during the Cultural Revolution, they were ruthlessly castigated in public wall posters and official media outlets. In 1968, Liu, who since the mid-1930s had been recognized as second to Mao within the Party, was publicly branded China's "number one capitalist-roader," stripped of all Party and state posts, and jailed. He died wrapped naked in a bed-sheet on the floor, due to a lack of proper medical treatment for pneumonia. His wife was tortured and jailed for twelve years. Those who were able to avoid this fate and remain in Mao's favor generally remained in the Party's top leadership positions until their death.

Other Party leaders who fell out of favor were stripped of their official posts and punished (often with banishment to the countryside to engage in manual labor). But, if the political winds shifted and they regained official favor, these individuals could be "rehabilitated" and brought back into Party leadership positions. This happened most notably to Deng Xiaoping, who was criticized and punished but subsequently "rehabilitated" three times before he finally consolidated power and assumed control of the Party from 1978 through his death in 1997. During Mao's Cultural Revolution, which spanned 1966–1976, a large percentage of Party leaders were castigated and punished (including Liu Shaoqi and Deng Xiaoping). Mao believed that these cadres lacked sufficient "redness," or communist commitment, and were too supportive of pragmatic policies that focused on success more than ideological correctness. Although Deng had supported many Maoist policies in the past, he was at heart a pragmatist; his pragmatic outlook was encapsulated in his famous statement that "it doesn't matter if the cat is black or white, as long as it catches the mouse." As Mao became increasingly ill in the early 1970s (he had amyotrophic lateral sclerosis (ALS), also known as "Lou Gehrig's Disease") and CCP Vice-Chair and State Premier Zhou Enlai increasingly took the administrative helm of the Party, most of the pragmatic cadres who had been punished earlier in the Cultural Revolution were "rehabilitated" and regained their prior posts. These cadres became key supporters of Deng's rise to become the most powerful leader within the Party in the years following Mao's death.

When Deng Xiaoping assumed the Party helm, he instituted a number of important changes in the Party's leadership selection and succession process, with the intention of making these processes more predictable and regularized, and of bringing new blood into the Party's top positions. To consolidate the Party's revised goal of economic modernization and reform, Deng also spearheaded an effort to bring in new and younger leaders, as well as cadres with more technical expertise. Among the membership of the CCP Central Committee of 1982 – the first to meet after the 1978 NPC Plenum at which Deng was recognized as the Party's most powerful leader and his reform program was endorsed – 60 percent were first-timers on the CC and nearly 56 percent were college-educated (as opposed to less than 24 percent in 1969). Since then, the percentage of college-educated members of the CC has grown to nearly 100 percent, and the percentage of new CC members on each CC has hovered between 60 and 65 percent. In terms of expertise, for roughly the first twenty years of the post-Mao period, the percentage of CC members with a technocratic background (in particular, engineering) rose – from 2 percent in 1982 to 51 percent in 1997. Since 1997, there has been a decrease in CC members with a technocratic background (36 percent in 2007) but a commensurate increase in those with a social science background. Among the seven members of the current (18th) SC of the Politburo, three are econo-mists by training. The average age of CC members went down from roughly 67 in 1982 to approximately 58 in 1985, and the average age has remained in the high 50s since that time.[8] Thus, a different kind of person – younger, more educated, and more pragmatic – has come to occupy the Party's top posts in the post-Mao period.

Deng also worked to regularize leadership succession at the very top – the Politburo, the SC of the Politburo, and the position of Party General Secretary. Although Deng remained the Party's most powerful leader until his death in 1997, he never took on the title of Party "Chair" or "General Secretary," and in fact abolished the title of Party "Chair" that Mao had used. Deng also stepped down from the SC of the Politburo. To encourage other elderly leaders to do the same, Deng created a new Party "Central Advisory Commission" (CAC) comprised of elderly leaders who were still very powerful, but would no longer sit on the SC of the Politburo. The CAC was designed to temporarily serve as a way to transition these elderly leaders out of formal positions of power. Deng wanted to end the Mao-era practice whereby leaders remained in office until their death. Deng served as Chair of the CAC until 1987, when he stepped down from both this post and the

Politburo. In 1992, the CAC was abolished entirely. Deng remained the chair of the Party/state Central Military Commission until the fall of 1989, but upon his retirement from that post he no longer held a high-level position within the Party. Though he remained the Party's most powerful leader through his death in 1997, he purposefully did not retain commensurate Party titles, due to his resolve to end the norm of lifetime leadership practiced under Mao.

During the 1980s, movement toward a more institutionalized succession of power at the top was fitful at best. Deng's first chosen successor to the position of Party General Secretary – Hu Yaobang – was dismissed from this post in 1987 due to his perceived support of student-led demonstrations for greater political reform. It was Hu's death two years later that sparked the massive student-led protests of April-June 1989. And the person that Deng had chosen to replace Hu as Party General Secretary – Zhao Ziyang – was dismissed from this post in June of 1989 for his perceived support of the student-led demonstrations that had been sparked by Hu's death. As noted earlier, Zhao remained under house arrest until his death in 2005.

From the 1990s through the present, the leadership succession process has stabilized, to the point that it is now quite regularized – at least relative to the past. The person chosen to replace Zhao as General Secretary in June of 1989 was Jiang Zemin. Once Deng felt secure in this choice (in November of 1989), he stepped down as chair of the Central Military Commission and Jiang assumed this position. At the 16th National Party Congress in 2002, Jiang voluntarily stepped down as Party General Secretary – the first time in CCP history that a person in the top Party post did not either die in office or be forced out and punished. Hu Jintao became the new General Secretary. As Deng had done, Jiang did not immediately retire as chair of the Central Military Commission; rather, he remained in this position for two years, until the fall of 2004. Thus, for this period there was some confusion as to who was the more powerful leader, Hu or Jiang. When

Jiang stepped down as CMC chair in 2004, Hu assumed this position. After serving two five-year terms as General Secretary, in the fall of 2012 Hu stepped down and was replaced by Xi Jinping, who is also expected to serve two five-year terms. Unlike Deng and Jiang, Hu did not hold on to the position of CMC chair after retiring as General Secretary; since the fall of 2012 Xi has been both Party General Secretary and CMC chair. Assuming that these most recent succession practices continue, the Party will have come a long way in terms of regularizing its leadership transition process.

The Party also has slowly moved toward a clear retirement age for senior Party leaders. At the 15th National Party Congress in 1997, all Politburo and SC members over the age of 70 – with the exception of then Party General Secretary Jiang Zemin – stepped down. At the 16th and 17th NPCs (in 2002 and 2007), all over the age of 68 stepped down. Regarding the most recent NPC in 2012, the official media reported that there is now a "rigorous rule" that Politburo SC members must retire by age 68. The stated aim is to "ensure political stability and set an example for the transfer of power in the future."[9]

For most of the post-Mao period, the occupants of Party posts have been chosen by Party leaders one level higher than the post in question. Thus, central leaders have chosen provincial leaders, and so on. At the lowest level of the Party – the village or neighborhood Party branch/committee – leaders at the next higher level (the township, city or county) have chosen candidates for the local Party Secretary. However, in both rural villages and urban neighborhoods, mechanisms of popular consent have been built into the local Party leader selection process over the past decade or so. In the countryside, since the late 1990s it has become increasingly common for villagers – including non-Party members – to participate in the selection process for village Party Secretaries. In many areas, a "two-ballot" system has been implemented, whereby all adult villagers get to vote their approval or disapproval of potential candidates for village Party Secretary. Only those candidates receiving 50 percent or more of the villagers' votes can be selected by the township Party committee as a candidate for the position. Village Party members then vote their approval or disapproval of this candidate. In other rural areas, a person can be eligible for the position of Village Party Secretary only if s/he is first elected to the village council, which, as will be discussed in more detail below, is chosen via the popular vote of all adult villagers (again, including non-Party members).[10] Similarly, in urban areas, since the early part of the new millennium, the Party has recommended that local Party Secretary candidates only be allowed to fill this post if they first are elected by the neighborhood residents to serve as the head of the neighborhood residents' committee.[11] Via these mechanisms, the Party has been making an effort to ensure that local Party leaders have the support of the people within their jurisdiction. In other words, the Party has made the selection of its leaders at the local level more democratic.

At higher levels efforts also have been made to increase popular input in the selection process. In the Mao era, in Party committee elections at the county, municipal, and provincial levels, there was only one candidate per seat on the ballot (thus rendering the election nothing but a formality). In the post-Mao period, the Party has introduced the requirement that there be "more candidates than seats." Although typically there have been only about 10 percent more candidates than seats, if a candidate's vote count has been within the bottom 10 percent, s/he has not been elected. This has been a way for the Party to weed out candidates that are opposed by the constituents of that body. In other words, it represents a small move toward the more democratic end of the political spectrum.

The process by which delegates to China's provincial Party congresses and National Party Congress (NPC) are chosen also has become more regularized, competitive, and consultative, but still remains highly politicized. Roughly eighteen months prior to the year in which a new NPC is scheduled to meet (which, as discussed in

Chapter 2, occurs every five years), Party committees at the provincial, municipality, county, and township level undergo a renewal and/or change in their membership – a process that involves some thirty million Party cadres. As noted above, cadres one level above choose new cadres to fill the positions below them. However, also as noted above, there have been some mechanisms introduced to make this process more open to input from below.

The NPC includes representatives from China's thirty-one provinces and provincial-level administrative units, as well as delegates from nine central Party-state organs (including delegations from the central organizations of the Party, the ministries/commissions of the state, state-owned enterprises, state-controlled banks, the People's Liberation Army, and the People's Armed Police) and special constituencies (including delegations of ethnic Taiwanese, and representatives from Hong Kong and Macao). A few dozen "special delegates," such as elderly retired Party leaders, also are invited to attend. For all but the "special delegates," the constituencies from each of the bodies listed above are given the power (at least on paper) to elect their delegates.

Officially, this election process begins with candidate nominations made by members of local Party branches, whereupon Party committees at the next higher level (the county or municipality) decide on a proposed nominees list, after which the standing committees of the Party committees decide on the final nominee list and submit that to the Party committee at the next higher level. Next, the Organization Department at that level conducts in-depth background checks on the potential nominees (remember that each individual has an official dossier detailing his/her life history, as well as that of his/her family). After this, the list of candidates is made public so that members of the constituency can voice their opinions. Following this, members of the full Party committee for each constituency discuss and vote on the candidates. Subsequently, the list is submitted to the Central

Organization Department for investigation. Finally, the existing Party Congress for each constituency holds elections.[12]

During the Maoist period, the ultimate slate of candidates included only one candidate per position. Thus, the final "election" of NPC delegates was only a formality. During the post-Mao period, an effort has been made to introduce at least a modicum of competition into the electoral process, with the requirement that "more candidates than seats" be on the final list. Progress has been slow but perceptible: in the elections for the 16th Party Congress in 2002 there were roughly 10 percent more candidates for seats; for the 17th Party Congress in 2007 there were about 15 percent more candidates than seats; and for the 18th Party Congress in 2012 ballots were required to have at least 15 percent more candidates than seats. However, the process remains subject to manipulation by powerful Party leaders. For example, if an individual favored by a high-ranking leader does not make it through the regular selection/election process, that individual often will become a delegate nonetheless.[13]

As noted in Chapter 2, although on paper, the National Party Congress meets every five years to choose a new Party Central Committee, whereupon the Central Committee chooses a new Politburo, and so on, in reality these high-level Party bodies are chosen by the existing members of Politburo and its SC. The summer before a new NPC convenes, these members meet privately at a beach resort (called *Beid-aihe*) near Beijing to determine who will be the new members of the Party CC, Politburo, and Politburo SC, as well as the new Party General Secretary. Both before and after this meeting, the existing SC also confers with retired former Party leaders, such as Jiang Zemin (and for future meetings, Hu Jintao, who stepped down as Party General Secretary in 2012). The Politburo and SC typically meet again a few weeks before the November meeting of the new NPC, to finalize their decisions. When a new NPC convenes, these selections are presented for "approval" (the new NPC approves the choices for the new

CC, the new CC for the new Politburo, the new Politburo for the new Politburo SC, and the new SC for the new General Secretary). In the post-Mao period there have been "more candidates than seats" for the CC, such that not all candidates have been elected (usually about 8–9 percent). For the Politburo and its SC, however, there have been no more candidates than seats, and all have been unanimously approved.[14]

Beyond publicized stipulations regarding age and term limits, relatively little is known about the rules (either formal or informal) that govern the discussions that occur among top Party leaders at *Beidaihe* and other sites. In his memoir (secretly written while under house arrest), former CCP General Secretary Zhao Ziyang refers to a sort of vote taken by Politburo SC members.[15] However, even the most knowledgeable and well-connected scholars of Chinese politics have been unable to confirm the process by which top-level CCP decisions are made. Thus, the specific process by which membership on the CC, Politburo, Politburo SC is determined – and by which the Party General Secretary is selected – remains unclear.

Overall, the selection method for Party leaders is much more regularized, consultative, and competitive than was the case during the Mao era. At the local level, electoral mechanisms have been put into place that give both rank-and-file Party members and non-Party members input into the choice of local Party leaders, including the ability to effectively veto potential candidates. At higher levels (up to the Central Committee, but not including the Politburo or its SC), although candidate slates typically are pre-determined by leaders one level up, there have been "more candidates than seats," such that the most unpopular candidates have not been elected. Thus, the Party leadership selection process has become more democratic.

However, it is important to emphasize that these changes were implemented not with the goal of ultimately instituting liberal democratic electoral procedures at the highest levels; to the contrary, these mechanisms have been intended to strengthen Party leadership by ridding it of unpopular cadres and allowing it to better represent the wishes of the people. Moreover, apart from the local level – where there has been real progress in terms of making Party leadership selection more democratic – the "more candidates than seats" elections have continued in the post-Mao era to feature only about 10 percent more candidates at best. There has not been a continual trajectory toward higher percentages of "extra" candidates. Apparently, top Party leaders have decided that this modicum of democracy is enough to ensure sufficient public input to guarantee continued political stability, and as a result, they have moved no further in this direction. Further, although leadership succession at the Party's highest levels has become much more regularlized than it was in the Maoist era, the specific process by which decisions are made regarding top Party posts remains largely opaque. Given that the real power within the Chinese government lies in the hands of those who occupy these top Party positions, this lacuna is not trivial.

PARTY LEADERSHIP SELECTION CRITERIA

The criteria by which individuals have risen through the Party ranks from the status of a regular member to a leader at the local level or higher also have changed relative to the Maoist period. Under Mao, ideological "correctness" (as defined by Mao) and astute political networking and maneuvering were key in enabling a person's political rise. During the post-Mao period, political networking and maneuvering have remained important, as has Party loyalty and adherence to the Party "line," but pragmatic success in achieving economic growth and political stability in a leader's area under governance (village, city, province, etc.) has eclipsed prior concerns with ideological purity. In keeping with Deng's maxim about catching mice, in the Reform period pragmatism has been the Party's guiding principle, and experimentation below the central level has been encouraged as a way to find the "best practices" that are appropriate to a given locality, and might be models for wider emulation. The catch-phrase summarizing this attitude is "crossing the river by feeling for stones;" in other words, it is a gradual movement forward, involving continual testing and re-orienting.

Candidates for Party positions at all levels below the center are selected based on their perceived ability to ensure economic growth and political stability in the area under their purview, as well as their political connections. Since 2002, all Party officials have been subject to an annual review. The appraisal includes interviews, questionnaires, public opinion surveys, on-the-spot investigations, exams, and person- nel records.[16] Each year, these local officials are evaluated based on their success at engendering economic growth and maintaining political sta- bility. In the summer of 2013, Party General Secretary Xi Jinping publicly called for more comprehensive evaluation criteria, including the "people's livelihood" the "development of local society," and the "quality of the environment" in the area under an official's purview.[17] According to official *Xinhua* reports in 2014, Hebei province and Ningxia Hui Autonomous Region have ended GDP-based assess- ments of officials in poor counties and cities, instead focusing on success in poverty reduction. And Fujian provincial leaders announced that in nearly three dozen counties, evaluations of GDP growth would be replaced by measures of agricultural development and environmen- tal protection. How effectively these new directives will be imple- mented, and whether or not such changes will become more widespread, remains to be seen.[18] Regardless, overall, at lower administrative levels, merit (as defined by the Party's dual goals of economic growth and political stability) has become a key leadership selection criterion within the Party – a major change from the Mao era. However, as was the case under Mao, political ties continue to be important; family and personal connections not infrequently trump other considerations, including prior performance.

Further, at the highest levels of the Party – when a person moves from a provincial Party position to a position on the CCP Central Committee or higher, ties with high-ranking Party leaders have remained extremely important – often more so than any other factor. More specifically, as top leaders have vied for power at the Party's pinnacle, they have tried to get members of their own political "faction" (Party cadres loyal to that top leader) promoted, and to prevent members of rival factions from rising through the Party ranks. Related to this phenomenon, the sons (and sometimes daughters) of former high-ranking Party leaders – called "princelings" – have had a clear advantage in the promotion process. On the current Standing Committee of the Politburo, at least four of the seven members are considered "princelings" – including CCP General Secretary Xi Jinping.[19] Yet unlike the Maoist period, education (specifically, a college degree) and a proven history of astute fiscal management (i.e. robust tax collection) also have been important factors in promotion to central leadership positions.[20]

The combined effect of these changes in leadership selection criteria and processes in the post-Mao period has been a top CCP leadership that has been remarkably united in its support of economic reform and modernization (and its rejection of the prior Maoist economic model), and in its focus on pragmatism and results over ideology. This is because leaders loyal to the pre-Reform period Maoist faction were systematically moved out of positions of power, and those loyal to the Dengist faction were moved in. This was one of Deng's primary goals during his long dominance of the CCP from 1978–1997. Since Deng's death, there have been factions within the CCP (e.g., the Jiang Zemin faction and the Hu Jintao faction), but they differ more in emphasis than in fundamental ideology or orientation. The Jiang faction is seen as more focused on economic growth and liberalization, whereas the Hu faction is seen as more concerned with economic inequality and "social harmony," but both are firmly committed to the pragmatic, pro-reform program initiated by Deng. This change is reflected in the demographic features of top Party leaders, regardless of faction: they are younger and much more educated than was the case in the Maoist period. Yet even so, the CCP remains a profoundly *political* organization, wherein loyalty to and personal connections with the right Party leader continue to make or break a person's career at the highest levels of the Party hierarchy.

As is the case with politicians everywhere, Party leaders in China ultimately are more concerned with maintaining their own political power than they are with economic (or other kinds of) results. In China, when higher-level leaders look one level down for potential leaders to promote, the higher-level leaders tend to select those who will enhance the higher-level leader's power through their loyalty to that leader. For, it is a higher-level leader's ability to get personal support from other high-level leaders that determines his (or potentially in the future, her) ability to gain and maintain a position on the Politburo or its SC, or be chosen to be General Secretary.

CHANGES IN STATE INSTITUTION SELECTION PROCESSES AND DEMOGRAPHIC COMPOSITION

As should not be surprising given the intertwinement between the CCP and the Chinese state, in the post-Mao period the leadership selection processes and demographic composition of China's state institutions have changed in an almost mirror fashion to those that have transpired in the CCP. The most dramatic change has occurred in local state institutions, where popular elections have been instituted. In the countryside, in 1987 a new law gave villagers the right to nominate and elect village council (VC) members, who serve three-year terms. Beginning in 1988, the Ministry of Civil Affairs established province-level guidelines for implementing the new law, and organized publicity campaigns, election work teams, and training classes. In 1998, a revised version of the law gave even more "democratic" rights to rural residents. To begin, the law stated that VCs should allow village assemblies – comprised of all adult village residents – to discuss and decide on matters such as village expenditures and revenues, applications, plot allocations, family planning actions, and collective contracts. On paper, these rights amount to a form of direct (as opposed to representative) democracy. In this respect, the legal rights of Chinese villagers exceed those given to citizens in most liberal democracies. The 1998 law also instructed VCs to publicize local government allocations and decisions. In addition, all adult villagers were given the express right to run for election, to directly nominate candidates, and to recall VC members before their term of office is complete.[21]

By 2002, virtually all Chinese villages had elected VCs. Moreover, the quality of VC elections appears to have improved over time. In 1990, an estimated 15 percent of VCs were operating in accordance with central policies. By 2003, (according to the Carter Center, an international election monitoring organization), 40 percent of VC elections were considered to be free, fair, and competitive according to Western standards.[22] Voter turnout has been high, with many reports of voting rates exceeding 90 percent. Moreover, in villages where VCs have *not* been elected according to central policies, local residents often have appealed to central leaders to enforce proper electoral procedures. And not infrequently, central authorities have done so, even annulling the results of fraudulent or unfair elections.[23]

At the same time, it is important to emphasize that CCP leaders did not initiate local rural elections because they saw such elections as a first step toward implementing liberal democratic elections at the highest governmental levels. Rather, local rural elections were instituted because rural uprisings were growing in intensity and number in the 1980s and 1990s, as rural residents protested what they viewed to be arbitrary and unjust taxes and fees levied by corrupt local officials. Rural residents also resisted unpopular central policies, such as those regarding birth control. Thus, central Party leaders saw village elections as a way to force out corrupt local officials and install officials that the local populace viewed as legitimate, and therefore worthy of respect and obedience. In other words, in the eyes of CCP elites, village elections were a way to *strengthen* CCP power, not weaken it. And indeed, their calculation seems to have paid off: in localities where central policies have been followed and free and fair elections have occurred, residents appear to be more willing to comply with government policies, and appear to be happier with their local leaders. Indeed, in some villages, former activists against corrupt village officials have themselves run for and won VC seats. And, in localities where election problems have arisen and villagers have successfully appealed to central leaders for help, the legitimacy of the central regime has grown.

These developments encouraged CCP elites to press for similar elections in China's cities. In 1990, another new law called for the election of residents' committees by residents of urban neighborhoods. In 2000, central leaders stipulated that residents' committee leaders should be directly nominated and elected by local residents. As of late 2003, only an estimated 10 percent of residents' committees had been elected via free and fair competitive elections, and more recent evidence suggests little improvement. However, the right to participate in these elections remains on the books, and top CCP leaders tout them as important innovations in the political system. Further, in recent years, the central regime has allowed higher-level political units – such as townships and cities – to experiment with direct elections.[24]

Overall, the institution of elections in rural and some urban localities has made the Chinese political system more democratic – both in the procedural sense, and in the broader sense of representing the wishes of the people. As a result, the political system has become more responsive to popular demands, grievances, and desires. Thus, somewhat paradoxically, the infusion of some elements of liberal democracy into the Chinese political system has made CCP rule more legitimate and stable.

Even so, there is evidence that with the institution of local elections have come some of the less "democratic" aspects of elections that have appeared in some liberal democracies – particularly in the United States. In a word, money has come to play a role in the electoral process. The actual role of money in Chinese elections is quite different from that in the US, however. In the US, money is used by candidates to buy ads that enhance their ability to attract votes. And in part because wealthy individuals have a greater ability to fund their own campaigns and/or network with wealthy potential donors, most politicians in the US are quite wealthy prior to their move into politics. Similarly, in China since the early 1990s, VC elections increasingly have been dominated by the relatively wealthy. This is not because of the need to buy ads, though. Rather, in poorer rural localities, this has been because there has been so little money that cadre salaries cannot be paid; the result has been that only individuals with independent income have been able to afford to serve. In addition, village governments and residents increasingly have relied on the resources of prosperous villagers. In some cases, candidates have even given payments to villagers in expected return for their votes.[25] Beyond these more pragmatic reasons, in many villages, wealthy individuals are among the most well-known and respected in the community. As a result, they are more likely to be nominated and elected.

Turning to other state bodies, the selection process for officials higher than the local level mimics that for Party officials. As discussed in Chapter 2, the Party-state's Organizational Affairs *xitong* decides who will be appointed to state and Party positions. In each territorial unit (e.g., province, county) the Party and state entities charged with overseeing organization and personnel work together to select officials one level below them. In general, the same criteria that are used to evaluate potential Party appointees are used for potential state appointees. However, one difference regarding the consideration of state appointees is that loyalty to particular Party leaders has been much less important than has a person's record of success at maintaining political stability and economic growth. Whereas within the Party, appointment to the highest central level positions has continued to be based largely on political ties with top Party leaders, within the state, promotion from the provincial level to the central level has been based much more on performance. Further, even though the vast majority of appointees to state positions are also Party members, not all are. Overall, although the process by which individuals are appointed to state positions is almost identical to that within the Party, the selection criteria are somewhat different, with the result that the state is slightly less politicized and slightly more merit-based and focused on matters of administration than is the Party.

That said, there have been numerous documented cases where individuals actually have bought positions in the state bureaucracy. To name one prominent example, following a major crash on China's new bullet train in 2011, it came to light that many jobs in the Railway Ministry had been purchased; reportedly, the going price to be a train attendant was $4500, while the position of supervisor required $15,000.[26] Although the official media portrays occurrences such as this as aberrations, it is hard to gauge how common they really are.

China's other major state bodies are the people's congresses that exist at the national level, the provincial level, and the county/township level. In terms of membership selection processes, on paper, county/township level congress members are elected by the population in that locality; the elections are organized by elections committees in each village and urban residential area, and all adult residents 18 and older are eligible to vote. County/township congresses then elect provincial level congresses, and provincial level congresses elect delegates to the National People's Congress (which, as noted in Chapter 2, meets once every year). However, also as noted in Chapter 2, these elections generally have not been free, fair, or competitive. In the Maoist period, candidates for these elections were pre-selected by the Party, and there was only one candidate per open seat. In the post-Mao period, as with elections for Party congresses, some effort has been made to make people's congress elections more competitive, with "more candidates than seats." Further, unlike Party congresses, which are open only to Party members, non-Party members have been eligible to run for people's congress seats. Technically, if a potential candidate can document the support of at least ten voters, s/he can become a tentative candidate (subject to official approval). Voters also may write in the names of candidates who do not appear on the official ballot.

At the provincial, county and township levels, roughly 30–40 percent of people's congress representatives are not members of the CCP. In the National People's Congress, about 70 percent are not Party members. Although this marks an improvement relative to the Maoist era, it is not representative of the population at large; nearly 95 percent of China's citizens are not Party members. Further, more than 50 percent of the seats on people's congresses at all levels are filled by Party and state officials. And, roughly 10 percent of National People's Congress seats are occupied by members of China's armed forces.

Moreover, even among the non-Party members who have been elected to people's congresses, it has been a very rare occurrence for a truly independent candidate to run and win a seat. And, this has happened only at the county and township level. Additionally, when an independent candidate has been elected, Party authorities typically have worked to annul the results, pressure or intimidate the candidate into resigning, or otherwise ensure that the successful candidate will not be subsequently re-elected. In the late 1980s, there were a number of such cases; perhaps most notably, during the 1986–1987 student demonstrations that ultimately led to the downfall of former Party General Secretary Hu Yaobang, students and other independent candidates attempted to run for people's congress seats. From the late

1990s through the present, a handful of independent candidates have run for election and won. One of the most well-known is Yao Lifa, an elementary school teacher. After unsuccessfully running for his local township people's congress (in Hubei province) for over a decade, in 1998 Yao was elected. In the process, however, he was punished with the loss of his job and other harassment. Since his election, he has been subject to frequent detention, and his election bids have been countered with manipulative practices on the part of the authorities to ensure that he does not again win a seat (which he has not). A 2006 book about his experiences was banned and pulled from Chinese bookshelves just two months after its publication. In the past few years, well over 100 independent candidates for local people's congresses have announced their candidacies online. Though they have been able to get their messages out via the Internet, none has been successfully elected, and most have been harassed or detained – with criminal charges of "sabotaging elections" levied against at least one. Some of those who have been detained have simply gone missing, with their family members and friends unaware of their whereabouts.[27] Overall, although the possibility of independent candidacies for people's congresses, as well as the opportunity to spread an independent message online, is an improvement relative to the Maoist period, people's congress elections remain far from any kind of democratic ideal.

Moreover, it appears to be increasingly common for wealthy individuals to use their economic influence to become candidates for people's congresses. In 2012 reports surfaced that the wealthiest seventy members of the National People's Congress were worth nearly ninety billion US dollars. As noted by journalist Evan Osnos, this staggering figure is "more than ten times the combined net worth of the entire US Congress."[28]

Finally, although the CPPCC is not an official part of the Chinese state or the CCP, but rather a separate consultative body comprised of political parties and other groups that supported the CCP during

China's civil war (1945–1949), the selection process for its members is controlled by the CCP. Roughly six months before a new CPPCC convenes, Party-state cadres discuss and decide on a candidate list for the CPPCC that will be submitted to the existing CPPCC Standing Committee (SC) for approval (remember that the Chair of the CPPCC SC also sits on the SC of the CCP Politburo). Little is known about the exact way in which this process occurs, or precisely who within the Party-state is involved. Each of the constituencies that comprise the CPPCC is given a quota for its number of representatives. As a way to coopt and incorporate private entrepreneurs into China's governing structure, in 1999 the CPPCC added a special "economic" constituency that includes roughly 100 private entrepreneurs, some of whom sit on the CPPCC SC. The opaque nature of the CPPCC selection process has been criticized by some leading Chinese academics in recent years. In 2010, two CPPCC delegates revealed that they had not been told of their appointment to the body until they read about it in the media. Some also have questioned the appointment of various celebrities to the CPPCC (including a Hong Kong actress known for her porn films and a young man who won the TV contest "China's Got Talent" with his break-dancing act).[29] Unlike the institutions that comprise the Party and the state, the CPPCC selection process and criteria have not become more open, democratic, or merit-based in the post-Mao era.

FORMULATING PREFERENCES AND PERCEIVING TASKS

The way in which Party and state officials formulate their preferences and perceive their tasks has changed substantially relative to the Maoist period, in line with the commitment of top Party leaders to pragmatic policies that result in economic growth, and their acceptance of experimentation in doing so. At the same time, Party and state officials have been given a much greater ability to voice their opinions and help to shape Party-state policies. Overall, policies have been created through this back-and-forth between input from below and directives from above.

Policies are formulated via a process that is much more consultative than was the case under Mao. During the Maoist era, Mao was the ultimate decision-maker, and deviation from or opposition to his "line" was a risky undertaking. Further, many of Mao's pronouncements were vague, such that it was not clear how to properly implement Mao's "line." Often, one found out only after the fact that his/her behavior was not acceptable. In the post-Mao period, and particularly since the passing of Deng Xiaoping, decisions made at the top level of the Party have been much more collective. When Deng was still alive, he remained the ultimate arbiter of policy, but he consciously attempted to move away from one-man rule by stepping down from his official Party and state posts. Since Deng's passing, there has been no single leader who can dictate or determine policy. Rather, top Party leaders have had to negotiate and compromise among one another. At the top, these leaders include both members of the Politburo SC and retired top Party leaders, such as Jiang Zemin and Hu Jintao. Though we have little information about what considerations are at the forefront of these leaders' minds as they engage one another in debate and decision-making, as noted above, it is clear that their various views are colored as much by factional maneuvering as they are by clear policy differences. Overall, at the highest level of the Party, the process by which decisions are reached is highly informal and personal – just as was the case during the Maoist period. However, relative to the Maoist period, which was characterized by virtual one-man rule, in the post-Mao period the circle of top decision-makers has widened.

In terms of formulating general Party policy, which is articulated in each new meeting of the National Party Congress, an extensive process of consultation occurs. Early in the year before a planned fall meeting of the NPC, the Party Central Committee (CC) constitutes a "drafting group" to formulate a draft of the new NPC document, and calls on all Party committees within China's various provinces and provincial-level administrations, as well as all other central Party organs, to discuss the draft and submit opinions and recommendations for revision. Opinions are also solicited from other political parties. According to official sources, over one hundred written memos typically are submitted in response to this call. Subsequently, the drafting group sends out investigation teams to China's provinces, holding meetings with local officials, and conducting field studies in villages and enterprises. The drafting group also asks the central organs of the state and the CCP to research and report on specific issues. In the summer, the Party CC distributes a revised draft to delegates to the existing Party Congress and retired Party leaders. Based on their feedback, hundreds of changes may be made to the draft. Next, the Party General Secretary meets with the non-CCP representatives on the CPPCC to solicit feedback. In the early fall, the Party CC further discusses and revises the draft. Throughout the process, the Politburo and its SC hold meetings to discuss the draft and the various opinions that have been received. Before the November meeting of a new Party Congress, the document is finalized.

Because the draft will have been widely circulated by this time, most delegates are already quite familiar with its contents. And because opinions have been solicited and incorporated prior to the final drafting of the document, typically little to no substantive discussion or opposition arises at the actual NPC meeting. Following NPC approval, the document becomes the general Party "line" governing policy-making. Although it is not clear how much substantive debate and revision occurs during the consultative process that leads up to the finalization of the document, the ultimate result reflects compromises made based on input from and negotiations among all major Party constituencies and top Party leaders. Thus, although the drafting process is not democratic in the Western liberal sense, it does involve a significant amount of consultation with the goal of reaching consensus.[30]

The final document shapes the way in which individual Party and state officials formulate their preferences and perceive their tasks. In addition, Party and state officials pay close attention to more specific directives, suggestions, and statements made by top Party leaders and higher-level Party and state bodies. Some of these appear in the official media, and some come down to lower-level officials through official documents or meetings with higher-level leaders. Individuals occupying positions in the Party and state who wish to move up the political ladder must work to follow and implement these (often somewhat unclear) directions, and conversely must be sure to not obviously contravene them.

The Party school system also serves as a way to both indoctrinate governing officials and seek input from them. Since 2006, all Party officials have been required to undergo at least three months of training every five years. At the pinnacle of the training system is the Central Party School (CPS) in Beijing, which oversees nearly 3,000 Party schools at lower administrative levels across the country. In 2005 three new training academies were established – two in China's interior (in the cities of Jingganshan and Yan'an), where the focus is on Party history and matters related to China's interior, and one in Shanghai's dynamic and capitalistic Pudong area, where the emphasis is on China's reform and opening, innovation in system reform, human resource management, and leadership methods. The CCP's Organization Department determines which cadres will be trained where. Whereas the sessions at most of these schools feature top-down instruction, they also offer the possibility for officials to discuss mutual problems and voice their concerns. At the CPS, more substantive discussion and debate often has occurred; indeed, it is referred to as the Party's main "think tank." In the early part of the new millennium, for example, the CPS served as a the key site of debate over Jiang Zemin's proposed

"Three Represents" theory, which was extremely controversial due to its proposed inclusion of private entrepreneurs in China's "communist" Party.

At the same time, Party and state officials pay close attention to the criteria upon which they are evaluated. Like politicians everywhere, their major concern is to maintain their position, and /or to rise through the political ranks. Cognizant of the fact that they will be reviewed according to how well they have promoted economic growth and ensured political stability in their locality, these considerations pre-dominate their formulation of preferences and their perception of their most important tasks. In terms of promoting economic growth, in some cases this has worked to the benefit of the community. But in other cases, this focus has had harmful effects. The main way in which officials have striven to promote economic growth is by striking agreements with private entrepreneurs to establish new business or construction projects in the area. Not infrequently, this has involved confiscating the land of local villagers, with inadequate compensation. It also has led local officials to turn a blind eye to environmental degradation that is caused by lucrative local businesses and construction projects. In terms of maintaining political stability, rather than trying to resolve or sympathetically respond to public grievances, many local officials have attempted to repress popular discontent – even capturing and detaining local petitioners who attempt to take their cases to higher-level authorities. In addition, many local protests have been violently crushed by local authorities. When publicized, these actions sometimes have backfired for local authorities, as such publicity has brought to the attention of higher officials the corruption and unpopularity of local leaders. A significant recent example occurred in the southeastern town of Wukan, where local authorities were punished for their repressive response to public protests. When not publicized, however, such actions on the part of local leaders have successfully stifled public discontent.

Turning to the people's congresses that exist at the provincial, county, and township levels, the formulation of preferences and perception of tasks have been quite different. For, people's congress delegates work for only a few days a year in this capacity, and otherwise have different regular occupations; most are not politicians seeking to climb the political ladder. Members of people's congress standing committees meet more frequently, but still for only one or two days every other month. Only about 30 percent of people's congress standing committee delegates work in this capacity full time. For the vast majority of people's congress delegates, since the position is only temporary and part-time, the way in which they form their preferences varies according to the reason why they were chosen as a delegate in the first place. Most were selected by higher level Party leaders to represent a specific constituent group (e.g., women, rank-and-file workers, peasants, intellectuals, private entrepreneurs) or to represent the Party or state office where they hold a regular position. The vast majority of these see their primary task as advocating for the group that they represent. Some intellectuals have taken a more active role in trying to provide policy advice. In recent years, private businesspeople have shown the greatest interest in becoming people's congress delegates, since they see it as a vehicle by which they can cultivate good relations with Party and state officials, and as a way to gain protection from arbitrary treatment by the authorities. In order to secure their position as a delegate, many private businesspeople have made donations to public works projects. Since the early 1980s, people's congress delegates also have been tasked with "bridge-building" with the public, which includes soliciting information about and responding to residents' problems. These problems typically include concerns with public facilities, the local environment, education, medical care, unemployment, resident disputes.[31] Overall, even though people's congress delegates are not democratically elected, most make an effort to represent and attend to the needs of the people in their constituency. Indeed, recent research based on over 5,000 interviews with local people's congress delegates finds that the vast majority "view themselves and act as 'delegates'" of their constituents – working hard to provide their constituents with tangible public goods.[32]

CONCLUSION

In sum, relative to the Maoist period, the manner in which Party and state officials are selected has become far more meritocratic and regularized in the post-Mao era. And, the people who occupy leadership positions in the Party and state are much more pragmatic and educated – and far less ideologically driven – than was the case under Mao. Similarly, CCP members are more educated and include a wider array of socio-economic groups – including private entrepreneurs and intellectuals. In this sense, the Party has shed most of its "communist" features and become a catch-all Party in terms of demographics and instrumental in terms of its policy focus – "whatever works" to bring economic growth and ensure political stability has become the Party's guiding principle.

Further, some attempts have been made to make Party and state leadership selection processes more democratic. On the state side, village council elections regularly occur in virtually all of China's villages, with perhaps half operating in a manner that is free, fair, and competitive by Western standards. And, the quality of these elections overall has been improving over time. Similarly, popular elections for urban residents' committees have been instituted, though far less extensively. On the Party side, too, efforts have been made to give common citizens more input, particularly in terms of local leadership. Local Party leaders increasingly have been subject to public assessment, either by the ability of local residents to vote out undesirable candidates or by the requirement that local Party leader candidates first demonstrate their popularity by being elected to the locality's village council or residents' committee. The result has been local state and Party leadership that is more representative of the wishes of the people. At higher levels of the Party and state, somewhat more democratic procedures have been implemented as well. In particular, the practice of having "more candidates than seats" has brought a modicum of competition and the ability to weed out particularly unpopular candidates.

Yet these reforms have not been intended as first steps toward transforming the Chinese political system into a multi-party liberal democracy with elections at the highest levels. To the contrary, the Party's goal has been to use these reforms as a way to *strengthen* the CCP's leadership and *stabilize* the political system. And overall, this aim has been achieved. Party leaders thus seem to have decided that, above the local level, no more "democracy" is needed; a few more candidates than seats will suffice. But at the same time, inasmuch as local-level democracy has been implemented, the Party and state have become more open and responsive to the public – and thus more democratic – even as they have become stronger and more stable. The result has been a new kind of political system that differs substantially from both the Maoist system and liberal democratic systems in the West, and may remain more or less as is for the foreseeable future.

The big question in this regard is the degree to which Party and state leaders are pragmatic and competent. Thus far, they generally have exhibited these important characteristics – particularly relative to the Maoist era. But to the extent that political connections and/or money overshadow demonstrated merit when it comes to selecting political leaders, the ability of the Chinese Party-state to fulfill the key functions of government – and thus remain stable – will be imperiled.

4 Maintaining Public Relations

As detailed in the preceding chapters, China's state and Party structures – and the types of people who occupy them – have changed over time. In some ways, these changes have made China's political system more open, inclusive, democratic, and meritocratic. But, in other respects, the system has remained closed, exclusive, authoritarian, and personalistic. This chapter examines the ways in which the various parts and features of the Chinese political system have facilitated or undermined the regime's ability to govern well (or at least adequately), and thereby elicit the public's support (or at least tolerance). And, it assesses how the system's ability to do so has changed over time.

As noted in Chapter 1, one of the key requirements of a stable governing regime is satisfying key demographic groups and responding to public grievances. This chapter investigates how well the various components of China's ruling regime have fulfilled this basic governmental function. More generally, the chapter considers the ways in which the "democratic" and "non-democratic" aspects of the Chinese Party-state have influenced the political system's ability to respond to the needs and complaints of the people, and what the trends in this respect have been over time.

RESPONDING TO PUBLIC GRIEVANCES

Despite the Chinese Party-state's many closed and authoritarian features, there are numerous legal avenues by which Chinese citizens may voice their concerns and seek redress for their grievances. One such venue that has attracted a great deal of attention in the West is China's court system. In the Maoist period, China had no courts in the Western sense of the word, and lawyers were virtually non-existent. Attorneys re-appeared in China in 1979, spurred by the CCP-led trial of the Maoist "Gang of Four" who were accused of orchestrating the excesses of the Cultural Revolution. That year, CCP elites restored the Ministry of Justice, which had been eradicated from the state apparatus in 1959. In addition, the Party-state began to recruit lawyers to work for the government as "state legal workers." Most had little to no legal training. Private lawyers still did not exist. Beginning in the mid-1990s, this situation changed: virtually all law firms were privatized, and lawyers became private sector workers. Since 2001, all new lawyers have been required to pass a "bar" exam before engaging in work as an attorney. In 1994, citizens were given the legal right to sue government officials for abuse of authority or malfeasance, and in 2011 citizens gained the right to sue the government for the release of information.

Despite these positive developments, lawyers and the court system in China generally serve at the behest of the Party-state, and do not challenge it or hold it to external legal standards. As with all organs of the state, the Chinese legal system exists to serve the interests of the CCP. Further, the number of lawyers remains extremely low compared to the size of China's population.[1] Yet because CCP elites know that in order to maintain stability, political authorities must be apprised of public concerns and then satisfactorily respond to them, efforts have been made to encourage citizens to adjudicate their grievances through the courts. Use of the court system increased in the mid-1990s, but has since plateaued. Overall, although courts are available for citizen use, they are rarely viewed by the public as a likely site for the sympathetic hearing of citizen grievances.

An alternative to resolving disputes through the court system is the use of community mediation committees (CMCs). Since 1982, every village and urban area has been charged with establishing an elected CMC comprised of local residents. Committee members are paid a small stipend by the Party-state, and the use of CMCs is free. CMCs hear millions of cases every year, and are reputed to have a 90 percent resolution rate. However, nearly all of these cases center on conflicts among citizens, and not disputes between citizens and Party-state officials or entities.

With regard to informing regime authorities about public concerns and then resolving them, a mechanism that appears to work better than both the courts and CMCs is China's "letters and visits" (or *xinfang*) system, which has been in existence since the Maoist period. This system encompasses a wide-ranging set of bureaus and offices that are part of all governments at the county level and above, and public and semi-public agencies within all courts, higher education institutions, and state-owned enterprises. Whenever a citizen feels aggrieved, s/he has the legal right to submit a letter or make a visit to these offices. The system is free, legal, and does not require the complainant to submit formal evidence. *Xinfang* offices must accept and respond to all petitions to their office. They regularly dispatch investigation teams to assess the validity of the aggrieved's claims. The CCP created these offices to facilitate communication between ordinary citizens and political leaders, allowing for the direct transmission of information regarding popular grievances and attitudes. In other words, *xinfang* offices are seen by Party elites as a form of political representation.

By all accounts, the *xinfang* system is an inefficient and often ineffectual means of resolving citizen complaints. Yet, most citizens take the charge of these offices seriously, and begin with voicing their grievances in this manner. Complainants regularly are met with stalling by the receiving office, and not infrequently elicit repressive responses on the part of the local authorities that are the subject of the complaint. When this occurs, aggrieved citizens can – and often do – move up the political hierarchy, submitting their complaint to higher levels of authority, be it at the provincial level or even traveling to Beijing to contact central *xinfang* offices. In numerous cases, accused local authorities have tried to punish and stop complainants, through fines, having their homes demolished or ransacked, confiscating their property, beating them (and/or their family members), and capturing and detaining them in informal (and illegal) "black jails." A study of rural residents undertaken in 2003–2005 found that over 60 percent of petitioners had been subjected to one or more of these forms of repression.[2] In large part, this behavior on the part of local authorities has derived from the fact that their performance review includes the number of petitions lodged against them. By early 2013, this behavior had become so prevalent that central authorities announced that they would no longer produce monthly lists of local authorities who have been criticized in large numbers of petitions.[3] However, local officials have continued to be evaluated in part based on their petition record, and citizens have continued to submit millions of petitions to letters and visits to offices every year. For, despite the many abuses described above, the system is viewed by both the central regime and citizens as an important legal venue for the expression and resolution of popular discontent.

Typically, it is only when citizens have become frustrated with their efforts to seek redress through the letters and visits system that they turn to other (more overtly conflictual and less clearly legal) methods of protest – including street marches, demonstrations, and sit-ins. These kinds of collective actions are categorized by China's ruling regime as "mass disturbances." In 2005, the last year in which Chinese authorities released figures, there were 87,000 such protests. Scholars and observers have estimated that roughly the same number has occurred in each subsequent year. Despite their differences in terms of specific grievances and the particular demographic groups involved, over the past decade most protests have displayed the same general chronology: localized and specific grievances; attempts, for some, at amelioration via formal means of political participation (such as letters and visits offices or the courts); localized mass protest; local reprisals at the hands of lower-level officials; and attempts at amelioration by higher-level officials.

As this typical chronology shows, China's governing regime has responded to popular protests with a mixture of repression and sympathy. Whereas local authorities generally have reacted to popular protests with repression, punishment, and at times violence, higher-level political leaders typically have made at least some effort to address the concerns of the demonstrators and to reprimand lower-level officials for malfeasance. Perhaps for this reason, for at least the last decade, even the biggest and most violent protests have not been directed against central governing authorities or the political system as a whole. Instead, mass demonstrations in China have focused on specific, local grievances, and have been directed against local officials, businesses and employers. Further, there have been many cases wherein local officials – usually those who have been popularly elected – have supported the cause of aggrieved residents, and worked to oppose the other local officials who have perpetrated the offense in question.

Somewhat counterintuitively, to the extent that authorities (usually at the central level, and sometimes at the local level) have responded sympathetically to popular protests, disgruntled citizens have felt more encouraged to protest. Indeed, many Chinese have come to believe that "A big disturbance leads to a big solution, a small disturbance leads to a small solution, and no disturbance leads to no solution." In other words, although protests skirt the boundary of what is legal/permissible and what is not, they have become accepted by both the central regime and citizens as a relatively normal means of expressing and resolving collective grievances. They are an inefficient, and sometimes violently conflictual, mechanism for doing so, but they have become a key contributor to the regime's ability to fulfill this basic governmental function. Although it may seem strange to view protest as something that serves to *stabilize* CCP rule, this indeed appears to be the case.[4]

Another mechanism used by the populace to vent grievances – and by regime authorities to simultaneously monitor, control, and respond to the public's complaints – is the Internet. Although the regime works hard to restrict the ability of the populace to access or disseminate via the Internet information that central leaders perceive as threatening, Chinese citizens are allowed what many Westerners would find to be a surprising amount of freedom of expression online. As of 2012, China had nearly 570 million Internet users – more than two times the number of Internet users as the US (254 million). Although this represents a much smaller portion of China's population than America's (42 v. 81 percent, respectively), by any measure this is a sizeable number. Further, adept Internet users in China are able to get around the government's "Great Firewall" if they so desire.[5] Most Chinese netizens appear to be satisfied with their ability to use the Internet to voice and share their opinions, and generally do not oppose the government's attempt to regulate it. In one recent survey, for example, 80 percent of mainland Chinese respondents stated that "the Internet should be controlled or managed," and 85 percent of those respondents believed that the Chinese government should be the only entity in charge of doing so.[6]

What is and is not acceptable Internet communication in the eyes of the Chinese Party-state varies, and is not always clear. Government offices regularly transmit memos to media outlets (including websites), delineating forbidden topics, phrases, words, and numbers. Some are perpetually forbidden (such as 6-4, a reference to the June 4 repression of the massive student-led demonstrations of 1989), while others come and go. The contents of these memos regularly become known to the public; indeed, the website China Digital Times maintains an archive of forbidden terms, which it updates on a daily basis.[7] Subscribers (including those living in China) are even able to have these updates e-mailed to them.[8] As a result, each day, Party-state authorities charged with Internet censorship play a cat-and-mouse game with Chinese netizens, who constantly come up with substitute words for forbidden ones. Moreover, millions of mainland Chinese Internet users participate in the online parody (*egao*) of government statements and policies. Although these discussions often involve quite acerbic political criticism, they are allowed to persist.[9]

In general, as with the letters and visits system, central political elites view the Internet as an important medium through which they can find out about local abuses and popular concerns, and then respond to these problems before they escalate into regime-threatening crises. So, central authorities do not wish to censor and control the expression of all public opinion via the Internet. Corrupt, illegal, and inappropriate behavior on the part of government officials regularly is uncovered by Chinese Internet users, with the result that the wrong-doing officials are tracked down and punished. In the summer of 2012, for example, dozens of nude photos were posted of Anhui province county officials and various women, on Weibo, the Chinese equivalent of Twitter. Though the central State Council Information Office later ordered all Chinese websites to cease posting materials related to this "incident," the offending officials reportedly were expelled from the Party and dismissed from their positions.

This is not to say that those who disseminate critical information or opinions about the government are always protected; if a posting is critical of powerful central leaders, or of the political system as a whole (and, if it is significant enough that it draws the attention of political authorities) or if a posting calls for collective public action – then repression is likely. For example, in 2008 over three hundred well-known Chinese academics and activists signed and posted online a manifesto called "Charter 08," which called for the fundamental transformation of China's political system, including an end to one-party rule, the establishment of an independent legal system, and the right to association free from CCP control. The main instigator of the Charter – Liu Xiaobo, a professor of literature – was detained and sentenced to eleven years. In 2010, he was awarded the Nobel Peace Prize, but he was not allowed by Chinese authorities to attend the ceremonies. Liu remains behind bars at the time of this writing. Roughly seventy of the original signatories also have been harassed and punished. However, the other original signatories, as well as the more than 10,000 others who have signed since the original posting, do not appear to have faced sanction. Similarly, if a posting calls on citizens to take to the streets or otherwise engage in a collective action directed toward political authorities, the source of the post is likely to be subject to repression. In other words, while Party-state leaders encourage citizens to voice their grievances online, political elites will not tolerate calls for public action to ameliorate those grievances.

Overall, use of the Internet in China illustrates both the regime's tolerance of freedom of expression and its limits. The system is neither entirely closed and totalitarian, nor entirely open and free. But on balance, the amount and types of political criticism and discussion that are allowed appear to be perceived as satisfactory in the minds of the majority of Chinese citizens.

SATISFYING KEY DEMOGRAPHIC GROUPS

Related to a government's ability to respond adequately to public grievances, in order to remain stable, a political system must satisfy groups within the society whose support (or at least tolerance) of the political status quo is essential. If a powerful demographic group turns against a regime, it will be difficult for the regime to maintain its power. A group's importance can lie in its numbers, or in its resources, or in its motivation to effect change. Historically (both in China and elsewhere), groups with substantial political importance have included private businesspeople, college students and graduates, rank-and-file workers, and small farmers. Although relations between some of these groups and some parts of the Chinese Party-state have been conflictual at times, in the post-Mao period the governing regime has done an adequate job of satisfying these groups' basic needs, and in most cases has done so increasingly well over time. As a result, particularly since the early 1990s, none of these groups has had an interest in pressing for fundamental change in the political system.

PRIVATE BUSINESSPEOPLE

One key group in China today consists of private entrepreneurs. Relative to all other major socio-economic groups in China, private entrepreneurs' relationship with the ruling Party-state has changed perhaps the most dramatically over time, and in the most positive direction. As discussed in Chapter 3, during the Maoist era, private enterprise was castigated as "bourgeois" and "capitalist," and private entrepreneurs were virtually non-existent. In the post-Mao period, capitalist economic reforms have led to a fundamental transformation in the economic, social, and political status of private entrepreneurs. According to official statistics, as of 2011, China had roughly 52 million private enterprises (defined as privately owned businesses with eight or more employees), employing approximately 160 million workers. As of 2012, private enterprises produced more than 60 percent of China's GDP.[10]

Thus, even though private enterprise owners comprise only a tiny portion of China's population (roughly one percent), they carry great economic weight. Accordingly, they are a key demographic group with the potential to influence the stability of China's governing regime. Many in the West have believed (and indeed hoped) that China's private entrepreneurs will come to oppose the CCP-dominated system. This view is based on the belief that private entrepreneurs' economic liberty inevitably will be restricted by China's lack of Western liberal freedoms and rights, including the freedom of the press. Also underlying this Western view is the historical experience of England, where private entrepreneurs pressed for political liberalization as a necessary means to break the power of an authoritarian state that limited their economic prosperity and opportunity.

Yet this chain of events has not transpired in post-Mao China. To the contrary, as the post-Mao period has progressed, China's private entrepreneurs have become only more embedded in, and supportive of, the CCP-dominated political status quo. One measure of this is the percentage of private enterprise owners in China who are CCP members. In the late 1980s, only one percent was a member of the Party, and virtually all of these had been Party members before entering into private business. By 1993, 13 percent of private entrepreneurs were Party members (again, all of these had been members prior to becoming businesspeople). After the 2002 change that allowed private entrepreneurs to join the CCP, the percentage jumped even higher; by 2011, 40 percent of all private entrepreneurs were Party members. In fact, private entrepreneurs currently have the highest percentage of CCP members per capita of any socio-economic sector. Further, those who are not Party members report that they have made this choice not because they oppose the CCP, but because they believe that they already have sufficient connections with the Party (through friends or family members). As a result, they do not feel that it is worthwhile to go through the effort of applying for and maintaining membership.[11]

In addition, private entrepreneurs appear quite willing to join government-sponsored business associations, and to work within existing political institutions. The CCP-dominated state has numerous government-sponsored business associations related to private entrepreneurs (e.g., the Self-Employed Laborers' Association, the Private Enterprises' Association, and the Industrial and Commercial Federation). These organizations are designed both to maintain state control over private entrepreneurs and to represent their interests. Surveys show that roughly 70 percent of private enterprise owners are members of at least one government-affiliated CCP-created business association.

And, the vast majority of these members say that they "actively" participate in the associations' activities. Importantly, these private entrepreneurs do not perceive any incompatibility between the associations' dual functions of state control and member representation. To the contrary, they see themselves "as partners, not adversaries of the state."[12] In addition, surveys show that a substantial percentage of candidates in rural village council (VC) elections are private entrepreneurs. Moreover, one survey found that nearly 68 percent of private business owners agreed that if a non-CCP member were elected to a VC, then s/he should join the CCP.[13] Private entrepreneurs also have displayed substantial interest in joining other state entities. According to official sources, as of 2002, more than 17 percent of National People's Congress members, and just over 35 percent of CPPCC members at various levels, were private entrepreneurs.[14] As these statistics suggest, rather than seeking to change the existing political system, private business-people have chosen to become part of it. Indeed, private entrepreneurs appear to be more supportive of, and intertwined with, the CCP-led political system than any other social group.

Why, contrary to prevalent expectations in the West, have private entrepreneurs chosen to embed themselves within the existing political system, rather than opposing it? The answer is that the regime has leveraged some of its still communist and non-democratic features to coopt and entice private entrepreneurs to join and support it. At the same time, the regime has shed many of its Mao-era communist controls over the economy, and its prior "communist" opposition to private enterprise – policies and attitudes that previously had constrained and punished private entrepreneurs.

As discussed in Chapters 3 and 5, over the course of the post-Mao period, the Party has moved away from its prior "communist" control over the entirety of the economy, as well as its "communist" disdain for private enterprise. During the first decade of the post-Mao era (the late 1970s through the late 1980s), very small private enterprises were tolerated. During the latter half of the 1980s, somewhat larger-scale private enterprises were allowed to emerge. Nonetheless, throughout the 1980s, private businesspeople were subject to periodic castigation by central authorities and discrimination at the hands of local officials, especially when competing with "communist" public sector enterprises for resources such as supplies, land/buildings, and access to utilities. Among other things, local state representatives levied exorbitant taxes and imposed fees related to sanitation, urban construction, transport, and weights and measures. During this period, the Chinese Communist Party remained uncomfortable with the idea of private enterprise, and as a result, private entrepreneurs remained politically vulnerable.

The material and social status of private entrepreneurs improved dramatically from the early 1990s through the start of the new millennium. As noted in Chapter 3, following Deng Xiaoping's famous "Southern tour" of special economic zones in Southeastern China, private enterprise was encouraged and praised by the Party-state. Further, because local officials now were evaluated on the basis of their ability to promote economic growth, they became eager to cooperate with private entrepreneurs who could provide that growth. Whereas earlier in the post-Mao period many private entrepreneurs were subject to official discrimination, since the early 1990s they often have enjoyed preferential treatment. Private entrepreneurs routinely are leased public land at low prices, enjoy low tax rates, and are granted licenses at low cost and with ease.

Moreover, beginning in the 1990s the Chinese Party-state dismantled its prior "communist" controls over labor, resulting in the creation of a seemingly unending supply of potential employees willing to work for minimal pay and to endure relentless working conditions. To begin, the regime eased the internal migration restrictions that had been strictly enforced throughout the Maoist period, and that had loosened only slightly in the late 1970s and 1980s. The result was a massive movement of rural residents to the cities. The pool of unskilled labor available for private business owners was further increased in the late 1990s, when the regime's privatization of most state-owned enterprises resulted in the lay-off of tens of millions of former state sector employees. Further, again because local political officials are evaluated based on the economic performance of their locality, they generally have turned a blind eye to the exploitative (and often illegal) employment conditions of private enterprise workers. Overall, these policies and practices have kept labor costs low for private enterprise owners, further buttressing their profits.

Meanwhile, as discussed in Chapter 3, the political and social status of private entrepreneurs was transformed with the CCP's endorsement of then Party General Secretary Jiang Zemin's theory of the "Three Represents" in 2002. Since that time, private entrepreneurs not only have been allowed to join the Party, they have been actively recruited into it. And, as noted earlier, they have responded enthusiastically. The reason is not that private entrepreneurs believe in communism; rather, they view Party membership instrumentally, as a way to ensure their protection and prosperity. Simultaneously, the Party has proven itself to be adaptable and open enough to incorporate the interests of private entrepreneurs, rather than working against them. When private entrepreneurs join the Communist Party, they do not have to subject themselves to any material constraints, and they do not have to hide or apologize for their entrepreneurial activities. To the contrary, they are praised for their success, and they are able to use their Party connections to further their material gains. In the early 2000s, the Central Party School even began to offer special classes and programs for private entrepreneurs, and top CCP leaders invited private business-people to accompany them on trips abroad. These actions have derived in part from the Party leadership's desire to coopt private entrepreneurs, but equally from the recognition that the interests of private business owners largely converge with those of the CCP. In other words, cooperation and intertwinement have become a win–win relationship for both the CCP and private entrepreneurs. A similar logic has driven private entrepreneurs' willingness to join associations affiliated with the Party-state, and to work within Party-state bodies, such as people's congresses and rural village councils.

This situation is almost completely opposite to the relationship between private entrepreneurs and the English state around the time of the Industrial Revolution. In England at this time, the non-democratic state acted as a parasite on members of the newly emerging entrepreneurial class, levying heavy taxes on them and forcing them to loan large amounts of money to the state with little to no return. Facing such economic abuse, private entrepreneurs in England pressed for democratic rights in order to protect their property and ensure their ability to grow and profit. In China since the early 1990s, in contrast, private entrepreneurs have benefited materially, socially, and politically from the policies of the state, and from their personal connections to the state. As a result, they have had no reason to press for fundamental political change, and many reasons to support the political status quo.

COLLEGE STUDENTS AND GRADUATES

A second key demographic group includes college students and graduates. Historically, both in China and around the world, college students and graduates have acted as critics of authoritarian regimes, and have pressed for democratic change. In fact, in China in the 1980s, relations between college-educated individuals and the state were increasingly attenuated, and at times flared into outright confrontation. The dramatic student-led demonstrations of the spring of 1989 were the most severe of these conflicts. Yet from the early 1990s through the present, college-educated individuals have evidenced a general decline in support for fundamental political change, and a greater interest in embedding themselves in China's current system – a development that has been both surprising and puzzling to Westerners, who have assumed that the further liberalization of China's economy would inevitably lead college students and graduates to press for liberal democratic political change.

In the late 1970s and 1980s, the relationship between China's Party-state and college students was somewhat schizophrenic. On the one hand, the political and social status of college-educated individuals rose dramatically, as the CCP (under Deng Xiaoping's leadership) dropped its Mao-era denigration of intellectuals, instead viewing educated individuals as valued drivers of China's economic and technological modernization. Yet on the other hand, the economic status of intellectuals and college students did not rise commensurately. This was because college students in the early post-Mao period still received jobs in a "communist" fashion: they were assigned to positions by the government, and they typically did not receive much more pay than did uneducated workers in the public sector. Meanwhile, as private enterprises slowly grew in the 1980s, individuals without college degrees increasingly were earning more than university graduates with state sector jobs. College students believed that many uneducated private businesspeople were profiting from their political connections; consequently, college students were increasingly frustrated with the status quo. Further, when the Party-state lifted price controls on some goods and services in the late 1980s, inflation spiraled, and the material conditions of most college-educated individuals declined. Concomitantly, top CCP leaders swung between policies that ceded greater autonomy and power to college students, and policies that repressed and constricted their freedom.

As a result, during the late 1970s and 1980s many college students did not feel that their needs were being adequately met by the Party. Indeed, at times their dissatisfaction was so great that they engaged in outright protest directed at the central political system. One notable case occurred in the winter of 1986–1987. During this time, then Party

General Secretary Hu Yaobang expressed the belief that economic modernization required further educational, political and administrative reform. Students responded by airing their grievances. Demonstrations began at the University of Science and Technology (UST) in Anhui province, when students protested their inability to nominate candidates for the local people's congress. Students at UST and other schools also complained about the students' poor living conditions, and expressed indignation at the gap between their educational attainment and their low salaries upon graduation. Campus protest activities spread across the country – including roughly 40,000 students at 150 higher education institutions in seventeen cities. While Party General Secretary Hu Yaobang quietly indicated his support of the students, the CCP's most powerful leader – Deng Xiaoping – declared that the movement must be put to an end. Subsequently, General Secretary Hu was forced to resign from his post (but remained on the Party's Politburo). Zhao Ziyang became the new General Secretary. In official media outlets, the protestors' demands were criticized as "bourgeois liberalism," and participants were described as having been led by a "handful of lawbreakers who disguised themselves as students," bent on fomenting nationwide chaos and disrupting stability and unity. Yet even so, the student participants generally were not punished. Further, central authorities responded to some of the protestors' grievances. Perhaps most importantly, they announced that candidates for local people's congresses would now be nominated by the electorate.

When former General Secretary Hu died on April 15, 1989, spontaneous popular mourning developed into renewed activism by college students. Exacerbating the grievances that had not been resolved by the protests of 1986–1987, inflation had soared into the double-digits. Students again drew attention to their poor living conditions, especially in contrast to "corrupt" cadres who used their political connections to profit from market reforms. Students also demanded democratic rights such as freedom of association and speech. By the end of May, protests had spread to virtually every major Chinese city, involving millions, and including workers, intellectuals, and citizens from nearly all walks of life. Along with street marches, sit-ins, and hunger strikes, students and workers formed autonomous organizations free from CCP control. Their collective actions persisted for more than one and a half months, due not only to the determined efforts of the participants, but also to a factional battle between more sympathetic Party elites, led by General Secretary Zhao Ziyang, and more hardline figures, such as Premier Li Peng. In early June, Deng Xiaoping ordered the military to clear out the remaining demonstrators at Beijing's central Tian'anmen Square, and violent force was used to remove anyone who stood in the soldiers' way; up to thousands of innocent civilians were killed, and many more were seriously injured.[15] Zhao was dismissed from his post and placed under house arrest, where he remained until his death in 2005. The official verdict in the media was vehement: a "small handful" had incited "chaos" and "pandemonium," resulting in a "shocking counter-revolutionary rebellion" – a "struggle involving the life and death of the Party and the state."

Thus, as the 1980s came to a close in China, it appeared that the CCP-led regime was not adequately satisfying the needs and demands of college students (as well as other social groups), and as a result, it was facing a rebellion. Many in the West assumed that the regime's violent repression of the protests would only further alienate and mobilize the population – particularly given the impending fall of communist regimes in the Soviet Union and Eastern/Central Europe. Yet, this did not occur. To the contrary, since the early 1990s college students have been remarkably quiescent, and have displayed an increased interest in joining the CCP. As noted in Chapter 3, by 2013, over 40 percent of all Party members were college graduates. Moreover, rather than seeking jobs that are distant from the Party-state, many young people have reported "a strong desire" to be employed in a government or Party position.

Further, from the 1990s through the present, when college students have engaged in public protests, they have not pressed for political change, but rather have defended China – and the Chinese government – against its foreign and domestic detractors. In 1999, student protests were sparked by the American military's bombing of the Chinese embassy in Belgrade. For three days, tens of thousands of students marched through the embassy districts of major cities and gathered in front of the embassy compounds of the US and other NATO countries. Their slogans – such as "down with the Yankees" and "sovereignty and peace" – echoed the CCP-controlled media's castigation of NATO countries, particularly the US. In 2005, student protests arose in response to the Japanese government's approval of a new middle school history textbook that diminished Japanese atrocities in China during WWII and portrayed Japan as a "benevolent liberator." When several anti-Japanese websites called for mass demonstrations in early May, government officials announced that future "unauthorized marches" would be illegal, and warned that police "would mete out tough blows" to those caught vandalizing property. Shortly thereafter, the protests ended. In 2008, student protests emerged in the context of a clash that occurred in Tibet, wherein Tibetan street demonstrators calling for greater autonomy were linked to the destruction of Han Chinese businesses, and CCP authorities responded with force. At the time of this occurrence, the Olympic torch was making its way around the globe in anticipation of the Beijing Olympics. As the torch traveled its route, foreign protestors criticized China's ruling elites and interfered with the progress of the relay. In China, students erupted in protest – defending China's integrity, and castigating foreign media outlets, groups, and individuals critical of China's response to the demonstrators in Tibet. When the French government did not intervene to block protestors from disturbing the progress of the Olympic torch relay in France, students and other mainland Chinese citizens joined a boycott of the French "Carrefour" stores in China. As with the other student protests since the early 1990s, participants voiced no criticism of China's governing authorities or political system; rather, they amplified the stance of the official media.

Why have college students apparently moved from criticism of and distance from the political system in the 1980s, to support for and embeddedness within it from the 1990s through the present? The answer, as with private entrepreneurs, lies in the post-1989 combination of market reforms and continued CCP dominance of the political system. To begin, since the early 1990s, China's higher education system has been marketized. In the Maoist period, college was virtually free, and parents had little choice as to the elementary, middle, and high schools that their child would attend. As a result, although disparities in college preparation existed between urban and rural areas, during the Maoist period, college admission was equally open to all young people, rich or poor. Since the early 1990s, colleges have charged tuition, and wealth increasingly has determined a student's ability to enter the prestigious "feeder schools" that substantially improve a student's likelihood of being admitted to college. By the end of the first decade of the millennium, for example, fees for premier "feeder schools" in Beijing reportedly had reached US$16,000 – a figure that exceeds the average yearly per capita income in Beijing.[16] Further, even if a student from a less privileged background succeeds in getting admitted to university, the required tuition and fees have become prohibitive for most families: the average annual expense for a college student now exceeds the average yearly per capita income in China. Consequently, since the early 1990s, university students in China increasingly have come from financially privileged families.[17] Inasmuch as the Party-state has been seen by these well-off students as facilitating their economic affluence and educational attainment, college students have been satisfied with the existing political system.

Meanwhile, the end of government job allocations for college graduates has dramatically changed their perception of the Party-dominated political system. Since they are no longer required to enter state sector jobs with limited pay, the private sector has offered educated individuals opportunities for affluence. Further, because the state sector has had to compete with the private sector to attract university graduates, government-affiliated employers have offered higher pay for skilled positions than was the case under the allocation system that remained largely in place in the 1980s. Consequently, in comparison with the 1980s, a college graduate's "return" on education has more than doubled. Coupled with the fact that college students today typically come from affluent backgrounds prior to their admission to college, the overall result has been that degree holders from the 1990s through the present have experienced a reduced gap between their educational attainment and their material prosperity.

Concomitantly, the Party-state has expanded the number of college admittees. In the early 1990s, the total number of university students in China was around 2 million; by 2013, the total number of students *graduating* annually from college was nearly 7 million. Within the population as a whole, the percentage of people with college degrees has more than tripled as compared with the 1980s. Although the expansion in university admissions can be seen as a welcome development, one negative result is that it has vastly intensified the competition for jobs among college graduates.

This situation has fueled frustration within this group. Although in 2011 and 2012 more than 90 percent of college graduates had found jobs within six months, the figure for 2013 graduates was closer to 80 percent. And, the surplus of college graduates has put downward pressure on the salaries and wages that they can command. Yet, although these circumstances might be expected to lead college-educated individuals to turn against the governing regime, they have instead turned toward it.

The reason, as with private entrepreneurs, is that the CCP simultaneously dominates the political system and has become more open and responsive to those with a college education. As a result, and as discussed in Chapter 3, college students and graduates have come to view connections with the CCP as an important means to getting a good job. At the same time, the Party (unlike in the Maoist period) welcomes college graduates into its ranks, and does not require that they articulate a belief in communist ideology, or otherwise sacrifice their moral or ideational beliefs. Party membership, in other words, has virtually no down-side, and many positive benefits. Overall, since the early 1990s, the existing political system generally has worked in a way that has favored the interests of college students. Even so, frustration with the dearth of good jobs for college graduates – a shortfall that in recent years has been growing – remains high, and has the potential to lead college students and graduates to become dissatisfied with the political status quo.

It should be noted that a small number of college-educated intellectuals have remained highly critical of China's CCP-dominated political system, and have engaged in both public and private acts of dissent. As discussed earlier, Nobel Peace Prize winner Liu Xiaobo and the other signatories of "Charter 08" represent one important example. Other quasi-dissident actions have been undertaken by intellectuals, lawyers, and journalists involved in what is known as the "rights protection movement" (*weiquan yundong*). These individuals represent and seek redress for those who have been victims of wrong-doing by local officials. Most well-known participants in the movement have been subjected to surveillance, harassment, threats, and physical violence. Many of the lawyers have been barred from practicing law, and some have been jailed.[18] The other most significant instance of collective political dissent in the post-1989 period occurred in 1998. That year, some of the leaders of the student protests of 1989 and the "Democracy Wall" movement of 1978–80[19] formed a true opposition party – the China Democracy Party (CDP). At its peak, the CDP had local committees in 24 provinces and cities, as well as a "preparatory" national committee. The CDP maintained a public appearance on the mainland for roughly six months before its leaders were arrested and the group was forced to cease its public activities.[20] Some of its founders were punished with lengthy prison sentences, but have since been released and exiled overseas. They continue their activism from a distance, and claim that the CDP remains active underground in China. As courageous as these individuals undoubtedly are, they represent only a miniscule portion of China's total population, and they have not been able to attract more widespread participation on the part of the general public.

RANK-AND-FILE WORKERS

Rank-and-file workers (or manual laborers) form a third key demographic group whose support is needed in order for the Chinese Party-state to remain stable. In part, this is because of their numbers – they, along with farmers, comprise more than 85 percent of China's population. Moreover, because the CCP still portrays itself as a *communist party*, to some extent its legitimacy rests on its claim to represent the interests of workers. And, workers (particularly in the public sector) have taken this regime claim quite seriously. In China, rank-and-file workers are divided into two types, each with different backgrounds and experiences. Their difference in background traces back to the fact that everyone in China has a residential registration card (known as a *hukou*) that stipulates whether they are a rural or urban resident, and in which specific location. Virtually all rank-and-file public sector workers are urban *hukou*-holders who are from the city and work in the city, while the vast majority of rank-and file private sector workers are rural *hukou*-holders who are from the countryside but have migrated to the city to find wage work. This basic difference coincides with quite substantial differences in the social, political, and economic experiences of rank-and-file public and private sector workers in the Maoist and post-Mao periods.

From the late 1970s through the early 1990s, public sector workers (who at the time made up roughly 42 percent of China's industrial workforce, and 46 percent of all employed urban *hukou*-holders) continued to enjoy the "iron rice bowl" benefits that had been afforded them during the Mao era. Along with a guarantee of lifetime employment, the "iron rice bowl" included subsidized meals in on-site cafeterias, ration coupons for consumer goods and daily necessities, housing with extremely low monthly rents, medical care, child care, a complimentary set of work clothes and shoes each year, and eligibility for state-provided loans. In addition, workers were allowed to retire at a relatively young age, supported by fairly generous pensions. Concomitantly, the Party-state's toleration of the emergence of private enterprise in the early post-Mao period increased the number and quality of consumer goods and services available to state sector workers. Thus, overall, the needs of state sector workers were met increasingly well from the late 1970s through the early 1990s.

In the mid-1990s, however, this situation changed dramatically, and for the worse: approximately one third of state-owned enterprise (SOE) employees were laid-off when the Party-state ordered large-scale reforms that privatized most SOEs. Many other SOE workers were forced into early retirement, and did not receive their full pensions. Meanwhile, still-employed state sector workers experienced cuts in pay and benefits, as well as more exacting and undesirable working conditions. This reality fuelled great dissatisfaction, and indeed sparked massive protests on the part of former SOE workers in the late 1990s and early 2000s. In 2002, for example, protests in the Northeastern industrial cities of Daqing and Liaoyang drew tens of thousands of laid-off workers from state-owned oil plants. At least ten of China's twenty-three provinces witnessed similar large-scale and protracted protests by former SOE employees.[21] However, these workers did not call for liberal democratic political reform; rather, they implored the ruling regime to make good on its communist promises. Even so, at the time, it seemed possible that this group might pose a challenge to the stability of China's political system.

Yet this possibility did not come to fruition. Since the middle of the first decade of the 2000s, protests by current or former state sector workers have been exceedingly rare. The reason is that China's governing regime has done an adequate job of attending to their basic needs. Even more so than with private entrepreneurs and college-educated individuals, the Party-state's ability and willingness to do so has derived from its still somewhat "communist" nature. For example, in the context of SOE privatization, public housing units previously provided at nearly no cost to urban state-sector workers were privatized as well. Yet, in keeping with the Chinese Party-state's "communist" commitments, existing tenants were allowed to purchase the units at prices that were so low (far below market price) that most were easily able to buy with cash. Consequently, although many SOE workers lost their jobs in the mid-to-late 1990s, virtually none have had to worry about housing. In addition, former state-sector workers have been eligible for an array of state-provided aid, including basic living expenses, job training assistance, and preferential hiring and tax benefits and loans for those starting private businesses. Further, as will be discussed more fully in Chapter 5, since the start of the new millennium the CCP has worked to put in place a new pension system. And, most urban state-sector workers appear to be satisfied with the results. Overall, although many former state sector workers have experienced a decline in living conditions relative to the early 1990s, their basic needs have been adequately met, and they show no sign of desiring or seeking an end to CCP rule – particularly because the CCP has retained at least some of the "communist" policies and practices that have been of aid to rank-and-file state sector workers.

As noted above, the situation for rank-and-file *private* sector workers – the vast majority of whom are rural migrants to the cities – has been quite different. In general, their living conditions have improved dramatically relative to the Maoist period, and over the course of the post-Mao period. Most rank-and-file private sector workers were forced to live in the countryside as farmers during the Maoist period, due to the regime's tight restrictions on residence enforced through the *hukou* system. During this time, Party-state policies favored urban workers over rural farmers (for example, forcing farmers to sell their produce to the state at very low prices so that the regime could provide low-cost food to urban workers), and did not allow farmers (or anyone, for that matter) to engage in private enterprise. As a result, most rural residents lived in poverty. Indeed, at some points during the Maoist era (most notably during the Great Leap Forward of 1958–1960) millions of farmers starved to death. Since 1978, migration restrictions have been progressively (though incrementally) loosened, allowing rural *hukou*-holders to travel to the city to set up small-scale street-side businesses, or to find waged work in the private sector. Manual laborers in the private sector typically have had to endure exacting and oppressive working conditions. However, they have earned far more in these jobs than they could have back in the countryside, enabling them to enjoy a standard of living that – while very rudimentary by Western standards – far exceeds that of the past, and has improved continually over the course of the post-Mao period. Moreover, as will be discussed in the section that follows, they have had a safety net of land rights back in their home villages in the event that things go awry in the city.

Further, when rank-and-file private sector workers have collectively protested against physical and economic abuses perpetrated by their employers and local political authorities, central political authorities not infrequently have intervened on their behalf. Typical private sector worker grievances have centered on wage arrears and wage underpayment, as well as draconian workplace rules and related fines. These abuses have led private sector factory workers to seek redress via direct requests to the employer. When these attempts have been met with intransigence, and especially when they have led to violent acts of reprisal on the part of the employer, workers sometimes have engaged in mass protests. In the case of self-employed private sector workers, such as pedicab drivers and street peddlers, mistreatment by local authorities has in some cases sparked immediate mass protests, without any prior attempt to seek redress via other methods, such as petitioning local political authorities. These types of protests by rank-and-file private sector workers have shown no sign of abating.

However, although many rank-and-file private sector workers are angry about their mistreatment by their employers, as well as by local political authorities who work as allies to these employers, central regime policies and actions have worked to their benefit. This is in part because the central regime has dismantled its prior "communist" controls over the economy, allowing for easier internal migration, as well as the rise of private business. At the same time, the central regime's continued "communist" commitment to satisfactory working conditions for manual laborers has led it to step in when the most egregious cases of abuse have been brought to its attention by protests. And, the central regime's "communist" guarantee of land rights to rural *hukou*-holders has served as a crucial safety net for rank-and-file private sectors with this residential status. Overall, the result has been that the basic needs of rank-and-file private sector workers have been adequately met by the central regime. Thus, their dissatisfaction with their employers and local political authorities has not been translated into discontent with the political system as a whole.

FARMERS

Farmers comprise another key social group whose support (or at least tolerance) is necessary in order for China's governing regime to remain stable. The importance of farmers lies partly in their numbers: as of 2013, just under half of China's population lived in the countryside, engaged in agricultural pursuits. Yet farmers' importance also lies in the history of China and the CCP: peasants formed the backbone of the communist rebellion that brought the CCP to power, and farmers have been at the forefront of perhaps a majority of the "mass disturbances" that have been prevalent in China since the 1990s. Central authorities are aware of these realities, and as a result have tried (albeit with mixed success) to respond satisfactorily to farmers' grievances and attend to their basic needs. Yet many farmers remain dissatisfied with the political status quo, and collective protests continue to arise in China's countryside.

The general situation of China's farmers mirrors that of rank-and-file private sector workers. As discussed above, during the Maoist period, farmers (as rural *hukou*-holders) were forced to live in the countryside, and were told by Party-state authorities what to grow, and for how much it could be sold. Most lived in abject poverty; at times, farmers suffered to the point of starvation. In the post-Mao period, the central Party-state's policies toward rural farmers have changed dramatically, in a way that has worked immensely to their benefit – particularly relative to the Mao era. Yet, farmers have continued to endure corrupt and abusive practices on the part of local political authorities. Further, their material improvement has not been steady over time or consistent geographically, and they have continued to have a far lower standard of living than do those who hold urban residence permits.

Overall, the economic freedom of farmers has increased dramatically relative to the Maoist period, and their material status has improved substantially. Whereas during the Maoist period all land was collectivized and all agricultural products were bought and sold through the state-planned economy, in the post-Mao period rural residents have been allowed to lease their own plots of land (for 30-year, renewable terms); to determine (in consultation with political authorities) what to produce from the land; and to sell their produce in free markets. Central authorities also have allowed non-agricultural local government-affiliated rural enterprises (known as Township and Village Enterprises, or TVEs) to emerge, which have offered local wage work to rural residents otherwise engaged in agriculture – work that typically has been more lucrative than agriculture. Similarly, with the loosening of internal migration restrictions and the rise of private enterprises in the cities, former farmers have moved to the city, earning wages and sending their savings back to their families still living in the countryside. Starvation is no longer a possibility. In this sense, China's post-Mao political system has satisfied farmers' most basic human need to survive – something that the Maoist government at times failed to do.

Beyond this, however, during the post-Mao period the living conditions of farmers have varied according to geographic location, and have waxed and waned over time. Thus, the political system has been inconsistent in its fulfillment of farmers' basic needs. When Mao-era agricultural collectives were replaced by the leasing of land to individual families in the late 1970s and early 1980s, local authorities lost their main source of revenue. In rural areas located in coastal provinces near the Special Enterprise Zones (SEZs) that were first established in the late 1970s, and that became a hothouse for very profitable export-oriented private enterprises, TVEs were very successful. In these areas, TVE profits provided local Party-state authorities with a new source of revenue to replace that lost by the dissolution of China's Mao-era agricultural collectives.

TVEs in China's central and western areas were far less successful. In these areas, township and village officials responded to their shortage of funds by adding to legally sanctioned taxes various supplemental fees, assessments, fines, and forced contributions. Peasants were required to pay for government services such as licenses and birth registration, and were penalized for both minor and major infractions – including fines that exceeded the average farmer's yearly income for having a second child within five years of the first. In addition, compulsory assessments were exacted for school and road construction, water projects, power station building and maintenance, medical facilities, and public security. Farmers in these areas resisted, engaging in collective protests that in some cases turned violent. Many local authorities responded with force, ransacking farmers' homes, taking their grain, livestock, and other belongings, and in some cases beating them to the point of serious injury, or even death.[22]

Central Party-state authorities did not ignore these problems; to the contrary, they made concrete and quite effective moves to resolve them. First, as discussed in Chapter 3, they called for the institution of local village council (VC) elections. The central leaders' goal was to root out corrupt local officials and bring in those who would better satisfy farmers' needs, and who – due to their greater legitimacy deriving from their popular election – could more effectively implement unpopular central policies, such as those regarding birth control. As discussed above, in localities where free and fair VC elections have occurred, popular satisfaction with local authorities has increased. And, in areas where there have been corrupt or manipulative electoral infractions on the part of local authorities, central authorities not infrequently have responded to local residents' demands for resolution. Further working to satisfy the demands of the rural population, in 2002, central Party-state authorities banned all local taxes and fees. Importantly, this ban has been effectively implemented. Since that time, rural protests and petition efforts revolving around excessive taxation have disappeared, as farmer grievances with this issue have been addressed.

Subsequently, however, new farmer concerns have arisen. In search of new sources of income, and aware that they will be evaluated based on the economic vitality of their locality, local rural authorities have requisitioned farmers' land and leased it to private businesses. Since 1990, land requisitions have affected at least 100 million farmers. The impact of these requisitions has been uneven. In some locations, land revenues have been used to provide public services, or even give villagers regular stipends that provide them with a higher and more stable income than they had earned from farming. Yet, in many cases farmers' compensation for their lost land has been viewed as inadequate and unfair. Accordingly, protests against such practices have been targeted at local political authorities. Not infrequently, these authorities have responded to farmer protests with repression and violent force.[23]

Since 2006, central political leaders have tried to address this issue. Along with directing provincial governors and local officials to reduce land requisitions, central leaders have stepped in to resolve farmer grievances as expressed in their collective protests. In some cases, these central government actions have been effective, and farmer satisfaction has increased. But in many other cases, under-compensated land requisitions have continued, and farmer unrest has continued to emerge. In these areas, farmers' basic needs are not being satisfied by the existing political system, with the result that farmers have remained a volatile political force. At the Third Plenum of the Eighteenth Central Committee in late 2013, top Party leaders publicly underscored their resolve to abolish unfair and unwanted land acquisitions by local authorities, prohibiting them from confiscating land without the permission of the household, and requiring that the household be compensated at full market value. Yet as long as the central Party-state does not address the underlying impetus for these acquisitions – the shortage of funds for local leaders, and the emphasis on local economic growth – problems of this sort are likely to continue.

In a broad attempt to address some of the underlying problems in the countryside, in 2006 the central government launched the "New Socialist Countryside" initiative. As will be discussed more fully in Chapter 6, this has included the abolition of educational fees for poor families, the expansion of agricultural subsidies, the creation of a rural "welfare" system for the poor, the expansion of rural healthcare, and the initiation of new rural consumer subsidies for home appliances.[24] Further, following the economic crash that began in the US in 2008, China's central government passed a large-scale stimulus package that included roughly US$60 million in rural infrastructure expenditures.

Though problems remain, these policies represent a significant and much-appreciated effort to address the needs of China's rural population.

In sum, when looking at all of the major social groups whose acceptance of the political status quo is key to the stability of China's CCP-led political system, in the post-Mao period – and particularly since the 1990s – central authorities have done an adequate job of satisfying the needs and demands of the populace. And, for most members of most of these groups, the political system's willingness and ability to do so have improved over time. As a result, key groups within China's citizenry have shown little to no desire to overturn or fundamentally change the political system. Some members of some groups – particularly farmers who have continued to suffer unfair land requisitions – remain highly dissatisfied. But, as with other groups that have expressed grievances since the early 1990s, their anger has been directed at local political authorities and businesses, and not at central leaders or the political system as a whole. Indeed, to the extent that central authorities have stepped in to support aggrieved citizens and sanction corrupt local officials, the legitimacy of the central government has improved in these citizens' eyes.

ETHNIC MINORITIES

The groups described above almost exclusively consist of China's dominant Han ethnicity, which includes more than 90 percent of China's population. In contrast to most Han Chinese, members of some of China's non-Han minorities (particularly Tibetans and Uighurs, and to a lesser extent Mongolians) have been highly dissatisfied with the CCP-led government's rule – some to the point of demanding political separation. The underlying grievance articulated by Tibetan, Uighur, and Mongolian groups has been the CCP-encouraged influx of Han

Chinese into once minority-dominant regions. Causing particular ire has been the resultant economic and political dominance of Han Chinese in these regions, as well as the repression of local minority cultures and lifestyles. For Uighurs – who are ethnically Turkic Muslims, and who mostly live in the Xinjiang Uighur Autonomous region that borders Pakistan – further fuel has been added to the fire since September 11, 2001, as the Chinese government has ramped up efforts to assimilate Uighurs under the pretext of fighting "terrorism."

In recent cases of Mongolian protests, central CCP authorities have made attempts to address the minority protestors' grievances. Demonstrations in Tibet and Xinjiang, in contrast, typically have been met with unapologetic repression. The most recent significant incident involving Tibetans occurred in 2008. In April of that year, hundreds of Tibetan monks took to the streets on the 49th anniversary of a Tibetan uprising against Chinese rule. They called for the release of fellow monks who had been detained for publicly celebrating an award given by the US government to the Dalai Lama. As protests escalated, violent clashes with public security forces ensued; human rights groups estimate that at least 140 were killed. Collective action on the part of Uighurs also had involved violence, and has included incidents far outside of the Xinjiang Uighur Autonomous region. In 2009, over 200 were left dead in Xinjiang in clashes between ethnic Uighurs and local Han Chinese. In October 2013, in front of Beijing's Tian'anmen Square, an SUV was set aflame and ran into a group of bystanders, killing two of them. In March 2014, individuals of Uighur ethnicity wielding knives and axes indiscriminately attacked passengers at a train station in the southeastern city of Kunming, killing roughly thirty. Within the next two months, in Xinjiang, a train station was bombed and a car crashed into bystanders at a public market and launched explosives, killing at least 46 and injuring more than 200. In July 2014 armed clashes between Uighur protestors and government forces in Xinjiang resulted in approximately 100 deaths.

These events have sparked great concern among CCP elites; in May 2014, Xi Jinping made a widely covered visit to Xinjiang, meeting with Party leaders there. Alongside some positive directives – most notably, that at least one-fourth of Xinjiang's state-owned enterprise employees be ethnic Uighurs – the need to take strong and decisive action against Uighur "terrorists" was emphasized. The latter is likely to only further exacerbate tensions among Uighurs, Han Chinese, and CCP authorities. To the extent that this transpires, violent attacks and clashes are likely to continue.

Although deadly incidents such as those listed above represent some de-stabilization of the polity – particularly in Tibet and Xinjiang – they are unlikely to pose a serious threat to the CCP-led political system as a whole. For, politically active members of these ethnic minority groups typically are not viewed with sympathy by members of the majority Han ethnicity. As discussed earlier, the Chinese government's repression of Tibetan demonstrators in 2008 was vocally supported by Han Chinese. Recent acts of violence against innocent civilians attributed to Uighur separatists have only accentuated Han Chinese fears of collective contention on the part of ethnic minorities, and further increased Han Chinese support of strict measures to control them.

ENVIRONMENTAL PROTESTS

Other public grievances that have emerged in the post-Mao period have not been associated with a particular ethnic or socio-economic group, but rather have attracted people from various walks of life who share similar concerns. Perhaps the most notable grievance of this nature has centered on environmental damage. Unlike regime responses to collective action on the part of Tibetans and Uighurs, yet similar to regime responses to popular contention on the part of the major socio-economic groups discussed above, the public expression of environmental concerns generally has been met with sympathy and redress on the part of central authorities, even when the source of the environmental problem was corrupt or careless behavior on the part of local political officials. Further, as with other kinds of public protests, in some cases local authorities (particularly those who have been popularly elected) have worked with their constituents to oppose environmentally harmful actions undertaken by local businesses and approved by other local officials. This reality underscores the fact that although in many ways China's ruling regime remains closed, corrupt, repressive, and "authoritarian," in other respects the regime has been responsive to public concerns.

Almost always, environmental protests have been preceded by failed attempts to seek redress via formal political processes. Some aggrieved citizens have filed environmental lawsuits, but nearly all have been rejected by China's courts.[25] A more common tactic has been writing joint letters of complaint and launching petition drives. As with other kinds of collective grievances, when attempts at redress via this method have failed, citizens have engaged in street protests.

A notable recent example of environmental protest occurred in 2011, in Haining city, Zhejiang Province. In this instance, local residents targeted a solar panel company whose discharge was believed to have caused an unusually high number of cancer cases in the community. Although the local environmental protection bureau had found the river water to be contaminated and had ordered the factory to halt operations, the company had not followed through. When a massive die-off of fish was discovered, roughly 500 residents rushed to the factory, overturning vehicles, breaking windows, and ransacking offices. For four days, the protestors remained in front of the factory. The demonstrations were forcibly ended when riot police arrived to clear the site. The factory subsequently was shut down and required to clean up its environmental damage.

Another example occurred the same year in the northeastern city of Dalian. The demonstrators' main concern was the threat of future environmental damage caused by a factory jointly owned by the city and a private company. The Party chief in Dalian had approved the factory. When a film crew from the Party-state-affiliated China Central Television (CCTV) that had come to investigate the safety of the plant was beaten and the crew's news report was pulled, outraged online discussion spread. Following an anonymous Internet call for citizens to gather in the city's central square, more than 10,000 demonstrators appeared. Both the new Dalian CCP chief and the Mayor of Dalian announced to the crowd that the factory would cease production and be moved out of the city.

These cases show that even when the Chinese political system's more regular channels of grievance resolution fail, mass protest can result in a sympathetic government response. Even when some local leaders engage in behavior that is harmful to the population, other local leaders – particularly those who have been elected – may respond to resident concerns with sympathy and support. And when central leaders have been made aware of mass protests, central authorities not infrequently have intervened in a way that satisfies the complainants.

CONCLUSION

Overall, although the Chinese political system remains authoritarian in many ways, in the post-Mao period it has done an adequate – and generally improving – job of responding to public grievances and satisfying the needs of important demographic groups. The Chinese public can articulate its concerns and request redress via a number of venues, including those that are an official part of the political system (such as the courts, letters and visits offices, and local elections), and those that are not (namely, collective protests). To the extent that these official venues are open and responsive to popular input, they may be viewed as more democratic elements of the system. And to the extent that collective protests have been allowed, and even viewed with sympathy by central Party elites, the Chinese public has been able to use this mechanism to express and gain redress for its grievances.

Simultaneously, some of the more authoritarian and "communist" features of China's political system have helped to satisfy the needs of some key demographic groups. For private entrepreneurs, the Party-state's continued control over many aspects of the economy has benefited the sizeable percentage of entrepreneurs that enjoy close connections with the CCP. Because the CCP now embraces private entrepreneurs and supports their desire to earn profit, private entrepreneurs have gained as a result of the CCP's political monopoly. Meanwhile, for public sector workers, the Party-state has continued to provide some valued benefits (such as pensions and affordable housing) that derive from its still "communist" commitment to the well-being of the working class. And for farmer and private sector workers (the vast majority of whom hold rural residential permits), the CCP-led regime's guarantee of land adequate for survival has attended to this very basic human need.

Even so, the Chinese Party-state has fallen short in many respects, and its political support among some key demographic groups is shaky at best. Perhaps most importantly, illegal and under-compensated land acquisitions approved and undertaken by local officials have yet to be brought to an end; until this occurs, farmer discontent will remain widespread. And although central (and some local) authorities have been making real efforts to halt practices that degrade the natural environment and harm local populations, China's environment remains severely compromised, and popular discontent with the harmful effects of this degradation continues to run high. To some extent, because China's governing system remains authoritarian at the apex, central authorities have the ability to move relatively quickly in their efforts to resolve these problems. However, the underlying cause of both land acquisitions and environmental destruction is the overwhelming quest for economic growth. Consequently, central political leaders have faced competing pressures to allow practices that spur economic growth (which generally has benefited all citizens) while simultaneously responding to citizen grievances about some of the ill effects of these practices. Thus far, the regime has done a satisfactory job of walking that line – due both to its open and somewhat democratic characteristics, and to its closed and authoritarian features.

5 | Managing the Economy ———

While China's ruling Party-state has done an adequate, albeit mixed, job of responding to public grievances and attending to the needs of key social groups, when it comes to managing the economy and promoting economic growth, the Party-state's record is much more impressive. Further, with regard to this latter essential requirement of a stable governing regime, China's authoritarian and "communist" features seem to have played a more beneficial role than has been the case regarding the first essential requirement. Indeed, in some important respects, these features have helped to enable China's economy to not only grow at an astounding rate, but also to avoid severe crises.

All governments are involved in the economy to some degree. Regardless of ideology or regime type, since the time of the Industrial Revolution, most political leaders have sought to promote economic growth and vitality within the territory under their governance. And, in virtually all countries, the populace has tended to attribute its nation's national economic health or weakness to its political leadership. But, just as countries can be more or less democratic, governments can be more or less involved in the economy, and their level of involvement can shift over time. Further, there are different ways in which a political regime can try to shape economic outcomes. And, these methods often change with time.

In China, the level and type of government involvement in the economy has shifted quite dramatically from the Mao era through the present. For most of the Maoist period, the Chinese economy was almost entirely state-run. In the post-Mao era, significant portions of the economy have been privatized and liberalized. But, many "communist" and Party-state-dominated features have remained. Simultaneously, China's economy has exhibited the highest sustained growth rates that the world has ever seen.

This chapter examines the ways in which CCP and state entities have intervened in, regulated, and transformed the Chinese economy over the course of the post-Mao period, and in contrast with the Maoist era. In so doing, the chapter assesses the success of post-Mao governmental efforts to maintain economic stability and growth. Moreover, the chapter examines the ways in which the post-Mao Party-state's mixture of democratic and authoritarian features, as well as its pragmatic embrace of both "communist" and "capitalist" economic practices, have shaped China's economic results.

ECONOMIC POLICY IN THE MAOIST ERA

The Chinese Party-state's current efforts to effectively intervene in the economy can only be understood in reference to the economic policies undertaken under Mao. Overall, although China's economy did grow during the Maoist era, it did so only very fitfully and unevenly. In general, urban residents enjoyed relative economic security and stability, while rural residents – who made up the vast majority of the population – endured very difficult living conditions. Indeed, during some portions of the Maoist period, the rural economy suffered so severely that large numbers of farmers literally starved to death. Thus, on balance, the Chinese Party-state did a poor job of maintaining economic stability and growth under Mao.

The main factor that undermined the Party-state's effectiveness in fulfilling this governmental function during the Maoist era was Mao's prioritization of ideological correctness over economic pragmatism. In other words, Mao believed that it was more important to adhere to "correct" communist principles than it was to achieve economic growth and stability. This was because, in Mao's view, the only way to achieve economic growth and stability in an equal and non-exploitative manner (i.e., a "communist" manner) was through the communalization of land, factories, and all other forms of property. Further, Mao believed that a communist economy could not thrive until the populace had become wholly imbued with a communist culture. As a result, he prioritized cultural transformation over economic gain.

In the cities, these ideological precepts dictated that all businesses must be owned and controlled by the representative of the "masses" – the CCP-dominated government. Following the victory of the CCP in 1949, under the leadership of Mao, virtually all private businesses in China disappeared, and all industry and enterprise were placed in the hands of the Party-state. During the early Maoist period, the CCP closely adhered to the Russian communist model of urban industrial growth. Urban residents were assigned to jobs in various types of Party-state-owned and -operated enterprises, which were subject to the Party-state's plans for production and distribution. Urbanites almost invariably worked for the same enterprise for the entirety of their career; it was nearly impossible to get fired, or to move to a different place of employment. Within each enterprise, all workers were assigned to a "work unit" (*danwei*), through which they received access to the "iron rice bowl" benefits discussed in Chapter 4. The standard of living experienced by these urban workers was stable and secure,[1] but rudimentary and stagnant: rental housing was practically free, but the units were very small and spare; food was adequate, but of limited variety and quality; and consumer goods were scarce. Nonetheless, as discussed in Chapter 4, most urban workers were satisfied with their economic status, and felt very little stress related to their personal finances.

Economic conditions for rural residents in the Maoist period were quite different. Ever-changing policies created continual and tumultuous economic changes that left most farmers in abject poverty. Although the Party-state's land reform policies in the early Maoist period raised farmers above the subsistence line for the first time in China's history, leading to remarkable satisfaction among rural residents, later policies caused rural living standards to decline.

The most extreme of these later policies were those associated with the "Great Leap Forward" of 1958–1960. During this period, all rural land, housing, and property were collectivized into gigantic communes including thousands of households. Residents were compensated in "work points" assigned to different kinds of tasks. Communes were told to create their own steel through the creation of "backyard furnaces," into which residents tossed their metal items, using all available trees, boards, etc. to fuel the smelting fires. Lacking any technical know-how regarding steel production, what emerged from the furnaces was useless. Moreover, the central Party-state requisitioned a large portion of each commune's harvests to provide urban residents with subsidized food. Under pressure to reach or surpass the Party-state's high production targets, commune leaders regularly over-reported their harvests. When central authorities thus increased the central regime's grain requisitions, very little was left for the commune residents to survive upon. When bad weather hit and harvests suffered, mass starvation resulted. An estimated 20–45 million died.

Although the Party-state subsequently pulled back on some of these policies (for example, lowering the unit of agricultural production to a more manageable 20–25 households, and allowing farmers to privately use 5–10 percent of formerly collectivized land), the subsequent chaos of Mao's "Great Proletarian Cultural Revolution" (1966–1976) further destabilized the livelihood of China's rural residents. Along with having to house and feed Chinese youths encouraged by Mao to re-trace the steps of the CCP's famous "Long March" across China, rural residents had to take in and provide for millions of urbanites who were "sent down to the countryside" for education in manual labor so as to inculcate in them proper communist mentalities.

In sum, the economic policies of the Maoist period had a decidedly mixed impact on the population. Urban residents enjoyed an economically adequate and secure, albeit basic, standard of living, enabled in large part by the Party-state's procurement of foodstuffs from the countryside at low costs. The flip side for rural residents was a life of hard work for little to no gain, and in some years during the Maoist era outright starvation. Given that the vast majority of the population at this time lived in the countryside, overall, China's governing regime did a poor job of satisfying the second basic requirement of a stable government.

ECONOMIC POLICY IN THE POST-MAO ERA

This situation has changed dramatically in the post-Mao period. Although the Party-state continues to maintain some strict controls over the economy, in many important respects the economy has been privatized and liberalized. The result in terms of overall economic growth has been nothing short of phenomenal. As noted in Chapter 1, over the course of the post-Mao era, China's GDP has grown at a rate that is unmatched in human history. Between 1980 and 2005, China's GDP grew by more than 630 percent – more than ten times the global average during this period (53 percent). Moreover, this impressive economic growth has substantially increased the incomes and standards of living of virtually all Chinese citizens, who have experienced an average of 8 percent income growth every year for the more than thirty years that have passed in the post-Mao period. Over 500 million – far more people than the entire population of the United States – have risen out of poverty. Whereas during the Maoist period roughly 60 percent of the population (virtually all of whom lived in the countryside) lived in abject poverty, in the post-Mao era that figure has dropped to 10 percent.[2] Simultaneously, both rural and urban residents have been able to purchase a vast array of consumer goods (such as home appliances, televisions, and motorcycles) that were not only unaffordable but generally unavailable for individual purchase during the Maoist period. In sum, in the post-Mao era the Chinese Party-state has done an admirable job of maintaining economic growth and stability. However, the benefits of China's overall economic progress have not been evenly distributed, and the economic experience of some groups (particularly state-owned enterprise workers and farmers) has not been entirely positive. In addition, future high growth will require significant shifts in China's economy. China's political leaders have been working to address these issues, but their success in doing so remains to be seen.

Although a variety of factors have contributed to China's economic success since the death of Mao, the Chinese Party-state's economic policies have been critically important. China's post-Mao political leaders have reversed the priorities of the Maoist era: economic pragmatism now rules over ideological correctness. An encapsulation of this mentality is found in the famous dictum of the initiator of China's post-Mao reforms, Deng Xiaoping: "it doesn't matter if the cat is black or white, as long as it catches the mouse." Associated with this pragmatic focus on "whatever works" has been a great tolerance, and even encouragement, of local experimentation, accompanied by gradual change. This slowly evolving, experimental approach is captured in another phrase that has been followed by China's post-Mao leaders: "crossing the river by groping for stones" (*mo zhe shi tou guo he*). Such an approach involves no single set path, but rather constant testing and readjusting, and occasional retreats before resuming forward motion. The result has been an amalgam of "communist" economic features (such as continued Party-state ownership of most large enterprises as well as the banking system) and capitalist ones (such as thriving private enterprises and free-market Special Economic Zones). Simultaneously, the result has been substantial geographic variation in economic practices and outcomes.

RURAL ECONOMIC POLICIES AND RESULTS IN THE POST-MAO ERA

China's post-Mao rural economic reforms are emblematic of the pragmatic, experimental, and gradual approach undertaken by Party-state leaders since the death of Mao. They also exemplify the way in which China's economy has come to blend state-interventionist, communist, and capitalist elements, with results that generally have been quite satisfying to the Chinese public. As discussed above, during most of the Maoist period, virtually all land and property were collectivized, and China's giant rural population suffered. However, around 1978 (and by some reports as early as the late 1960s) political leaders in some villages began to experiment with allocating plots of land to individual households. As word spread that these practices were bringing increased farmer satisfaction and agricultural productivity, more villages began to do the same. Pleased with this positive development, in 1983 central leaders announced that a new "household responsibility system" (tudi chengbao zerenzhi) would be encouraged nationwide. By 1984, virtually the entire Chinese countryside had adopted this new system. According to official guidelines, plots were leased to families by the state for fifteen-year periods, with the allotment based on household size and labor supply. Among the various plot types sanctioned by central regulations, "grain ration" land was supposed to fulfill the basic consumption needs of the household. The Party-state made no claim to the produce of these plots. "Responsibility" land was granted in exchange for a fixed payment of grain or other agricultural items at a Party-state-stipulated below-market price. However, any additional produce from the "responsibility" plot could be used or sold as the household pleased. Similarly, "contract" land was allocated in return for a fixed cash payment, tantamount to rent. In addition, peasants could be granted small private plots over which they had nearly complete control.[3]

This system has been very popular, and has persisted through the present. The only major change has been to extend the lease period to thirty years. Agricultural productivity has risen dramatically, as have rural incomes. At the same time, basic sustenance has been assured in the countryside; the "grain ration" land allotted to every household has made impossible the famines of the Mao era. Importantly, this combination of benefits has been the result of the way in which the household responsibility system has blended "communist" and "capitalist" features. The system's communist facets include continued Party-state ownership of all land, a relatively equitable distribution of land based on household size, Party-state-set prices for produce from "responsibility" land, and assured basic sustenance for all rural residents. Its capitalist characteristics include individual control over production and sales, and market-set prices for most produce.[4] This combination has both fostered economic growth and ensured economic security for the vast majority of China's rural residents. This land allotment system also has been an important fallback for citizens with a rural residential *hukou* who migrate to the city in search of wage work. If things do not work out in the city, these migrants know that they can return to their home village where their family will have land and a home, and their subsistence will be assured.

Another important change in rural economic policy in the post-Mao period has been the development of Township and Village Enterprises (TVEs). These enterprises have been encouraged by the Party-state as a way to enable rural residents to earn wage income rather than relying on only agriculture. Reflecting a continued communist emphasis on state ownership and collective labor, these firms are collectively owned by a village or township. In the early post-Mao period, TVEs were extremely successful: between 1978 and 1990, the number of TVE employees rose from fewer than 30 million to more than 80 million, and their total output grew from approximately ¥50 billion to roughly 545 billion per year.[5] Indeed, much of China's phenomenal economic growth during this time span was attributed to TVEs.

The success of TVEs was made possible by China's opening to the global capitalist economy via the establishment of Special Economic Zones (SEZs), which in 1980 were created in a few southeastern coastal cities in Guangdong and Fujian provinces and the entire island province of Hainan. In 1984–1985 fourteen more coastal cities and their environs (in both the north and the south) were declared SEZs.[6] In villages located within or nearby such zones, access to supplies and markets was eased, and new opportunities arose to fulfill labor-intensive and low-tech needs within the production process. Consequently, although most villages tried to establish TVEs, these enterprises have been most prominent and successful in coastal provinces, and much less so in central and western areas.

Uneven TVE success has led to great geographic variation in the economic status of rural villagers in the post-Mao era. Geographic differences also have been the result of the central Party-state's rural taxation and spending policies. In the Maoist period, the central government exacted taxes from rural areas in the form of grain quotas taken from the communes into which the countryside was divided. With the dismantling of the commune system and institution of the household responsibility system in the late 1970s, the central government had to change the way it collected rural taxes. From the late 1970s through 1994, the central government negotiated remittances with each province, with a redistributive intent; wealthier provinces paid more, and got less in return, than did poorer provinces. Despite its beneficial intent to help even out rural living conditions, this negotiated tax process left the central government with increasing debt.[7]

Consequently, in 1994 the central government instituted a uniform national tax code. This change was a boon to wealthier provinces, as they no longer had to contribute more in taxes than they received back in central allotments. But in poorer provinces, the economic situation of most rural residents suffered. In these areas, as noted above, TVEs typically were not successful, and thus did not provide much revenue. When redistributive tax money from the central government declined, local officials became seriously strapped for cash. In response, they levied upon rural residents myriad fees, assessments, fines, and forced contributions. As discussed in Chapter 4, these practices led residents of poor rural areas (mainly in central and western China) to take to the streets in protest. The central government responded by banning all local taxes and fees in 2002. This ban effectively ended this source of rural discontent in poor inland areas.

In the middle part of the first decade of the 2000s, the central government launched a "New Socialist Countryside" initiative and passed a stimulus package designed to improve the economic well-being of rural residents through reduced educational charges, improved public goods and services, and spending on rural infrastructure. These policies have had a real and positive impact on rural residents, particularly those in poorer inland areas. However, in rural areas located closer to the coast, residents in many localities have continued to suffer from "land grabs" on the part of local officials. As noted in Chapter 4, in late 2013 top Party-state leaders prohibited local officials from confiscating land from peasants without their permission, and required that full compensation be given to them according to the market value of their land. However, more than pronouncements will be required to fully eradicate unfair land acquisitions.

Another major policy change that has had a highly positive impact on the economic situation of rural families has been a relaxation of the residential registration (*hukou*) system. During the Maoist era, this system prevented those with a rural *hukou* from leaving the countryside – even when, as during the Great Leap Forward, there was literally no food to eat. Over the course of the post-Mao period, the Party-state has slowly relaxed its internal migration controls – in a way that has been somewhat haphazard and decentralized, but that generally has greatly enhanced the economic status of those with a rural *hukou*.

Overall, rural economic policies in the post-Mao period have dramatically improved the livelihood of China's rural *hukou*-holders.

Between 1978 and 2012, per capita rural incomes rose from ¥133 to ¥7917 – a mind-boggling increase of nearly 6000 percent in only thirty-four years. From 1990–2006, rural residents' yearly per capita consumption of meat and aquatic products nearly doubled.[8] The purchase of household appliances also has become much easier for rural residents. For example, in 1985, less than one percent of rural households owned refrigerators. By 1998 this number had climbed to 9%, and by 2007 it had risen to 26%. Following the institution of government subsidies for appliance purchase by rural hukou-holders in 2007, the percentage of rural households with refrigerators more than doubled, rising to 61% in 2011.[9] In a nationwide survey undertaken by Han and Whyte in 2004, relative to other socio-economic groups in China, farmers exhibited some of the highest levels of optimism.[10] Nonetheless, significant causes of rural dissatisfaction remain – particularly, corruption on the part of local officials and unfair land acquisition practices.

The rural economic policies discussed above represent a combination of "free market" and "interventionist" mechanisms, and a continued dose of "communist" policies intended to address the plight of the poor and ameliorate the economic disparities that have accompanied China's economic growth. A key example is the household responsibility system, which features: (i) a "communist" guarantee of land to all rural residents, (ii) state intervention (in that all land remains owned by the state, and most categories of land require fulfillment of a contractual obligation to the state), and (iii) market mechanisms (farmers are allowed to sell much of their produce on in the open market). TVEs also represent a blend of state intervention (local government ownership) and the free market (where TVEs buy and sell their goods). Through these hybrid policies and practices – as well as through its willingness to allow local experimentation and to adapt in response to emergent problems – the CCP-led Party-state has done an admirable job of stimulating and managing China's rural economy in the post-Mao period.

URBAN ECONOMIC POLICIES AND RESULTS IN
THE POST-MAO ERA

As discussed above, China's urban residents led a secure but basic existence during the Maoist era. During that time period, the CCP-led Party-state's urban economic policies epitomized "interventionist" and "communist" approaches: all urban production, consumption, and labor were directed and controlled by the government, oriented toward ensuring high levels of economic security and equality. In the post-Mao era, some of the interventionist and communist elements of the Maoist period have remained intact. But others have gone by the wayside, as free market capitalist practices simultaneously have been encouraged. As in the countryside, the result has been a hybrid economy that has been incredibly dynamic and successful.

The private sector

In most respects, urban economic reform has occurred in the gradual, experimental fashion that generally has characterized China's post-Mao rural economic reforms. This is certainly the case with regard to private enterprise. In the Maoist period, private businesses simply did not exist: all rural residents lived on state-run collectives, and all urban residents worked in state-owned enterprises. In the early post-Mao era, the new CCP leadership – headed by pragmatist Deng Xiaoping – tolerated the emergence of very small-scale private enterprises. Initially, would-be entrepreneurs began to "test the waters" by setting up mobile, low-capital individual businesses, such as street-side fruit-stands, shoe repair services, and improvised taxis. Seeing these small businesses as a way to "fill up the gaps" left by the public sector in terms of consumer goods and services, central Party-state elites turned a blind eye to their emergence. However, private enterprises still remained suspect in the eyes of many local officials, and as a result were under constant threat of harassment and punishment. In 1982, central Party-state leaders explicitly sanctioned the existence of small-scale private businesses, by stipulating in the new state Constitution that "the state protects the lawful rights and interests of the individual economy." In the late 1980s, central leaders amended the Constitution to state that the government "encourages" and "supports" the private sector, and issued guidelines for medium and large-sized private businesses (defined as those with eight or more employees), including rules for establishment, dissolution, and employment.

During this early part of the post-Mao period, private enterprises were allowed to produce and sell their goods and services in free markets without government price or wage controls, but they often found it difficult to purchase needed inputs, as these generally remained under the purview of the Party-state's plans for the state-owned enterprises that still almost completely dominated the urban economy. Nonetheless, private enterprises mushroomed during this period. Further, although Party-state officials technically were forbidden to engage in private business, many did so anyway (typically calling their enterprises "collectives," in a practice known colloquially as giving a private company a "red hat"). These political cadres-cum-businessmen often capitalized on their insider political knowledge and connections to increase their profits. All of this occurred rather spontaneously, haphazardly, and from the bottom-up; it was not the result of an intentional plan on the part of central authorities, and was largely unregulated by the Party-state.

While these developments were occurring in cities across China, central Party-state leaders undertook an additional step to promote free markets in new Special Economic Zones (SEZs). Initially, SEZs were established in four coastal locations in southeastern China; they were to function as mini "free trade zones" wherein foreign investors could establish export-oriented joint ventures and operate free from most restrictions on trade and employment, and pay very little in taxes. Also, in these zones infrastructure was created to facilitate production and exports. Over the course of the 1980s, more SEZs were established. However, they remained islands within China's larger, still mostly planned, economy. In early 1992, Deng Xiaoping made a highly publicized "Southern Tour" of the initial SEZs. He declared the experiment a great success, and called for further economic liberalization. By the end of 1992, dozens of additional SEZs had been created, and in the years that have followed, many more SEZs of various types have appeared. At present, there are over 1,500 SEZs and similar kinds of free-market "zones" across China. In these areas, the central Party-state generally maintains a "hands-off," *laissez faire* acceptance of capitalist practices. Under China's current top leader, Xi Jinping, these policies should be expected to continue; indeed, Xi's first public trip after assuming office was to the SEZs that Deng Xiaoping visited on his famous 1992 "Southern Tour."

The Party-state's embrace of economic liberalization was enshrined in official doctrine at the Fourteenth Party Congress in late 1992, which called for the establishment of a "socialist *market* economy" (italics added) and touted economic growth as the country's highest priority. As the major engine of China's economic growth at the time, private business gained a much-elevated status. In 1994, China's first Company Law came into effect, allowing for the establishment of limited liability shareholding corporations. At the Fifteenth Party Congress in 1997, private enterprise was described as an "important" element of China's economy, and in 1999, the Constitution was modified to reflect this shift in categorization. Further, Party-state cadres no longer were restrained from engaging in private enterprise.[11] As a result, many opted to remove their "red hats" and register as privately owned businesses. Consequently, the official number of private enterprises skyrocketed. In 2004, private property rights became constitutionally protected. Whereas the prior version of the Constitution declared that only *public* property is "sacred and inviolable," the 2004 constitution (in Article 13) adds that "the lawful *private* property of citizens" also is "inviolable" (italics added). At the Seventeenth Party Congress in 2007, the Party Constitution was amended to place the non-public economy on equal footing with the public economy. This change gave private businesses access to some areas of the economy that previously were "off-limits," and ended preferential policies toward state-owned enterprises.[12] At the Third Plenum of the Eighteenth Central Committee in late 2013, further support for the private sector was indicated by an official statement that the market now plays a "decisive" role in the economy. Meanwhile, the tax burden on private enterprises has been quite low relative to the private sector's contribution to China's GDP. In 2011, private businesses made up roughly 75 percent of all industrial profits in China. However, their share of business taxes paid to the government was only about 15 percent.[13]

While hugely beneficial, these policies and changes alone were insufficient to ensure the success of private business. Perhaps the most important requirement for private sector profit growth has been the availability of cheap and motivated laborers. Due to the strict enforcement of the *hukou* system during the Maoist era, labor was immobilized; it was virtually impossible for individuals with a rural *hukou* to leave the countryside in search of wage work. In the post-Mao period, internal migration restrictions have been gradually loosened, such that rural *hukou*-holders increasingly have been able to move to SEZs to work for private firms. As of 2013, China had more than 260 million migrant workers – that is, Chinese citizens with rural *hukou* who have moved to the city for wage work. This number is four times higher than the entire population of the UK, and only about 50 million less than the population of the US. China's migrant workers comprise the vast majority of unskilled private sector workers in China's textile, garment, and construction industries. They also make up a significant portion of the private sector workforce in the service sector.

As with other economic policies, the Party-state's move to allow greater labor mobility was slow and gradual. In the 1980s, the central

Party-state created new residential statuses that enabled rural *hukou*-holders to reside in urban areas legally, and made it easier for them to obtain food (previously, all food distribution in the cities was limited to those with urban *hukou*). Even so, rural migrants to the city were routinely harassed by local authorities, and most lived in makeshift shelters, due to their inability to legally rent state-owned housing, as well as the lack of private housing. During this period, the vast majority of rural migrants to the cities were young men working in construction. Following Deng Xiaoping's Southern Tour of 1992, private firms, often funded in part by foreign investment, proliferated in China's SEZs. To attract laborers willing to work very hard for little pay, local authorities in most SEZs relaxed migration restrictions to enable rural migrants to fill this role. Many private factories set up dormitories and cafeterias on factory grounds, so as to provide shelter and food for rural *hukou*-holders employed by the firm (as well as to maintain control over these workers and enable the factory to more easily have them on the production line for many hours a day, virtually every day of the week). With this change, the demographic composition of rural migrants shifted, as tens of millions of young, unskilled women from rural inland regions moved to SEZs to take jobs in manufacturing, textile, and garment firms. By the middle of the first decade of the 2000s, roughly half of all private sector workers were female.[14]

In most private enterprises, unskilled workers work exceedingly long hours for very little pay; a 2001 survey of migrant workers in Guangdong province (within which roughly one-third of all industrial migrant workers were employed at the time) found that 80 percent worked more than ten hours per day, and more than 50 percent worked twelve to fourteen hours. Nearly half rarely had a day off.[15] As of 2011, the hourly wage for Chinese apparel workers was $1.26/hour, only about one-third of what is considered a "living wage" relative to the cost of living. However, these figures are much higher than they were ten years prior, suggesting that the pay for private sector workers has been improving over time.[16] Overall, China's "communist" Party-state has done a great deal to stimulate private enterprise and embrace free-market capitalist principles, and the results have been very impressive in terms of stimulating national economic growth and improving the economic status of rural *hukou*-holders. At the same time, wages and working conditions for rank-and-file private sector workers remain abysmal by Western standards.

The public sector

In some ways, the tolerance and later encouragement of the private sector were relatively easy changes for the Party-state to make. A more challenging task facing Party-state leaders was how to deal with the behemoth of state-owned enterprises (SOEs) that made up the entirety of the urban economy in the Maoist period, and the vast majority of the urban economy through the early 1990s. Because of the lifetime job security found in these enterprises, as well as the panoply of "iron rice bowl" benefits and services offered to the workers within them, the vast majority of SOEs were operating at a serious loss. Thus, they were a giant drag on economic growth. During the first decade and a half of the post-Mao era (1978–1994), the government did little to make SOEs more profitable. During this time period the only significant change in this direction was that, beginning in 1984, new state-sector workers were hired without guarantees of lifetime employment or "iron rice bowl" benefits. This reform generally was accepted by younger workers, many of whom welcomed the increased job flexibility. However, it did little to address the huge operating deficits of SOEs. Indeed, over the course of the 1980s, wages and benefits for SOE workers improved, but the profits of these enterprises did not grow commensurately; as a result, if anything, the financial health of the state sector declined.

In the mid-1990s, central Party-state leaders resolved to force SOEs to become profitable, or to become private. In 1995, the central Party-state announced its intention to "keep the large [SOEs] and let the small go" (*zhuada fangxiao*). Supporting this decision was the fact that, as of the mid 1990s, nearly three-fourths of small firms owned by local governments were unprofitable.[17] In 1997, the Fifteenth Party Congress introduced a plan to privatize SOEs. By the end of the following year, over 80 percent of state sector firms at the level of the county or lower had experienced some form of privatization.[18] This dealt with the multitudinous unprofitable small SOEs, but left many unprofitable medium-sized and large SOEs relatively untouched. To address this problem, in 1998 central Party-state leaders announced that all SOEs would have three years to become profitable. These leaders knew and accepted that this would require massive lay-offs; there were simply too many people employed at these firms for them to make a profit. And indeed, beginning in the late 1990s, tens of millions of middle-aged and older SOE employees were laid-off. Along with layoffs, SOEs reduced their workforce by forcing an estimated ten million employees into early retirement.[19]

This massive change was very beneficial to China's overall economic health, but it was devastating to the nearly 100 million SOE workers who were "downsized" in order to make SOEs profitable. These workers had been accustomed to working at a leisurely pace, with the expectation of job security for life and a generous pension. When they were laid off or forced into early retirement, they found it difficult to adjust. Surveys conducted in the late 1990s found that 90 percent of laid off SOE workers were dissatisfied with their economic and employment status, over 97 percent felt depressed, and about 74 percent were pessimistic and felt hopeless.[20] Most have been able to find only informal, temporary work that is not considered "real" employment, including urban sanitation, community service, secondary production services, and personal service.[21] For these individuals, the introduction of capitalism into the workplace has been hard.

However, the Party-state simultaneously has employed interventionist, "communist" measures to ensure some degree of economic security for these workers. As noted in Chapter 4, and as will be discussed in more detail in Chapter 6, the Chinese government has: (i) allowed current and former SOE employees to purchase their homes at far below market costs, thus enabling widespread debt-free home ownership; (ii) provided job training, tax breaks, and loans to laid-off SOE workers; (iii) provided welfare payments to those with incomes below a certain level; (iv) worked to ensure that pensions were provided to SOE workers forced to retire early (even when their former firm was bankrupt) and to create a new pension system to cover all urban workers.

Moreover, although all SOEs were forced to become profitable in the late 1990s, not all were privatized. To the contrary, the Party-state still owns and runs many very large enterprises in key industries. Whereas privately owned enterprises dominate China's retail and manufacturing in most competitive sectors, very large SOEs control all industries that the Party-state deems "critical," including: mining, gas, oil, nonferrous metals, steel, petrochemicals, telecommunications, transportation, utilities, banking and finance. Though these are all government-run entities, significant changes have been made in their operations relative to the Maoist era. When virtually all medium and small SOEs were privatized in the mid-1990s, the remaining large SOEs were "corporatized;" they were restructured to be more profit-driven, enabling most to be listed on stock markets. In 2003, they were placed under the control of the State-owned Assets Supervision and Administration Commission (SASAC), which sits directly under the State Council, the highest body within China's state structure. The SASAC exercises "quasi-trustee control" over the SOEs; along with overseeing government holdings, it appoints top personnel in central SOEs (in conjunction with the CCP's Organization Department), and directs all mergers, divestments, etc. In addition, because the Party-state also owns all banks and financial institutions, the SOEs under the control of the SASAC enjoy preferred access to loans, land and government subsidies. These decisions are informed by Party-state-run firms and research institutes that investigate markets and recommend projects that are promising yet risky or long-term, which may be best undertaken by SOEs.[22] Simultaneously, the National Development and Reform Commission (NDRC), which also sits under the State Council within China's state structure, helps to manage policy related to SOEs. In particular, it reviews and approves large projects, and sets prices for certain items. Perhaps most importantly, the NDRC sets energy tariffs; it does so with the goal of ensuring that SOEs in the energy sector will prosper.[23]

Through these measures of Party-state intervention and control, China's state sector is no longer the major drag on economic growth that it once was. Even so, in comparison to the dynamic and seemingly ever-more-successful private sector, the financial record of SOEs since the dramatic reforms of the mid-1990s has been mixed and unsteady. Initially, SOE performance improved dramatically; between 2002 and 2007, SOE profits quadrupled, and their contribution to China's GDP nearly doubled.[24] Since then, their performance has slipped, with many falling back into the red. However, this is not the case universally. Generally speaking, in sectors where SOEs maintain a near-monopoly position (namely, tobacco, oil and electricity), profits remain strong.

As noted above, the Party-state owns a variety of SOEs, including many in heavy industry, public utilities, and transportation, but also in banking. In fact, all of China's large banks are government-owned and controlled. The biggest and most important are the Industrial and Commercial Bank of China (ICBC), the China Construction Bank (CCB), the Bank of China (BOC), and the Agricultural Bank of China

(ABC). Each holds an enormous amount of "tier-one capital" (the value of a bank's stock and disclosed reserves): ICBC has US$161 billion, making it the largest bank in the world; the CCB ranks fifth in the world with US$138 billion; the BOC ranks ninth with US$122 billion; and the ABC ranks tenth with US$111 billion. These banks are very profitable, with net interest incomes that rank first (ICBC), second (CCB), third (ABC) and eighth (BOC) in the world.[25] Their scope is almost unfathomable: ICBC has over 400,000 employees and four million clients; CCB has approximately 14,000 branches.[26]

A major source of the profit earned by these giant banks is the savings placed in them by ordinary people. China's domestic savings rate (GDP minus total consumption) is extremely high – hovering just above 50 percent of GDP every year for the past ten years.[27] By way of comparison, the domestic savings rate in the US in recent years has been just under 15 percent, and in the UK it has been about 13 percent. Perhaps even more importantly, China's banks offer such low interest rates on domestic savings that they can use this money virtually for free. This is also part of the reason why SOEs in other sectors have been able to profit: they receive low-interest loans from China's state-owned banks. In contrast, China's large banks rarely loan significant amounts of money to private enterprises, or individual citizens. This perpetuates the cycle of high domestic savings.

With consumer credit hard to come by (whether it be auto or home loans, or personal credit cards), ordinary people typically need to save in order to buy. The contrast with the US is striking. Whereas less than one percent of China's urban *hukou*-holders rely on loans to purchase goods, roughly 47 percent of American families use consumer loans and carry a credit card balance. When it comes to purchasing a vehicle, about 6 percent of Chinese rely on loans, in contrast to more than 75 percent of Americans. The same is true for housing: only about 10 percent of Chinese homeowners have mortgage debt, as compared with roughly 70 percent of Americans.[28]

On the flip side, Chinese households save up to 50 percent of their income, whereas American households save only about 3 percent.[29] Along with the dearth of available consumer credit, which is a conscious Party-state policy followed by China's state-owned banks, other government policies somewhat more indirectly have propelled Chinese citizens to save. For example, the one-child policy, which since 1979 has prevented most couples from having more than one child, has created a situation where there are many more elderly parents than there are younger, working-age children to support them. As a result, parents have put more into saving for their own care in old age. Further, the privatization of most SOEs, and the dismantling of "iron rice bowl" benefits such as health care and pensions provided though the work unit, have spurred greater personal savings for these expenses. Though other factors may also lead Chinese to save their money, Party-state policies such as these have been key.

The Party-state's control over SOEs and banks has been beneficial to those entities. And to the degree that SOE and state-run bank profits have contributed to China's GDP, this control has had positive results for China's overall economy: in 2012, bank profits comprised nearly 3 percent of China's GDP. By way of comparison, in America, even when bank profits peaked (in 2006), they comprised only one percent of GDP. However, the consequences of government ownership of and intervention in SOEs and large banks have not been wholly beneficial. For one, because of the tight relationship between China's large SOEs and state-run banks, SOEs are almost assured of funding and support, which diminishes their competitive edge. Accurate figures are hard to come by, but it is widely believed that China's big banks are currently holding a significant amount of bad SOE debt. In addition, in response to the global economic slowdown that began in late 2008, central state-owned banks loaned extensively to local governments seeking to fund infrastructure and other projects designed to avoid an economic downturn. In early 2014, the total debt of China's provincial, county, and township governments was estimated at nearly US$3trillion.[30] Although official sources state that only about one percent of all state-owned bank assets are in non-performing loans, estimates by the investment bank Morgan Stanley run as high as 8 percent. Concerns about this issue seem to have spurred central Party-state leaders to diversify, particularly by seeking overseas investment. In 2012 alone, the overseas assets held by ICBC grew by 30 percent, more than double the overall rate of growth for the bank.[31] However, the non-performing loan debt held by large state-owned banks remains significant.

Further, private entrepreneurs and ordinary people have been disadvantaged by China's government-controlled banking system. For private entrepreneurs, the inability to obtain loans from banks has led them to seek financing from an array of sources in what is commonly known as the "shadow-banking" sector. This includes "off-ledger" lending activities by regular banks, insurance companies, pawnbrokers, and informal "Ponzi"-style schemes, as well as investments in them by regular citizens seeking a greater return on their money than the paltry interest that they can get from state-owned banks. As "shadow-banking" entities have increased their share of the financial market, both outside observers and Chinese political leaders have grown concerned about their potentially destabilizing effect on China's economy. In addition, as China's overall economic growth has slowed in recent years (from an average of 10 percent from 1979–2011 to 7.7 percent from 2012–2013), Party-state officials increasingly have spoken of the need to shift China's economy away from export-led growth and toward domestic consumer-led growth. With the largest population in the world (standing at 1.36 billion as of 2014), there should be plenty of opportunity for China to move in this direction. But if Chinese citizens continue to save most of their money in response to existing policies, this shift will be slow in coming.

Aware of this, the Party-state has made moves to facilitate above-board lending to consumers and private entrepreneurs. Since the late

1980s, joint-stock commercial banks (JSCBs) – which are held by various investors, including both state and private entities, but typically with public investors holding a minority of shares – have been allowed to operate in China. They have been a primary source of loans for small and medium enterprises. In recent years, such banks have grown dramatically as the demand for private sector and consumer loans has risen. Although these JSCBs remain much smaller than the "Big Four" state-owned banks (in 2012, two of the largest – China Merchants and China Minsheng – ranked 56th and 80th world-wide in tier-one capital, respectively), they now hold more than half of all banking assets in China.[32] In late 2013, following the Third Plenum of the Eighteenth Central Committee, central Party-state leaders suggested that in some cases fully privately owned small and medium-sized banks would be allowed. If this comes to fruition, it will further enable private firms to obtain formal bank credit.[33] Meanwhile, two giant Chinese Internet sellers – Alibaba and Tencent – have been starting to loan money to small and medium private businesses, and to offer consumers opportunities to invest in managed funds with potentially high interest. Moreover, in late 2013, Alibaba and China Minsheng bank signed an agreement to cooperate on banking services, including wealth management and credit cards.[34] To the extent that these developments – which have been tolerated and even encouraged by the Party-state – stimulate greater consumer spending, they will facilitate the Chinese economy's transition from dependence on exports to generate growth.

Even so, in order to fully transform the economy to reliance on consumer spending to stimulate high levels of economic growth, at least two additional challenges remain. First, if state-owned banks target more of their money for consumer loans, they will have less to loan to the massive state-owned enterprises that remain reliant on this financial support. Second, in order to fully tap into China's potentially vast consumer market, rank-and-file workers in the public and private sectors, and farmers – groups which together comprise roughly 85 percent of China's total population – will need to improve their financial situation such that they can afford to purchase non-essential consumer goods and services. At present, most of these individuals have very little "extra" money to spend.

In sum, the Chinese Party-state's urban economic policies have been characterized by a mixture of free-market capitalism and state-direction. Special Economic Zones have proliferated, wherein the state generally takes a "hands-off" attitude toward private business. And, most former SOEs have been privatized. Yet the Party-state retains control over key industries, including banking. Although even these SOEs have been listed on stock exchanges and are expected to turn a profit, they are largely protected from competition, and their activities ultimately are dictated by the government, rather than the market. This hybrid urban economic system has brought fantastic economic growth rates, and has greatly improved the standard of living enjoyed by urban residents. Further, although tens of millions of former SOE workers suffered a dramatic loss of economic security as a result of SOE privatization, the Party-state has provided them with a variety of "communist" safety nets and benefits – including very affordable housing – that has enabled them to weather their economic dislocation in a way that most have found to be satisfactory.

INTERNATIONAL ECONOMIC POLICIES AND RESULTS IN THE POST-MAO ERA

As is evident in the discussion above, China's urban economic policies have been deeply intertwined with its international economic policies – particularly those designed to facilitate exports. And, as with the Chinese Party-state's rural and urban economic policies, its international economic policies have featured a combination of state intervention and free markets. Together, China's hybrid domestic and international economic policies have resulted in astounding profits through exports.

In part, China's growth in exports was facilitated by its entry into the World Trade Organization (WTO) in late 2001. As the price of admission, China had to relax or remove thousands of tariffs, quotas, and other barriers to "free trade." At the time, there was great domestic concern that doing so would cause Chinese farmers and urban SOEs to suffer. With regard to SOEs, WTO membership actually helped China's political leaders to justify large-scale reform. Ordinary citizens were told that it was no longer possible for SOEs to be totally shielded from the global capitalist system. If SOEs did not become competitive and thereby profitable, there would be no alternative to privatizing them or shutting them down. With regard to farmers, WTO membership has indeed caused agricultural profits to drop within China. With a roughly 20 percent decline in agricultural tariffs and an end to agricultural export subsidies, Chinese farmers have been subject to much greater international competition. And because virtually all Chinese farmers work only small plots (a consequence of the household responsibility system), their ability to effectively compete on a global scale is very limited; most Chinese farmers sell only to domestic consumers. This is also why the Chinese Party-state has eased up on internal migration restrictions, making it easier for rural *hukou*-holders to leave the countryside in search of wage work. As a result, despite the hardships suffered by farmers as a result of China's WTO membership, their overall economic status has continued to rise. Moreover, WTO membership has enabled China to enjoy a reciprocal relaxation of tariffs and trade barriers levied by other countries against Chinese exports, thus facilitating China's export-driven economic growth.

China's growth in exports also has been facilitated by the government's encouragement of foreign direct investment (FDI) in joint ventures with domestic enterprises. Following Deng's endorsement of China's Special Economic Zones in 1992, FDI has grown exponentially – rising from just US$4 billion in 1991 to US$124 billion in 2013.[35] As of 2013, foreign-invested enterprises were responsible for nearly half of China's total exports and more than 80 percent of China's high-tech exports.[36] The Chinese Party-state's encouragement of FDI since the early 1990s represents a key way in which China's post-Mao international economic policies have differed from those in the so-called "developmental states" that governed Japan, South Korea, and Taiwan in the 1950s–1980s. Whereas these countries generally prevented FDI in their domestic economies, in post-Mao China, FDI has been a crucial source of capital and technology for export-oriented businesses.

A third contributor to China's export success has been the availability of low-cost workers who are highly motivated to work extremely hard and endure draconian working conditions for long hours, day after day. These workers almost exclusively have been rural *hukou*-holders whose families were forced to remain in the countryside during the Mao era, but in the post-Mao period have been allowed to migrate to China's cities to engage in wage work. The memory of the abject poverty faced by their families in the Maoist era, and their resultant eagerness to advance economically at almost any cost, have made them ideal employees for profit-hungry private business owners. And because the supply of such workers has been so large – numbering in the hundreds of millions – and local officials have been focused more on stimulating local economic growth than on enforcing China's labor laws, employers have been able to pay these workers very little. As a result, the price of China's exports has been able to remain relatively low. However, in recent years, wages for unskilled workers have been rising, and as a result, China's competitive advantage in this area has been declining. Even so, China is projected to have significant "excess" labor through at least 2020.[37]

Another source of China's export-led growth has been the Party-state's currency policy. Many foreign leaders – particularly in America

– have argued that China's fantastic export success has derived from the Chinese government's refusal allow the value of China's currency (the Yuan) to float freely. Indeed, the Chinese government has interfered with the value of China's currency to a larger degree than has been the case with the US and other advanced industrial countries. Normally, if a country exports more than it imports, the value of its currency rises, as the "demand" for its currency (needed to buy its exports) exceeds the country's "demand" for other currencies, and the supply of its currency increases due to its greater sale of exports than its purchase of imports. So, in the case of US–China trade, the value of the Yuan relative to the US dollar should rise, with the result being that the cost of Chinese exports to the US should become higher for US residents, leading to decreased demand for Chinese goods and a re-balancing of the trade deficit in America's favor. But, the Chinese government intervenes in this process by withdrawing some of the "surplus" dollars earned by Chinese exporters and compensating them instead in Yuan.[38]

Even so, since 2005, the Chinese government has done so to a lesser extent. While from 1995–2005, the value of the Yuan relative to the US dollar was "artificially" kept at one US dollar to about 8.3 Chinese Yuan, since 2005, the value of the Chinese Yuan relative to the US dollar has been allowed to drop, hitting 6.14 in 2014. And, Chinese leaders have signaled their intention to continue to diminish their interference in currency markets until the Yuan drops to its "natural" value. In 2013, a top Party-state leader announced that the government "plans to stop intervening in the currency market and allow for a managed floating exchange rate system. The stated goal is to reach full [Yuan] convertibility by 2020."[39] Also in 2013, central leaders announced the establishment of yet another new type of free-market zone – the Shanghai Pilot Free Trade Zone. One path-breaking feature of this zone is that, after a two-to-three year testing period, it is intended to allow for full currency convertability, as well as the use of Chinese currency across international borders.

However, debates over whether or not Chinese currency practices are "fair" are irrelevant to the question of how well the Chinese Party-state has managed its economy in the post-Mao era. With regard to this question, it is hard to deny that Chinese authorities have done a very good job of enabling export-led economic growth. They have done so via participation in the global capitalist system (including WTO membership), and a general embrace of "free trade." Yet simultaneously, Party-state leaders have engaged in state intervention in China's international economic affairs, including managing the value of its currency. Over time, the Chinese Party-state has decreased its currency "manipulation." And, to the degree that Party-state policies are successful in stimulating domestic consumer-led growth and shifting China's economy away from dependence on export-led growth, we can expect that it will feel even less impelled to intervene in the "free" functioning of global currency markets in the future. A trickier challenge for China's leaders will be to develop its international competitiveness in higher-tech products, and to move away from its reliance on the export of low-tech textiles produced by low-paid unskilled workers with insufficient income to contribute to an increase in domestic consumption levels.

CONCLUSION

Overall, China's post-Mao Party-state has quite adeptly fulfilled the general governmental function of providing economic stability and growth: the economy has grown at a phenomenal rate, and with remarkable stability. Party-state leaders have succeeded in doing so via the creation of a somewhat uniquely dualistic economic system that combines a large state sector characterized by "communist"/authoritarian "top-down" government control with an equally large "capitalist" private sector that operates from the "bottom-up" in response to free market conditions. This highly successful post-Mao economic system has become so powerful that it has been given its own name

– "Sino-Capitalism."[40] It is similar to Anglo-American-style capitalism in that both systems include some elements of the free market, yet also a degree of government intervention in and regulation of the private sector. Both also feature some government-run economic entities, and some political influence over banking. But in China these features are much more extensive and extreme. At the same time, Party-state policies have been anything but rigid; to the contrary, they have been highly adaptive, experimental, decentralized, and pragmatic.

Moreover, many of the "authoritarian," "state-interventionist," and "communist" features of Chinese economic policy in the post-Mao era actually have aided China's economic growth and stability. In a liberal democracy, policy-making is messy, shifts with the result of each new election, and is often stymied by divided government (particularly in the US, where each chamber of Congress can be dominated by a different party, and the party with which the President is affiliated may not be the same party that dominates one or both chambers of the Congress). Further, in a liberal democracy politicians are fundamentally driven by the desire to get elected/re-elected. This leads them to craft policies to appeal to voters, as well as to the wealthy donors and interest groups who provide the campaign funds that politicians need in order to bring their message to the voters.

In China, political leaders do not rely on monetary donations or popular votes in order to remain in power. As a result, if they are so inclined, they can craft policies that they deem to be in the best interest of the country overall, rather than policies that will appeal to the more short-term and/or individualistic concerns of voters and donors. And, they can implement policies over the long term, without starts and stops due to shifts in partisan control of the government, and without having to negotiate with conflicting political parties that have opposing ideological goals. This is not to say that politicians' lack of dependence on donations or votes in order to remain in power will make them choose to craft policies in this manner, but rather that it opens the possibility for them to do so without fear of losing their political position as a result.

It must be emphasized that this is not to argue that economic decision-making in non-democratic political systems is always better than is the case in democracies. To the contrary, non-democratic economic decision-making can be much worse than democratic economic decision-making if the political leaders are not motivated by a desire to improve the economic standing of the population as a whole, but rather their own financial improvement or that of only certain demographic groups. In addition, non-democratic economic decision-making can be disastrous if political leaders are incompetent, ignorant, or rigidly ideological. To a large extent, such was the case during the Maoist period. And, the economic consequences during this era were mediocre at best, and horrific at worst (e.g., during Mao's Great Leap Forward). But in the post-Mao period, China's political leaders have demonstrated a remarkable degree of flexibility and adaptability, as well as a pragmatic focus on figuring out what works best. Relatedly, they have allowed for local experimentation on the ground, free from ideological imperatives. Thus far, this combination of policy pragmatism, openness, and fluidity – without electoral pressures, and with a sizeable dose of state intervention, has helped China's economy to outperform all others in the world.

Further, these features of economic policy-making in China have enabled the Chinese economy to weather many crises. Perhaps most notably, this is demonstrated by the economic crisis that began in 2008. In the latter part of that year, ominous signs of economic downturn appeared not only in the US, but in China as well. By the end of 2008, China's real GDP growth had fallen to 6.8 percent, and industrial production growth had dropped to 5.7 percent.[41] With the US – the major importer of Chinese goods – falling only deeper into recession in early 2009, experts predicted 6 percent GDP growth in China in 2009, with the possibility of growth as low as 4 percent.[42] Although advanced industrial countries such as the US might have looked at such statistics with envy, a 4 percent growth rate would have been the lowest that China had experienced since 1990. Further, even 6 percent GDP growth would have fallen short of the 8 percent rate that is portrayed by Chinese officials as the minimum level required to prevent an increase in unemployment.[43] Yet almost immediately after China's economy began to slide in late 2008, Party-state leaders passed a US$585 billion economic stimulus package that included fiscal spending and tax reductions, and cut interest rates by a hefty 1.08 points. China closed 2009 with an impressive 8.7 percent growth rate for the year, and averaged 8.86 percent yearly economic growth from 2009–2013.

To be sure, the Chinese Party-state's ability to maintain such high levels of economic growth and stability is not guaranteed. Most importantly, China's capacity to prosper by exporting cheap low-tech exports made by poorly paid workers willing to endure relentless working conditions will soon run its course. Future growth will require an increase in domestic consumption and the development of competitive higher-tech exports. But, if Party-state leaders continue to approach policy-making with pragmatism and flexibility, and allow continued "bottom-up" experimentation and freedom, their simultaneous "top down" management of parts of the economy is likely to continue to bear fruit – despite, and in many respects as a result of, the Party-state's non-democratic features. Importantly, however, although freedom from electoral pressures has made it possible for China's post-Mao political leaders to engage in the policies that they have, it did not make them certain to do so. The case of China from the Maoist era through the present demonstrates that, particularly in an authoritarian system, the attitudes and quality of the political leadership are key in determining the system's success or failure at managing the economy.

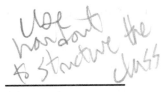

6 Providing Goods and Services

Along with successfully managing the economy and responding to public grievances, in order for a government to enjoy stability, it must ensure that the populace has access to necessary goods and services. Some of the most important are: health care, housing, poverty alleviation, education, pensions, infrastructure, and a healthy natural environment. There are a variety of mechanisms by which a government can try to ensure that important goods and services are available to the populace. First, a central government can offer a good or service directly. Perhaps most notably, virtually all advanced industrial countries have a national government-run health care system (the only exception is the US). Second, a central government can delegate key goods/services provision to lower levels of government – e.g., a state/province, county, or city. Third, a central government can allow private businesses or civic organizations to provide necessary goods and services. For example, private charity groups or religious organizations might run homeless shelters or food banks. And, private businesses might establish tuition-charging schools. In most countries, necessary goods and services provision occurs through a mix of these three mechanisms.

In China during the Maoist period, all public goods and services were provided by the government; no private businesses existed, nor did autonomous civic organizations. In areas where the government did not provide a key good or service, people were on their own. Over the course of the post-Mao era, the Party-state has moved away from complete governmental control over goods/services provision in most areas. During the 1980s, the provision of key goods and services by government entities virtually ceased in the countryside. This occurred not so much by design as by default;[1] when the agricultural collectives of the Mao era were dismantled and land was leased to individual households through the "household responsibility system," the goods and services that previously were provided by the collectives disappeared. With no plan for alternative provision, these goods and services deteriorated in much of the countryside. From the 1990s through the present, the CCP-led Party-state has made various efforts to remedy this problem, with mixed results.

In the cities, in contrast, state-owned enterprises (SOEs) provided basic goods and services throughout the 1980s and early 1990s. However, in the latter half of the 1990s, SOE privatization coincided with a loss of the "iron rice bowl" benefits that until that time had provided low-cost goods and services to virtually all urban *hukou*-holders. Further, many important goods and services, such as education and health care, were not available to the tens of millions of migrant workers who came to China's cities for work. From the late 1990s through the present, Party-state leaders have worked to create new mechanisms for the provision of key goods and services to urban residents. Although more successful than the new approaches that have been tried in the countryside, universal access to key goods and services remains far from being achieved.

Overall, the post-Mao Party-state has approached the provision of important goods and services in the same general way that it has managed the economy: with a mixture of governmental control and grassroots autonomy, experimentalism, and adaptability. In some respects, and with regard to some goods and services, this hybrid approach has been successful. Yet in other areas it has not. Indeed, in contrast to the post-Mao Party-state's history of managing the economy, it is far from clear that the post-Mao Party-state's hybrid approach to providing key goods and services has had better results than did the

affordability, access, comprehensivenss/quality

wholly government-directed approach of the Mao era. To the contrary, the provision of many key goods and services in the post-Mao period – in terms of affordability, access, and comprehensiveness – is much less impressive than it was during the Maoist era. Further, although there were times in the Maoist period when important goods and services were not adequately available, this was the result of detrimental policies emanating from Mao's ideological rigidity; it was not due solely, or even primarily, to the fact that the state was in charge of providing key goods and services. Overall, the experience of China from the Maoist period through the present leads one to question the degree to which state control is necessarily detrimental to the provision of important goods and services. More broadly, an examination of basic goods and services provision in China over time, and in comparison with other countries over time, allows us to assess the ways in which a political regime's "democratic" and "authoritarian" features may hinder or facilitate its ability to satisfactorily provide such goods and services.

GOODS/SERVICES PROVISION IN THE MAOIST ERA

Although the Maoist system exhibited serious shortcomings in terms of managing China's economy, when it came to the provision of many important goods and services, this system was fairly successful. Importantly, however, Mao's dogmatic focus on ideological "correctness" also bred policies that undercut the system's ability to provide important goods and services. The most glaring example is the Great Leap Forward of 1958–60, wherein Mao's refusal to acknowledge the development of severe food shortages led to the starvation of millions. Even the best health care system imaginable cannot enable people to thrive when they simply have no food.

Yet if it is possible to bracket off horrific experiences such as the Great Leap Forward (admittedly a difficult leap), the general system of goods and services provision in the Maoist era was impressive – especially when compared with that in other countries at similarly low levels of economic development. At the same time, there was significant variation in goods and services provision in rural and urban areas. And, due to the strict enforcement of the *hukou* system during most of the Maoist period, people living in the countryside could not move to the city in order to enjoy the superior goods and services available to urban residents.

In the countryside, great progress in the provision of key goods and services was made during the Maoist era – particularly in comparison with the pre-communist period. Perhaps the most significant example is health care. Prior to the communist revolution, rural farmers (who at the time made up nearly 90 percent of the population) had no health insurance whatsoever; if they fell ill or required medical attention, they had to pay for it out of pocket. They also typically had to travel a sub-stantial distance in order to find any kind of trained medical personnel. After the CCP came to power (under Mao), the Party-state implemented a new "cooperative medical care" system in the countryside. This occurred in tandem with the communalization of rural land. Over time, the countryside became organized into large-scale "People's Communes" comprised of smaller-sized "production brigades" that generally covered the territory of an individual village. Every commune was required to provide its production brigades with funds to establish a health station. Each health station had one or two medical personnel (called "barefoot doctors" in communist parlance) charged with taking care of the population within the brigade, and paid with commune funds according to the "work points" that they earned through their services. The over-arching focus of the "barefoot doctors" was preventive care. This included vaccinations as well as campaigns to eradicate diseases and remove disease-causing pests (such as the snails that cause schistosomiasis). At the "brigade"/village level, a clinic was available for residents. For more serious medical concerns, residents were referred to township or commune-level hospitals, or to more comprehensive county-level hospitals.

This system was far from perfect – perhaps most importantly, health station workers often had very little formal medical training or equipment. However, it provided free health care for the vast majority of China's citizens. By the end of the Maoist period, 90 percent of Chinese villages, including 80–85 percent of China's rural population, were covered by the cooperative medical care system. Morbidity and mortality rates for infectious diseases dropped consistently over the course of Mao's rule, and once-endemic diseases, such as schistosomiasis, cholera, and sexually transmitted diseases, largely were eradicated. Life expectancy rose from about 40 years in 1954 to roughly 62 years in 1978. As of the mid-1970s, the World Health Organization hailed China as a model of rural public health.[2] This health care system – though decentralized – was entirely public, and government-provided.

The Mao-era Party-state also made significant progress with respect to other key goods and services. In terms of housing/land, when the communist regime came to power, it confiscated most of the land and housing previously held by the gentry, and then redistributed it to the peasantry. As a result, landlessness was eradicated in the countryside. Not long thereafter, however, rural land was collectivized, such that individual households no longer had rights to a particular plot of land. Even so, all rural residents were supposed to be guaranteed a share of the fruits of the land sufficient for subsistence, and roughly equivalent to that of all other rural residents. As a result, dire poverty (in the sense of living on the edge of life and death) disappeared – again, with the significant exception of 1958–1960.

Infrastructure also improved dramatically during the Mao era, as a result of direct governmental actions. The central Party-state's Soviet-style five-year economic plans included major programs to control

China's water supply and to build basic road and rail systems throughout the country. Over the course of Mao's rule, the portion of irrigated farmland doubled, from one-fourth to one-half, and the use of fertilizer per hectare tripled. In addition, massive electrical grids were constructed; whereas in 1949 virtually no rural areas had electricity, by the end of the Maoist period roughly 60 percent of rural residents did.[3]

In terms of education, the Maoist Party-state dictated the content and focus, emphasizing basic elementary education, ideological indoctrination, and the reduction of illiteracy. But in the countryside, the central government did not provide funds for education; the commune or brigade was to be "self-reliant" in this respect. As a result, the quality of education varied depending on the financial situation of the locality. Even so, the literacy rate in China rose dramatically over the course of the Mao era, from roughly 20 percent (in 1949) to approximately 70 percent (in 1979).

The central government did virtually nothing with regard to pension provision for rural residents in the Maoist period. Those who were too old or otherwise physically unable to work were given minimum assistance by the commune or brigade, or by their families.

China's urban residents enjoyed much more extensive goods and services provision during the Mao era. Indeed, the social welfare benefits provided to urbanites were well above what would be expected given China's level of economic development. As discussed in Chapter 5, virtually all urban residents were employed in a state-owned enterprise (SOE) of some sort. Through either the government-affiliated union branch at their workplace or their work unit, they were provided with a myriad of goods and services, including free healthcare for themselves and their dependents. Pensions were also provided through the (state-owned) workplace. Full pensions were given at a relatively young age – 60 for men, and 55 for women in government and state-owned companies. Moreover, as a percentage of the worker's prior income, pensions were among the highest in the world – reaching up to 90 percent.[4]

Overall, although in China during the Maoist period wages were low (and significant raises were exceedingly rare), urban workers did not have to spend much on daily needs. During the workday, they ate highly subsidized meals in cafeterias on factory grounds. Many larger SOEs maintained plots of land that provided additional produce to workers, either free of charge, or through the enterprise meal hall.[5] Urban workers also received (through their workplace) ration coupons for consumer goods and daily necessities, (including foodstuffs, cloth and coal), as well as a free set of work clothes and shoes each year (worth about a month's wages). Child care was free, again provided through the (state-owned) workplace. Large housing units were constructed near factory grounds, such that most workers could walk or easily take public transport to and from work each day. Although all housing units were owned by the Party-state (via the SOE), monthly rents were extremely low – rarely amounting to more than one or two days' pay. For most workers, rent cost about as much as a pack of cigarettes. In addition, workers were eligible for state-provided loans.[6] Generally speaking, during the Mao period the average urban family spent only about 5 percent of its budget on necessities such as housing and food. By way of comparison, in 1982 the average American family spent 45 percent of its budget on necessities, and the average Japanese family spent 21 percent.

Education was free for urban *hukou*-holders in the Maoist period. As in the countryside, ideological indoctrination was emphasized, but basic education led to dramatically improved literacy rates. The quality of schools was much higher in urban areas than in rural. However, all urban schools were not equal; there were two types of urban schools – "key" and "non-key" – with the former given priority in terms of funding and other resources.

Higher education was free of charge, and open to any young person (urban or rural) who scored at a sufficient level on the national entrance exam. However, a student's chances of attaining the requisite scores for admission were greatly bolstered by a prior education in an urban "key" school. Thus, rural students and students in "non-key" K-12 schools were at a significant disadvantage. Generally speaking, however, although far from exhibiting truly "equal opportunity," the system was merit-based and open to youths regardless of *hukou* or other kinds of demographic status. One dramatic departure from this norm occurred during the latter part of Mao's Great Proletarian Cultural Revolution (particularly the first half of the 1970s), when China's universities were almost entirely shut down due to Mao's belief that they were hotbeds of "bourgeois revisionism" and other "counter-revolutionary" ideas. Thus, as with health care, despite the Maoist system's overall impressive provision of basic and very affordable goods to the vast majority of the urban population, during some periods of Mao's rule, his obsession with ideological "correctness" prevented the system from providing key goods and services.

Turning to the most collective and perhaps most important social "good" – a healthy natural environment – the Maoist era fell very short. Mao's drive to increase agricultural and industrial production at a super-human pace led to numerous policies and campaigns to "conquer nature." Citizens were mobilized in mass efforts to bolster grain production by clearing forests, building dams, diverting rivers, and reclaiming wetlands for agricultural use. Mao also pushed every town and village to develop its own industry, in an effort to bring "development" to the countryside, as well as to protect China from enemies that might seek to wipe out China's industrial base. Lacking sufficient technological know-how and environmental foresight (in part due to Mao's distrust and repression of educated intellectuals who might otherwise have been sources of more sound advice), massive swaths of China's land were subject to deforestation, erosion, flooding, desertification, and pollution.[7]

In addition, Mao believed that China's greatest economic and military resource was its people. As a result, the Party-state constantly exhorted couples to have as many children as possible – portraying procreation as part of a good comrade's patriotic and communist duty. Consequently, the population of China nearly doubled over the course of the Maoist period – from roughly 600 million to one billion. Such rapid population growth exacerbated the strains on the environment enumerated above.

Even so, the environmental degradation of the Maoist period did not engender the astronomical levels of pollution that have been a hallmark of the late post-Mao era.[8] In part, this was because during the Maoist period, the strict *hukou* system kept the vast majority of the population spread out in the countryside. In addition, the Mao era Party-state's industrialization strategy was not as successful at promoting rapid economic growth as has been the case in the post-Mao period.

Overall, the Maoist system of goods and services provision marked a dramatic and life-changing improvement relative to the pre-communist political system. Indeed, goods and services provision during the Mao era was much better than that for virtually any other country in the world at a similar level of economic development – particularly for urban *hukou*-holders. And, this was accomplished entirely through the Party-state; nothing was provided by private entities (apart from the family in some cases).

GOODS/SERVICES PROVISION IN THE POST-MAO ERA

In the post-Mao era, Party-state entities have ceased to provide many of the goods and services that they did in the Maoist period. For some periods of the post-Mao era, citizens have thus been on their own with regard to particular goods and services. The result has been a decline in their ability to enjoy those goods and services. Perhaps most notably, health care has become prohibitively expensive for most citizens. In the 1980s and 1990s, Party-state leaders only very slowly responded to this situation. Since the turn of the new millennium, they have ramped up their efforts to ensure that the populace has access to key goods and services. Party-state leaders have done so in the same way that they have worked to encourage economic growth – through decentralized experimentation, and through a hybrid mix of government control and privatization. However, as noted above, this approach to goods and services provision has been much less successful than it has been with regard to managing the economy. This suggests that the fulfillment of different governmental functions may require different approaches. More specifically, the case of China indicates that when it comes to ensuring access to key goods and services, state control can accomplish more than privatization.

POVERTY ALLEVIATION

During the early part of the post-Mao period (the late 1970s through the early 1990s), poverty was not a problem for China's urban *hukou*-holders, as virtually all were afforded a version of the "iron rice bowl." With large-scale SOE reform in the mid-to-late 1990s, tens of millions of urban workers – roughly one third of the SOE workforce – were laid off. Many other SOE workers were forced into early retirement, and did not receive their full pensions. The government attempted to implement a Reemployment Program to help those who had been laid off find new jobs, but it was a largely failed effort. Separately, in the early 1990s Shanghai experimented with an alternative method of attending to those who had been displaced by SOE reforms, as well as other urban *hukou*-holders with incomes below a designated line. In the late 1990s, this system was adopted in cities across China. Known formally as the Minimum Livelihood Guarantee and colloquially as the *dibao*, it provides very small monthly allowances for those whose incomes fall below a stipulated level. The level, as well as the allowance, vary by location, and have shifted over time. Generally speaking, city allowances have been far higher than rural allowances, but there has been wide variation from city to city as well. From the time of its initiation through the present, *dibao* eligibility levels and payments have decreased. Between 1998 and 2011, for example, the average *dibao* standard declined from nearly 21 percent of the mean wage in large cities to under 8 percent.[9]

In the countryside in the post-Mao era, initial efforts to attend to rural residents who remained poverty-stricken despite the institution of the "household responsibility system" involved direct state funding to rural counties that were officially designated as "poor." Although a fairly significant sum of money was allotted to these locales, an estimated 33–50 percent of poor rural residents did not live in these counties. Moreover, sizeable portions of the funds were used by local authorities for purposes other than direct payments to poor families. Overall, although an impressive number of rural residents were lifted out of poverty from the late 1970s through the 1990s, this was mainly due to increased agricultural productivity and profit, and not government efforts specifically targeted at rural poverty alleviation. In the first decade of the new millennium, as part of central authorities' new effort to "Construct a New Socialist Countryside" (*jianshe shehuizhuyi xin nongcun*), the *dibao* system that earlier had been established in China's cities was extended to rural residents.

These efforts at poverty alleviation have been barely adequate at best. Moreover, the decline in payments and eligibility levels since the time of the program's initiation has diminished what was even at the start only minimally helpful assistance. Further, the scope and level of *dibao* payments appear to have improved only in response to the mass expression of public grievances, such as the large-scale unrest that erupted in nearly two dozen provinces in the wake of SOE reform in the late 1990s, and the multitudinous rural protests that have emerged in the 2000s. The disappearance of street protests by urban *hukou*-holders has been accompanied by decreased *dibao* payments and eligibility levels, suggesting that the Party-state has engaged in poverty alleviation only out of a motivation to quell social unrest; regime leaders not appear to view poverty alleviation as a goal in itself. As long as this attitude persists, improvements to poverty assistance programs will occur only if China's poor continue to take to the streets in protest.[10] In the meantime, Chinese authorities also have encouraged citizen groups – including religious groups – to provide food and other forms of assistance to China's poor. Indeed, although Chinese political leaders generally are extremely wary of citizen organization outside of the direct oversight of the CCP, this is one area in which social groups that are not affiliated with the CCP have been granted some freedom.

However, the lack of satisfactory governmental assistance for the poor is not necessarily the result of the fact that China's political system does not feature elections at the national level. In the US as well, poverty alleviation efforts have been minimal, and have tended to improve only in response to social unrest.[11] Because voter turnout rates are very low among poor people in the US, and because poor people lack "extra" money to donate to politicians, they tend to be ignored relative to other socio-economic groups. Further, in the US, conservative political leaders – as well as large percentages of Americans – view governmental poverty alleviation efforts as illegitimate, as they are believed to "enable" or give poor people "incentives" to stay poor rather than to pull themselves up by their bootstraps and succeed. In China, in contrast, both Party-state leaders and prevailing public opinion retain the "communist" belief that the government has a duty to help the poor, as their poverty is seen as the result of factors beyond their control (such as being laid off from their SOE) rather than as the result of their lack of ambition. Even so, in both China and the US the government encourages civic groups to provide assistance to the poor.

PENSIONS

Relative to its poverty-alleviation efforts, the post-Mao Party-state has done a better job of ensuring the provision of adequate pensions. As with the *dibao* system, pension initiatives arose in response to public unrest, and have seemed to be directed more toward quelling such unrest than to providing an optimal pension system that best ensures the wellbeing of the elderly. At the same time, the limited success that has been achieved in pension provision has been the result of local experimentation.

During the early post-Mao period (roughly 1978 through the early 1990s), China's pension system for the urban elderly was unchanged from the Mao era. Retirement ages remained quite young by international standards, and payments as a percentage of prior pay were extremely high compared to international averages. Meanwhile, in rural areas, as was the case during the Maoist period, elderly residents received no pensions; generally speaking, they were on their own to provide for themselves in old age. However, unlike the Mao era, when government-run collectives controlled all of the fruits of agricultural land, in the early post-Mao period, the "household responsibility system" provided rural residents with plots of land from which they could grow food for their own subsistence as well as for-profit agricultural products that generated income that could be saved for old age. Moreover, in the early post-Mao era rural residents were able to engage in wage work in local TVEs or in the cities, and could save some of these funds for their retirement.

In the mid-1990s, pension provision changed dramatically for urban residents. As discussed above, when large-scale SOE reforms resulted in mass layoffs and forced retirements, protests erupted across China's major cities. A major complaint was the non-payment or under-payment of pensions. Scrambling to quell these protests, the central government stipulated that enterprises would no longer pay pensions.

Instead, new urban social insurance agencies (SIAs) were charged with this task. However, central authorities encouraged local experimentation.[12] The result has been a "patchwork" of locally based pension programs "with uneven rules," and with "few provisions" for people who migrate for work or when they retire.[13] Most involve something around an 8 percent monthly contribution from the employee and a roughly 20 percent contribution from the employer.[14] However, the low legal retirement ages for men and women that existed from the Maoist era through the early 1990s have remained unchanged. And although the average ratio of pre-retirement pay to pension has dropped to 75–80 percent for still-employed SOE workers, it remains far higher than the international average. As of 2011, roughly 280 million urban workers were covered by urban pension programs, all of which involve some contribution on the part of the worker.[15] Although this amounted to only about 40 percent of all urban residents at the time, this number includes migrants to the city with rural *hukou*, who prior to the mid-1990s generally were offered no pension coverage at all.

A viable pension program for rural residents has been much slower in the making, yet since the middle of the first decade of the 2000s has progressed much further in terms of coverage. From the late 1970s through the mid-1980s, the central government made virtually no effort to address the lack of a pension system in rural areas. However, as has been the case with antecedents to the "household responsibility system," local authorities in some rural areas began to experiment with new ways to provide for the elderly. In 1987, Party-state leaders allowed the central Ministry of Civil Affairs (MOCA) to oversee experiments drawing from existing approaches, and proposed six potential models. In 1991 a Temporary Office for Rural Social Insurance Pensions was established by MOCA, and through the early 1990s, experiments continued. By the end of 1998 all provinces but Tibet had in place some sort of voluntary rural pension scheme. However, the contributions and payments tended to be exceedingly small, and coverage remained limited to just over 80 million farmers, or about 10 percent of the rural population.[16] From 1998 to 2006, central authorities paid little attention to improving rural pension systems, and rural pension coverage actually dropped to just over 50 million, or about 7 percent. Finally, in 2006, central authorities focused serious attention to the issue, as part of the government's initiative to "Construct a New Socialist Countryside." Experiments continued, and in 2009, a national pension program was enacted to cover all elderly rural residents. Under this system, rural workers can voluntarily contribute to personal accounts that are subsidized by the government (both at the central and local levels).[17] By the end of 2012, the program had made impressive strides, with approximately 460 million rural residents – 70 percent of the rural population – participating.[18]

The long-term viability of this system is uncertain. Most troublingly, because (a) current pension payments have been made from the contributions of current employees, and (b) the ratio of workers to pensioners has been decreasing, China's new pension system faces a huge unfunded future debt. Further, the new power of local governments to collect pension contributions had bred cases of extreme corruption. The most dramatic example occurred in Shanghai, where urban authorities collected fees far above what were necessary, and then diverted the excess revenue into loans to various real estate and financial firms.[19]

Yet on balance, the pension reforms of the late post-Mao period have been quite successful. Overall (and unlike *dibao* payments), pension payments have risen dramatically – even in, and often especially in, the most "corrupt" localities. Indeed, Shanghai's new pension system is the most generous and extensive in the country, extending even to migrant workers and residents in surrounding counties. Moreover, surveys indicate that both urban and rural residents are satisfied with the new status quo.[20] Finally, and importantly these popular pension schemes are entirely state-run; pension provision has not been privatized.

3 HOUSING/LAND

Another key good is housing. In this area, the post-Mao Party-state's record is mixed. Those who have been eligible for government-provided land and/or housing have enjoyed both affordability and security in this regard. Whereas in the 1980s only about 20 percent of all Chinese households owned homes, by 2010 that number had climbed to 85 percent. This is a much higher percentage than is the case even in countries with highly developed economies. However, demographic groups that have had to rely on the private sector for housing have been unable to enjoy affordable, secure housing.

In the countryside, since the late 1970s the "household responsibility system" has guaranteed every family a plot of land sufficient for subsistence, as well as additional land for profit-oriented use. Virtually no other country in the world – democratic or not – provides this kind of guarantee. This system has been extremely popular with rural residents. In cases when farmers' land has been appropriated by local authorities, this guarantee has been violated. However, although residents in this situation are often poorly compensated for the loss of their land, they are always offered monetary compensation and alternative low-cost housing. In many instances, the residents are not happy with the alternative housing, as it is in cramped, low-grade apartment complexes. However, the fact remains that the government is expected to, and does, ensure that rural residents have affordable housing. And as a result, there is virtually no homelessless in China's countryside.

Simultaneously, the Chinese Party-state has ensured affordable housing for the majority of urban *hukou*-holders. Prior to large-scale SOE privatization in the mid-1990s, urban *hukou*-holders were able to rent very low-cost housing through their work unit. When urban housing was privatized in the mid-1990s, urban *hukou*-holders were sold these units at far below market prices. By the early 2000s, 70 percent of households with urban *hukou* owned their own homes.

Moreover, most were able to purchase their unit with cash. Thus, the vast majority of middle-aged and older urban *hukou*-holders own their own homes free and clear.[21]

In contrast, demographic groups that have had to rely on the private sector for housing have found it nearly impossible to afford a decent place to live. In large part, this is because in the period since urban housing was privatized, urban housing prices have skyrocketed – roughly tripling between 1999 and 2009, and continuing to rise (albeit more slowly and fitfully) since then. For those who live in the city but were not able to purchase housing at below-market prices at the time of urban housing privatization, urban home prices have been prohibitively high. As of 2008, the ratio of average house price to average income was even higher in China than it was in the US – meaning that housing was even less affordable for new home buyers in China than it was in the US at the peak of America's housing "bubble." Further, although the central government's State Council requires local governments to commit no less than 10 per cent of funds coming from land conveyance to affordable housing, the number of low and middle-income housing units in China has flatlined, and even slightly declined since 1999, while the number of luxury housing units has more than tripled.[22]

The largest group that has been negatively affected by these developments includes China's more than 250 million migrant workers. As of 2012, less than one percent of migrant workers owned homes.[23] Migrant workers with construction jobs typically live in ramshackle shanties erected next to the work site. Those who work in factories usually reside in dormitories constructed on factory grounds, often adjacent to or above the shop floor. In most factories, a small residential fee is deducted from the worker's wages. Living conditions are rudimentary at best; the average dorm room measures 26 square meters, and is shared by roughly twelve people.[24] The factory compound is typically gated and locked, and in some cases the dormitories are locked from the outside during certain hours. In these circumstances, fires have been particularly dangerous. To name but one example, in 1993, close to two hundred young women workers burned to death at the Zhili toy factory in Shenzhen because the steel-mesh doors of their dormitory had been sealed.[25] However, almost no migrant workers are truly homeless. For, if they are unable to find work or housing in the city, they have the option of returning to their home village, where their family is assured land/housing through the "household responsibility system."

The other significant group that lacks secure and affordable housing includes recent college graduates and young professionals. Though most come from families that were able to purchase former urban SOE housing at below-market prices, if they do not live with their parents, they are on their own for housing. And even though they generally earn more than do migrant workers, housing prices are so astronomical in most cities that individuals in this demographic group also tend to live in cramped, shared, substandard housing.

4   HEALTH CARE

With regard to health care, China's trajectory parallels that of pensions. Through the early 1990s, most urban *hukou*-holders were provided practically free health care through their work units, while rural *hukou*-holders had little access to formal health care. In the latter half of the 1990s, SOE privatization ended free health care provision for most urban residents. Since the start of the new millennium, the government has attempted to formulate new health insurance schemes to provide medical care to both urban and rural residents. However, unlike the new pension system, which has virtually no private sector involvement, the health care system has been privatized to a large extent. Under this mixed system of health care provision, affordable quality care has not been available to most regular citizens.

In the early post-Mao period, the "iron rice bowl" remained intact for most urban *hukou*-holders, including free or very lost-cost health care. However, in the mid-1980s, preventive care facilities had their state subsidies reduced, and were allowed to charge patients on a fee-for-service basis. For SOE workers, this was not a problem, as their medical care was covered. But for the SOEs that employed them, this became a huge financial strain. Indeed, the rising indebtedness of most SOEs in the early post-Mao period was a major reason why the Party-state moved to privatize them in the mid-1990s.

When SOE privatization led to mass lay-offs, tens of millions of former SOE workers were left almost entirely on their own for health care. By 2005, government expenditures as a percentage of total health-care spending had dropped by more than half in comparison with 1990. During the latter half of the 1990s, local experiments with new urban health care systems were undertaken in Zhejiang, leading in 1999 to a central government recommendation of a new plan that was supposed to cover all urban employees. As of 2004, only about 40 percent of urban employees were covered. Further problems resulted from the privatization of funding for doctors and hospitals. Although the Party-state required doctors and hospitals to charge below-cost prices for basic, non-invasive care, this well-intentioned action had an adverse effect. Because, simultaneously, doctors and hospitals were made to rely on patients rather than the government for most of their income, they routinely began to under-utilize basic procedures, and to recommend unnecessary but expensive tests, prescriptions, and procedures. A World Bank study conducted in the early 2000s found that less than one percent of drug prescriptions in China were necessary, and that 20 percent of spending on appendicitis and pneumonia was unnecessary. Not surprisingly, and in marked contrast to the Maoist era and early post-Mao period, curative health spending outpaced preventive expenditures. An estimated half of all Chinese healthcare spending is on prescriptions, compared with 10 percent in the US and 15 percent in

Europe.[26] Per capita spending on health care has risen dramatically, with many spending exorbitant amounts and falling into debt.

In the countryside, the health care situation was even worse from the late 1970s through the early years of the new millennium. When the agricultural collectives of the Mao era were dismantled in the late 1970s, and land was allotted to individual families as part of the "household responsibility system," local government authorities no longer had a collective revenue source. As a result, rural medical collectives deteriorated. Whereas almost 80 percent of rural residents were covered by rural medical collectives in 1979, by 1987 only 2 percent were covered. For rural residents during this period, medical costs became a significant cause of poverty. Although experiments with a new medical cooperative scheme were undertaken in 1989–1990, they were limited to Sichuan province, and did not lead to any significant changes nationwide.[27]

By the middle of the first decade of the 2000s, China was ranked as one of the worst countries in the world in terms of fairness of financial contributions to health care. Earlier progress in disease eradication slowed to a halt, and in some cases regressed. It was not until the middle of the first decade of the 2000s that Party-state authorities took serious action to address the dire health care situation faced by rural and urban residents. Around 2003, central Party-leaders worked with local authorities to develop a new rural medical cooperative system. By 2006, it covered roughly half of all rural counties, reducing the percentage of rural residents without medical coverage from more than 75 percent in 2003 to about 57 percent.[28] In 2009, central authorities announced that a greatly expanded national health insurance plan would provide basic coverage to almost 100 percent of the citizenry. In 2011, the Party-state's new Five Year Plan promised "to add 150,000 new primary care physicians, build 2,000 new county-level hospitals, 29,000 new township-level hospitals, and upgrade another 5,000 existing hospitals and clinics."[29]

Even so, as with pensions, local governments were made responsible for the administration of health care. Consequently, there has been wide geographic variation. Moreover, medical care has remained extremely expensive for most citizens, and corruption has been rampant. The reason is that hospitals continue to receive little government funding, and doctors continue to earn very low salaries. Patients regularly are expected to provide "red envelopes" (hong bao) filled with cash when seeking treatment – often in amounts that exceed their monthly income. In 2010, for example, the average charge for medical consultation and medication fee in community clinics was ¥83, and the average price of in-patient services was ¥2,358.[30] The same year, the average monthly income in China was about ¥1,500. Further, the cost of procedures has continued to skyrocket in many places. For example, between 2000 and 2013, the charge for surgery for stomach cancer reportedly rose from roughly ¥9,800 to approximately ¥49,100.[31] Thus, despite the central government's admirable effort to expand health insurance, health care costs have continued to rise as a result of the privatization of health care provision. Although current CCP General Secretary Xi Jinping has initiated a campaign to eradicate corrupt practices, unless the underlying problem of underfunded hospitals and underpaid doctors is resolved, affordable quality health care is likely to remain out of reach for the vast majority of China's citizens.[32]

5 EDUCATION

In the realm of education, the Party-state's record in the post-Mao era is decidedly mixed. Primary education remains government-run and is supposed to be available free of charge, as was the case during the Maoist period. However, as in the Maoist period, severe inequalities between urban and rural hukou-holders exist. Moreover, in marked contrast to the Mao era, higher education has been largely privatized, with the result that socio-economic status has come to play a decisive role in determining access. Although colleges and universities have expanded and proliferated since the early 1990s – thus opening many more opportunities for youths to gain admission to higher education institutions – skyrocketing costs have made a college education prohibitively expensive for most Chinese youths. The situation was almost opposite in the late 1970s through the late 1980s, when only a tiny portion of college-age young people could gain a spot in a higher education institution, but tuition was virtually free, such that youths who had high scores on the national university entrance exam, but whose families had limited incomes, were able to go to college.

For the duration of the post-Mao period, all children have been officially guaranteed nine years of schooling in free public schools, beginning at age six. For urban *hukou*-holders, this has been a reality. For rural children, primary and middle-school education also has been available, but the quality has been far below that of public schools in the cities. For the children of migrant workers who live with their parents in the city, access to quality primary and middle school has been very limited. Although public schools in cities technically are open to children without a local urban *hukou*, many of these schools will accept a migrant child only if paid fees that typically are so high that they exceed the income of the parents. As a result, most migrant children in the cities attend cheaper private schools that are unregulated and unlicensed. Further, even private schools charge fees that hover around 10 percent of the parents' income.

When it comes to high school and college education, as noted above, the children of middle- and low-income families have been severely disadvantaged in the late post-Mao period. As a result of the marketization of higher education, a college education has become increasingly inaccessible to these children. In 1992, universities were allowed to "determine their own fee structures," and in 1993, universities were told to "move gradually from a system under which the government guaranteed [higher] education and employment to a system in which students were held responsible for both."[33] Meanwhile, the government contribution to education funding fell – dropping from 82 percent in 1993 to 62 percent in 2002. For kindergarten through the ninth grade, as of 2005 the regime still paid for more than 75 percent of the total cost. Yet at the high-school and university levels, government funding dropped to less than 48 percent. The balance has been made up by an increase in tuition and ad hoc fees.[34]

As a result of these changes, money has come to play a key role in university enrolment. In the words of political scientist Stanley Rosen, "money … has become the standard method by which – and often the only way – parents can get children into the [prestigious senior high] schools of their choice."[35] Since attendance of key high schools ensures good scores on the national university entrance examination, those who cannot afford to attend an elite high school have a greatly diminished probability of gaining a university education. Moreover, those with money are more likely to attend the leading middle and primary schools that feed prominent high schools. The exclusionary consequences of this reality are even more severely experienced by migrant children, who – as discussed above – often receive substandard K-12 education in unregulated private schools. The ability of migrant children to succeed on the university entrance exam is further undercut by the requirement that most migrant students take the university entrance exam back in their home town. Because each locality has a different curriculum, if a student has not had their K-12 education in that locality, it is difficult for them to excel in the exam.[36] Beyond the obstacle of the entrance exam, even if a student is accepted to university, the required tuition and fees have become prohibitive for most families. In 2000, the average annual expense for a college student was estimated at ¥8,000 to 10,000, while the average annual per capita income in China was slightly more than ¥7,000.[37]

Overall, due to the severe decline in government subsidization of higher education and subsequent marketization of higher education fees, since the early 1990s, university students in China increasingly have come from financially privileged families. Fewer qualified students from average and low-income homes have been admitted, and fewer have had the financial capacity to enroll.[38] At the primary and middle school levels, rural children and the children of migrant workers living in the city also have been significantly disadvantaged.

6 INFRASTRUCTURE

As discussed above, during the Maoist period the Party-state undertook massive efforts to improve China's infrastructure – including transit and electrical grid construction, and water control and irrigation projects. In the early post-Mao period (from roughly the late 1970s through the early 1990s), political leaders made little further investment in infrastructure development. In the late post-Mao period, and particularly since the early years of the 2000s, the Party-state has invested a massive amount of funds into infrastructure. As a result of these governmental efforts, at present, many elements of China's infrastructure are quite advanced, particularly relative to China's per capita GDP. Thus, especially during the past decade or so, China's government has done an admirable job of providing its citizens with affordable and fairly high quality infrastructure.

From the late 1970s through the early 1990s, infrastructure improvement was not a Party-state priority. Virtually all long-distance passenger and commercial transit was done via rail. Apart from major cities, roads were in poor condition. Citizens got around by foot, bike, public bus, or train. Travel between cities, towns, and villages that were not connected by rail was exceedingly slow. Private cars were almost non-existent. Through the early 1980s, only one relatively small subway line existed in the entire country, in Beijing. A second small subway line began service in Tianjin in 1984. No other cities had operating subways. In the late 1980s, construction on a national highway system began, but its expansion was very slow. As of 1993, only about 400 miles had been built.[39]

Beginning in the mid-1990s, but much more significantly since the early years of the 2000s, infrastructure construction has exploded as Party-state leaders have made this a priority. In the mid-1990s, the government opened new subways in Shanghai and Guangzhou. In 2004, central authorities made a significant investment in rural infrastructure, including efforts to provide safe drinking water and to ensure that all townships were accessible via paved roads.[40] Highway expansion was dramatically stepped up as well; by 2008, 33,500 miles of highway were in operation. From 2009–2010, the central government invested more than ¥4 trillion in infrastructure. In 2012, nearly ¥1 trillion more was allotted. New subway systems have been built apace; as of 2014, seventeen cities had a subway in operation, and fourteen more were under construction. Further, existing subway systems have been greatly expanded.[41] By January 2014, China's highway system had grown to 64,900 miles.[42]

These investments have been driven by Chinese leaders' economic concerns: following the economic crisis of 2008, infrastructure construction was seen as a direct way to stimulate the economy while simultaneously improving citizens' quality of life. Concomitantly, infrastructure expansion has been viewed as a necessary pre-requisite for further urbanization. And further urbanization has been seen by government leaders as being key in shifting toward domestic consumer-based economic growth and away from export-led growth. In early 2014, central Party-state leaders announced a new urbanization plan that seeks to increase the portion of urban residents in China to 60 percent by 2020 (as of 2014 it was roughly 54 percent). According to the plan, every city with more than 200,000 residents will be covered by standard railways by 2020, and cities with more than 500,000 residents will be connected by high-speed rail services. The civil aviation network will also be expanded to cover approximately 90 percent of the population.[43]

The post-Mao Party-state also has made great progress in electricity provision, again through state ownership, direction, and investment. Under Mao, electricity access significantly expanded, but even so, as of 1979 well over one-third of all rural residents – roughly 245 million people – lacked electricity. Through large investments, by the late 1990s the Chinese Party-state had brought electricity to nearly all rural residents. Between 1998 and 2002, central leaders led a further push to increase the quality and efficiency of electricity provision. During this period, the reliability rate for electricity rose from 87 percent to 95 percent, and the percentage of electric voltage that met national standards rose from 78 percent to 90 percent. In addition, rural electricity fees were reduced. Indeed, for both urban and rural residents, electricity is available at very low rates.[44] In 2012, the Party-state earmarked US$100 billion to construct new ultra-high voltage transmission lines, designed to increase efficiency and reliability. Government officials believe that these lines will provide four-to-five times the power of traditional lines, and will do so with much less lost energy during transmission. As of late 2013, nearly 5,000 kilometers of such lines had been completed, with a further 6,400 kilometers planned.[45] Overall, China's post-Mao advances in electricity provision have occurred entirely through government investment and control. Although China's national state-owned electric grid was broken up into separate, regional entities in the early 2000s, virtually all electricity generation and provision has remained owned and directed by governmental entities.

When it comes to access to safe drinking water, the Party-state's record is much less impressive. As of 2013, tests gave nearly three-fifths of all underground water supply stations ratings of "relatively bad" or worse. Approximately half of all rural residents do not have access to drinking water that meets international standards. In 2013, central

Party-state leaders announced that by 2015, the government would ensure that all of China's rural residents would have access to safe and affordable water. As of March 2014, government officials reiterated that this was a top Party priority, but admitted that despite bringing water to 63 million rural residents in 2013, roughly 110 million rural residents still lacked access.[46]

That government control and direction have been key in infrastructure development in China is without question. Yet, how have the Chinese government's authoritarian and democratic features influenced its success at infrastructure provision? In some ways, the authoritarian aspects of the political system have aided governmental efforts regarding infrastructure. Most importantly, when the government decides to build a new subway, road, or other type of infrastructure, it simply does it, regardless of the views of those whose lives may be disrupted in the process. As a result, new infrastructure projects typically are completed much more rapidly than is the case in more democratic countries.

Contrarily, however, the lack of transparency that is inherent in China's authoritarian system has enabled officials to engage in corrupt practices when it comes to infrastructure construction. Indeed, in numerous cases citizens have been harmed – and even killed – by faulty infrastructure that was caused by government authorities who cut corners with regard to safety and quality as a way to pocket some of the money earmarked for the project, or in their haste to impress higher-level officials by completing a project on schedule. Sadly, examples of this kind of tragedy abound. In the massive earthquake that struck Sichuan in 2008, dozens of school buildings crumbled, burying thousands of children alive. Nearby buildings survived virtually unscathed. It was later discovered that the school walls had not been properly reinforced. Another major case occurred in 2012, when three people were killed and five injured when a 320-foot section of an eight-lane bridge in northeast China broke off when four large trucks drove on to it, plunging the vehicles to the ground. The bridge supposedly had been designed to handle nearly 10,000 vehicles an hour.

Overall, very serious concerns about infrastructure safety diminish the Party-state's strong record in terms of infrastructure expansion and provision. At the same time, it is not at all clear that the institution of multi-Party elections at the national level would eradicate this problem. A more directly effective solution would be for higher-level officials to revise the evaluation criteria used to judge local authorities so as to place more emphasis on local safety and less on the rapidity with which local infrastructure expands. Further, more concerted efforts to increase local authorities' pay might reduce their drive to seek alternative sources of income.

7 NATURAL ENVIRONMENT

With regard to the "good" that is essential to all people in a fundamental way – a healthy natural environment – the situation in China is grim at best, and in some respects can only be described as horrific. Due to logging, erosion, and the depletion of water supplies, more than one-fourth of China's land is considered "desertified." Virtually every major body of water is polluted, and an estimated one-tenth to one-fifth of all cropland is contaminated with heavy metals as a result of water pollution. In some areas of China – Shanghai being a prime example – cadmium levels in nearby farmland are so high that rice grown locally is dangerous to consume. In almost every major city, drinking water contains arsenic and other toxic chemicals.

Air pollution also is extreme. The World Health Organization (WHO) recommends no more than 20 micrograms of PM2.5[47] per cubic meter of air. The European Union stipulates that any reading above 40 is unsafe, while the US level is 75. Most major cities in China regularly far exceed even the higher US standard. Beijing's particulate level often surpasses 300 for days on end; in January 2013, it surged to nearly 900. The same year, even more extreme readings of 1,000 were recorded in the northeastern cities of Harbin and Shijiazhuang. In online posts, residents of cities such as these have described the air as "postapocalyptic," "terrifying" and "beyond belief."[48]

Environmental degradation has had a severe impact on public health in China. In cities with the highest levels of air pollution, simply breathing the air for a day is equivalent to smoking two packs of cigarettes. A joint study by the World Bank and China's State Environmental Protection Agency in 2007 found that 600,000 to 700,000 people in China die prematurely from air pollution each year. Diseases related to water and land contamination abound as well. Treating people who fall ill as a result of environment degradation is also costly. These expenses, as well as others deriving from pollution and resource scarcity, are estimated by the World Health Organization to cause a loss of nearly 6 percent of China's GDP per year.[49]

China's central political leaders are well aware of the problem, and have made significant efforts to curb further environmental degradation and even roll it back. Some local authorities have worked to address environmental issues as well. Indeed, China's political elites have had little choice to do otherwise, as the public has demanded it – in recent years, environmental protests have grown in number and size. Local authorities have played varying roles in these mass actions. Some – particularly those who have been popularly elected through a free and fair process – have acted to champion the people's cause, even acting as protest leaders. Yet in most cases, local authorities themselves have been the target of the protestors' ire, and have tried to repress the participants. Higher level authorities, in contrast, generally have intervened in support of the protestors, in many instances sanctioning those involved in perpetrating the environmental harm and attempting to ameliorate the ensuing problems.[50]

Beyond simply responding to local cases of environmental degradation and public harm, central and province-level political leaders have undertaken an array of initiatives and policies to curb pollution. First, to better monitor air quality, by 2017 air particulate measuring stations will be established in all cities at the county level and higher, nearly tripling the total number of monitored cities to 338 (from 119 in 2014). Second, central authorities have been working to reduce China's use of coal and petroleum, which at present provide roughly 90 percent of China's power, and are leading causes of China's air pollution. In 2006, central authorities committed to reducing China's CO_2 intensity by 40–45 percent by 2020; as of 2014, China was on track to meet this goal. To help achieve this, China has (in the words of BBC columnist David Shukman) "embarked on the greatest push for renewable energy the world has ever seen."[51] According to government plans, China will add more electricity generating capacity from renewable sources by 2035 than the US, Europe, and Japan combined. China already has by far the world's largest hydropower capacity, exceeding that of the US, Canada, and Brazil together. China is also the world's largest producer of wind power. Further massive increases in all of these renewable sources are planned and in progress. By 2020, the current (2014) installed capacity of 75 gigawatts (GW) of wind power is slated to increase to 200 GW. The entirety of the European Union has just over 90 GW.[52] In addition, in 2013, China installed 12 GW of new solar capacity, by far more than any other country has installed in a given year (the prior record was 8 GW), and more than China had installed in all prior years put together. By way of further comparison, Britain has a total of 4 GW of solar capacity. In 2014, Chinese leaders plan to surpass the 2013 record by installing an additional 14 GW of solar energy.[53] Similarly, hydropower is on track to grow by 15 GW per year from 2011–2015. During the same period, hydropower capacity is slated to grow by only 1.9 GW in all of North America, 1.8 GW in South America, 0.5 GW in Europe and 0.3 GW in Africa.[54] Meanwhile, according to a central government plan announced in late 2013, coal consumption in three large regions (Beijing-Tianjin-Hebei, the

Yangtze River Delta, and the Pearl River Delta) is required to flat-line and then decline.[55] It remains to be seen whether or not this goal will be achieved.

A third group of government policies aimed at curbing further environmental degradation concerns vehicle use. To begin, by 2017, roughly 15 million "heavily polluting vehicles" – which according to government officials make up about 15 percent of all vehicles in China but discharge almost 60 percent of all vehicle pollutants – will be banned. In addition, the sulfur content limit of gasoline sold in China, which through the early years of the new millennium was an astoundingly high 800 micrograms/gram, was reduced to 50 in 2013, and will decline to 10 in 2017, such that it will equal the standard in Europe. In the US, the national limit is 30.[56] The sulfur content in diesel fuel, which is used by large, heavy-duty trucks and vehicles such as tractors, is slated to be reduced from a staggering 2,000 prior to 2013 to 50 in 2015.[57] In some cities, vehicle restrictions also are in place. For example, in 2013, Beijing announced that on high air pollution days, half of all vehicles (according to whether the license plate has an even or odd number) will be banned from the streets, factories will be closed, and construction work will be halted.[58] In addition, in four major cities, including Beijing and Shanghai, only 20,000 new vehicles may be registered (via a lottery) each month. An estimated 1.53 million potential buyers are vying to be chosen.[59] Although necessary and well-intended, these governmental efforts to restrict private vehicle use arose only after Party-state leaders realized that their earlier encouragement of private vehicle manufacturing and sales in the 1990s and early part of the 2000s had devastating effects on air pollution and created serious traffic blockages.

Government authorities have sought out foreign assistance and advice to support their environmental efforts. For example, in 2014, officials in Hebei province (which in 2013 had 236 days that exceeded air particulate safety levels) announced that they would spend US$20 million to hire two hundred "foreign experts" to develop projects on air pollution control.[60] In addition, NGOs (most of which are affiliated with international groups) have been allowed substantial input into environmental decision-making processes. The most notable is Friends of Nature, which became China's first officially recognized environmental NGO in 1994. Thousands of other environmental NGOs exist in China as well, and (in the words of leading environmental scholar Elizabeth Economy) are used by citizens to "push local officials to reveal accurate pollution statistics, work with Chinese journalists to investigate corruption, and launch public campaigns against corporations that break environmental laws and regulations."[61]

Though these activities represent a significant and impressive effort on the part of the Chinese Party-state to address China's severe environmental degradation, governmental actions have exhibited many serious flaws as well. One is short-sightedness and haste. For example, in some provinces with particularly bad air pollution (such as Hebei) aircraft have been dropping "smog-dispersing chemicals" to produce rainfall that decreases air pollution in the short term, but may contaminate land and water.[62] Similarly, authorities have rushed to plant large numbers of trees in desertified areas, so that they can tout their environmental progress, but have not considered that the trees' water use would only further the problem, and ultimately kill the trees as well.

Moreover, as with infrastructure, corrupt behavior on the part of profit-seeking Party-state officials has exacerbated China's environmental problems. Indeed, the main target of the tens of thousands of environmental protests that occur every year is local officials who collude with local businesses to allow practices that damage the environment and harm the local population, but enrich the officials and business owners. Relatedly, the central government's prioritization of economic growth over all else has spurred many local officials to ignore environmental problems that are created by lucrative businesses in their areas. At the same time, the decentralized nature of the political system – a feature that has helped to stimulate economic growth – has worked against the fulfillment of many central government initiatives. Because pollution flows across territorial boundaries, local authorities in a "polluting" locality may not have an interest in dealing with the pollution that affects neighboring areas – particularly if the polluter in their locality is a source of revenue for them. To try to address these problems, in 2014 the CCP's powerful Organization Department – which ultimately decides who holds positions of power within Party and state institutions – announced that it would begin to include in its personnel evaluations an assessment of whether or not an official achieved the environmental targets that had been given to them, and also if they had failed to respond to cases of "heavy pollution."[63] The potential effects of this new policy remain to be seen.

To what extent have the Chinese political system's democratic and authoritarian features aided or inhibited the Party-state's ability to provide Chinese citizens with a healthy natural environment? Certainly, at the local level, when officials have been popularly elected, they have been much more likely to champion the cause of their constituents, including by leading protests against other local authorities who have been involved in activities that have harmed the local environment and its residents. In contrast, local authorities who have not been subject to free and fair elections by the people often have ignored the environmental well-being of the people within their jurisdiction. In this sense, electoral democracy may be seen as having aided in the provision of this good, while a lack of electoral democracy may be seen as inhibiting it. At higher levels of China's political system, the evidence is more mixed. In recent years, despite the fact that China's top Party and state leaders are not subject to popular election, they have exhibited an impressive commitment to improving China's natural environment, including through significant investments (such as those for renewable energy sources) and regulations (such as those regarding fuel and vehicle use), and through their sympathetic response to many popular protests. Given this, it is unclear how higher-level elections might lead China's central leaders to better address China's environmental issues.

CONCLUSION

Overall, the post-Mao Party-state's record of ensuring access to key goods and services has been mixed, with impressive success in some areas but deterioration in others. Further, access to important goods and services has been unevenly distributed across the population. Urban *hukou*-holders have remained privileged relative to rural *hukou*-holders when it comes to housing, pensions, and health care, and the wealthy have enjoyed greater access to education. The one exception is the natural environment, the degradation of which has negatively impacted all who reside on the mainland.

With the appropriate will and prioritization on the part of top CCP leaders, it is possible for the present political system to address these issues. However, this will require a concerted and focused effort on the part of central authorities that is not simply a reactive and ad hoc response to the articulation of mass grievances. Moreover, central leaders need to make good on their assertion that economic growth will not be the only significant criterion upon which lower-level leaders will be evaluated as they seek to rise through the Party-state ranks. Until the provision of important goods and services is equally valued in the cadre evaluation process, lower-level authorities will continue to prioritize economic growth.

Research on Chinese villages in the late post-Mao period shows that goods and services provision is better in areas where free and fair local elections are the norm.[64] Thus, further efforts to protect and promote meaningful elections at this level are likely to enhance the regime's ability to fulfill this key governmental function, and thereby remain stable. At the same time, it is not clear that central-level elections would improve goods and services provision. Indeed, with regard to some goods and services (such as infrastructure), China's lack of elections may allow the regime to act more quickly and decisively than is the case in many liberal democracies.

Finally, the deterioration of many important goods and services in the post-Mao era has appeared to be an outgrowth of the economic privatization that has occurred during this period. Although economic privatization has played a key role in stimulating China's overall economic growth, it has been accompanied by decreased access and skyrocketing costs for some important goods, such as health care and education. In contrast, goods and services that have been subjected to direct governmental controls and oversight (most notably infrastructure, pensions, and the environment) have exhibited the greatest progress. Meanwhile, some groups (particularly middle-aged and older urban *hukou*-holders) have enjoyed affordable housing as a result of government intervention in the free market, while groups that have had to fend for themselves in the private housing market have suffered. Thus, in counter-distinction to the Party-state's record of managing the economy, wherein privatization has played a key role in China's success, when it comes to ensuring access to key goods and services, privatization has had many detrimental effects.

7 Stable Authoritarianism?

To β188 simple review

Although the structure of China's ruling Party-state has been altered very little in the post-Mao period, the composition and focus of its leadership have changed dramatically. In the Maoist period, ideological "correctness" (as determined by Mao) motivated the selection of Party members and leaders, as well as governmental policy. Since the death of Mao, ideology largely has gone by the wayside, replaced by a pragmatism oriented toward maintaining the Communist Party's political dominance. Importantly, in the post-Mao era top Party-state leaders have sought to enhance the Party's strength by becoming more competent and responsive to the public. And by all indices, they have succeeded in these efforts. As a result, the regime's popular legitimacy has been buttressed.

This pragmatism has led the Chinese government and its policies to exhibit a hybrid mixture of authoritarian, democratic, state-interventionist, and capitalist features. Generally speaking, this combination of characteristics has enabled the Party-state to adequately fulfill the basic functions of a government: responding to public grievances and satisfying key demographic groups; managing the economy; and ensuring the provision of key goods and services. Though China's post-Mao political system has been far from perfect in doing so – particularly with regard to the first and last functions listed above – even in these areas its performance has been satisfactory. And with regard to managing the economy, its accomplishments have been impressive.

Even so, there remain serious shortcomings in the post-Mao Party-state's performance. Assuming that China's leaders wish to maintain the legitimacy of the CCP-controlled political system, they will need to address these problems. Under the administration of CCP General Secretary and state President Xi Jinping, the Party has made some efforts to deal with pressing issues, particularly corruption. However, it is doubtful that Xi's anti-corruption efforts will eradicate the root causes of cadre corruption. Moreover, Xi Jinping simultaneously has moved to stifle the expression of public discontent, and these actions threaten to undermine the regime's ability to satisfactorily respond to public grievances.

With regard to the question of whether or not more "democracy" is needed to resolve existing shortcomings in the Chinese political system, the answer is both "yes" and "no." At the local level, it is clear that elections have improved governance. Conversely, local officials who have not been subject to free and fair elections have tended to be the source of popular complaints. Thus, the extension of free and fair elections at the local level is important. At the national level, however, it is not clear that free and fair multi-Party elections would improve the Party-state's fulfillment of the basic functions of government.

STATIS AND CHANGE IN CHINA'S POST-MAO PARTY-STATE

As noted above and discussed in detail in Chapter 2, the structure of China's political system has remained almost entirely unchanged from the Maoist era through the present. At the national level, the bottom of the Party's official structure is the National Party Congress (NPC). One level up is the Central Committee (CC), followed by the Polit-buro, and then the Standing Committee (SC) of the Politburo. Although according to the Party constitution, power flows from the NPC up, in reality power flows from the SC down. The members of the SC, as well as some Party elders who do not hold any key positions within the Party structure, are the true political power-holders in China. Those who occupy the most important posts within the Party also sit in the top positions within China's state structure – which exists as the mirror image of the Party, and was created by the Party to serve its ends. In addition, not unlike other kinds of political systems, China's political system includes numerous informal and unofficial entities that wield great political power despite their invisibility "on paper." In all of these respects, the structure of China's Party-state has evidenced virtually no innovation relative to the Maoist period.

However, the manner in which Party and state officials are selected has become far more meritocratic and regularized. And, the people who occupy leadership positions in the Party and state are much more pragmatic and educated – and far less ideologically driven – than was the case under Mao. Similarly, CCP members are more educated and include a wider array of socio-economic groups – including private entrepreneurs and intellectuals. In this sense, the Party has shed most of its "communist" features and become a catch-all Party in terms of demographics, and instrumental in terms of its policy focus – "whatever works" to ensure political stability.

Further, Party and state leadership selection processes have become more democratic, particularly at the local level. On the state side, village council elections regularly occur in virtually all of China's villages, with perhaps half operating in a manner that is free, fair, and competitive by Western standards. And, the quality of these elections overall has been improving over time. Similarly, popular elections for urban community residents' committees have been instituted in some localities. On the Party side, too, efforts have been made to give common citizens more input, particularly in terms of local leadership. Local Party leaders increasingly have been subject to public assessment, either by the ability of local residents to vote out undesirable candidates or by the requirement that local Party leader candidates first demonstrate their popularity by being elected to the locality's village council or residents' committee. The result has been local state and Party leadership that is more representative of the wishes of the people. At higher levels of the Party and state, somewhat more democratic procedures have been implemented as well. Most notably, the practice of having "more candidates than seats" has brought a modicum of competition and the ability to weed out especially unpopular candidates.

Over the course of the post-Mao period, the Chinese Party-state has remained in some basic ways "authoritarian" (particularly at the highest levels) but has become fairly democratic in other respects (particularly at the local level). And, this hybrid system generally has been successful at fulfilling the basic functions of a stable government. At the same time, however, there are some serious gaps in the post-Mao Party-state's performance. Resolution of these problems does not require the institution of procedural democracy at the political system's highest levels. Indeed, the authoritarian nature of the Party-state's apex opens the possibility for top political leaders to take quicker and more dramatic action than is the case in most liberal democracies. Yet, this possibility can come to fruition only if top political leaders make the resolution of these issues a priority. Further, their actions must be driven by the pragmatic goal of finding what works best, rather than ideological imperatives.

SUCCESS AND FAILURE IN THE THREE GOVERNMENTAL FUNCTIONS

Responding to public grievances and satisfying key demographic groups

In terms of the first key governmental function – responding to public grievances and satisfying important demographic groups – the post-Mao Party-state has done a satisfactory job. Through a variety of formal/legal/institutionalized and informal/quasi-legal/

uninstitutionalized mechanisms, China's post-Mao political system has allowed for a remarkable degree of openness to the expression of public grievances, and has made significant efforts to effectively redress these grievances. Formal, legal and institutionalized mechanisms include the official "letters and visits" (*xinfang*) system and local elections for rural village councils and urban residents' committees. Informal mechanisms that skirt the boundaries of what is legal include Internet posts and street protests. Together, these mechanisms have enabled the public to articulate and gain redress for most serious problems. In so doing, these mechanisms have strengthened public support for the CCP-led political status quo. However, recent moves by top CCP leader Xi Jinping to curtail popular expression threaten to undermine the government's ability to maintain this situation.

The post-Mao Party-state also has satisfied key demographic groups, including private businesspeople, college students/graduates, rank-and-file workers (in both the public and private sectors), and farmers. Although some of these groups have had strained relations with parts of the Chinese Party-state at times in the post-Mao period, overall, the governing regime has improved in its efforts to address the needs and desires of these groups. It has done so through a combination of inclusionary efforts (such as the admission of private entrepreneurs into the Party) and "communist" initiatives to provide safety nets – particularly through policies that guarantee land to rural *hukou*-holders and that have enabled home-ownership among many urban *hukou*-holders. As a result, China's major socio-economic groups have exhibited little desire to upset the political status quo.

Even so, support for the Chinese Party-state among some groups is tenuous. Most notably, farmers who have been subject to unfair land acquisitions have been extremely dissatisfied. Although central political leaders are aware this problem and have attempted to address it, these efforts have had little impact. In addition, public discontent with environmental degradation is high. Although the Chinese Party-state's authoritarian features open the potential for the regime to act quickly and decisively to address these problems, political leaders from the top level to the bottom have been hesitant to take pro-environment actions that might dampen economic growth.

Meanwhile, some of China's ethnic minority groups – namely Tibetans and Uighurs – are highly (and increasingly) dissatisfied with CCP rule, and in some cases have resorted to violent actions against not just governmental authorities but also regular civilians. However, these ethnic groups represent a tiny minority of China's total population, and do not enjoy the sympathy of members of the majority Han population. If anything, the Party-state's repression of these groups has strengthened the Han population's support for the CCP-led government.

Maintaining economic stability and growth

When it comes to the second key function of a stable governing regime – maintaining economic grown and stability – the post-Mao Party-state's record is impressive. Since the death of Mao, China has posted the highest GDP growth rates in world history, and it weathered the global economic recession that began in 2008 with minimal disruption. Despite the emergence of significant domestic economic inequalities, virtually all Chinese citizens have experienced a dramatic rise in incomes and living standards. This economic growth has been the result of the Party-state's decentralized, experimental, and pragmatic approach to economic policy-making, which has created a hybrid economic system that features both free-market capitalism and state direction.

The post-Mao Party-state's success at managing the economy has in some ways been aided by its authoritarian nature at the central level. As discussed in Chapter 5, a lack of electoral democracy at the national level in no way makes it inevitable that governing elites will pursue policies that benefit the populace as a whole. The economic record of the Maoist regime is a vivid illustration of the severe harm that can be done by authoritarian regimes. However, a lack of elections at the national level can open the possibility for political leaders to pursue policies that are more consistent and effective than may be the case in liberal democracies.[1] The contrast with the US is particularly striking. As of the time of this writing, the two dominant political parties in America espouse opposite ideological views, and control different parts of the government. As a result, economic decision-making often is stymied. Further, because American political leaders must constantly be concerned about election and re-election, and because their success at getting elected/re-elected turns on their ability to attract large sums of money from wealthy donors, US political elites must cater to the interests of these donors, even when those interests are not identical with the interests of the populace as a whole. In China, central Party-state leaders are free of these considerations. As a result – if they are so inclined – they are able to craft policies based on pragmatic considerations of what works best to benefit the economy as a whole. Generally speaking, China's post-Mao political leaders have exhibited this inclination.

It must be emphasized that problems with the American political system are not necessarily the "fault" of democracy; rather, liberal democratic procedures at the national level make possible the kinds of shortcomings that the American system currently exhibits. Political leaders in liberal democratic systems need not make the same choices as have those in contemporary America, just as political leaders in authoritarian systems need not make the same choices as have those in contemporary China. The point is that different systems open different kinds of possibilities and limit others.

Indeed, it remains to be seen how well China's Party-state officials will respond to present economic challenges. Perhaps most importantly, China's export-oriented economic growth has begun to run its course, and a shift toward domestic consumption-based growth is needed. Party-state elites are well aware of this imperative, and have started to undertake policies (such as allowing greater consumer credit) that will encourage this transition. However, it is a gargantuan task that will require a fundamental re-orientation of China's vast state-owned banking system, and may pose a threat to the massive state-owned enterprises that remain reliant on loans from state-owned banks. In addition, the economic standing of China's rank-and-file workers and farmers – who comprise the vast majority of China's population – will need to be much further raised before these groups can enjoy the financial ability to consume at a level that will engender high economic growth rates based on domestic consumption.

Providing goods and services

With regard to the third basic requirement of a stable government – ensuring the provision of key goods and services – the post-Mao political system has done a barely satisfactory, but improving, job. In recent years, Party-state leaders have stepped up their efforts to ensure popular access to health care, poverty alleviation, education, pensions, and a healthy natural environment. While in some areas, and for certain demographic groups, these efforts have been successful at improving goods and services provision, in other respects, and for other demographic groups, progress has been minimal.

With regard to housing, education, pensions, and healthcare, urban *hukou*-holders have been much better provided-for than have rural *hukou*-holders. Yet affordable, quality healthcare remains elusive for even urban *hukou*-holders. Party-state leaders have been moving in the right direction on this front, but the privatization of the health care system has spurred adaptive behaviors on the part of hospitals and health care professionals that have been harmful to the general public. Similarly, the privatization of China's higher education system has made it very difficult for the children of most families to afford to go to college. Meanwhile, China's natural environment is severely degraded, with horrific consequences for the health of all residents of China. Party-state leaders have made significant efforts to address this situation, and have made noticeable progress. However, the problem is so extreme that even the most knowledgeably crafted policies would not be able to bring China's natural environment to an acceptable level of health within the foreseeable future.

The authoritarian nature of the central-Party state in some respects makes it possible for China's top political leaders to take decisive action in the areas where goods and services provision is most lacking, namely, health care and the environment. With the proper will, and through pragmatic consultation with experts in these fields, effective policies can be crafted. Based on China's historical experience with goods and services provision thus far, such policies are likely to feature more state direction, and less privatization. In addition, progress in terms of goods and services provision will require stronger efforts on the part of the central leaders to ensure that local leaders will be evaluated on this criterion as much as on local economic growth. Finally, given that goods and services provision tends to be better in localities where free and fair local elections have occurred, top Party-state elites should focus on ensuring that all local elections occur in this manner.

NEW DEVELOPMENTS UNDER XI JINPING

How likely is the Chinese Party-state to continue with the policies that have worked well, to end those that have not, and to devise new policies to resolve existing shortcomings? Two new developments under Xi Jinping, who assumed formal leadership of the Party-state in late 2012 and is expected to remain in this position until 2022, are cause for a moderate degree of optimism, but also significant pessimism. Xi's first major campaign has focused on eradicating corruption. As part of this campaign, Xi has banned lavish expenditures by political cadres. In 2013, Xi announced the initiation of a "year-long effort to rid the Party of 'formalism, bureaucracy, hedonism and extravagance.'" Along with prohibiting expensive meals and purchases by Party and government cadres, central elites declared a five-year ban on the construction of new government office buildings, as well as entertaining and catering facilities affiliated with government offices. In addition, officials have been told to cease excessive spending on "galas, especially those organised with public funds, that are held just to show off grand scenery, or staging extravagant production elements," and to refrain from "competing for celebrities, lavishness and ostentation." In the short term, this campaign has been effective; indeed, expensive restaurants and high-priced goods have seen a noticeable drop in demand. However, the long-term effectiveness of these efforts is uncertain.

Another part of Xi's anti-corruption campaign has involved the investigation and punishment of corrupt officials. In a speech addressing political cadres, Xi asserted that "the style in which you work is no small matter, and if we don't redress unhealthy tendencies and allow them to develop, it will be like putting up a wall between our Party and the people, and we will lose our roots, our lifeblood and our strength." Further, Xi vowed that this effort will focus not only on "flies" (local officials) but also on "tigers" (higher-level officials). Numerous high- and low-profile cases have since been reported. Perhaps most notably, in August 2013 the enormous state-owned enterprise PetroChina became the subject of corruption investigations. Whether or not Xi's anti-corruption campaign succeeds in the longer-term remains to be seen. If these efforts ultimately focus only on officials who have fallen out of political favor, they will not have a significant impact on corruption.

Even if Xi's anti-corruption campaign does not substantially diminish corruption within the Chinese Party-state, it is benign at worst, and at best may help the political system to more successfully fulfill the basic requirements of a stable governing regime. Xi's second major campaign, in contrast, has worrisome potential to undermine the regime's performance. This second campaign has been directed toward the purification not of corruption, but of public thoughts and expression. In 2013, Xi ordered academics not to speak about "seven sensitive issues: universal values, freedom of the press, civil society, civil rights, past Party mistakes, crony capitalism and judicial independence." In apparent accordance with this directive, a planned article on "constitutionalism" was pulled from a well-known liberal magazine published out of the southeastern Chinese city of Guangzhou, the *Southern Weekly*. The original content, which argued that in order for China to become "free and strong," the political system must feature a "division of powers," was stripped of these references. In August 2013, the Party's General Office issued "Document 9," warning of the threat of "false ideological trends, positions and activities." These include: "promoting Western constitutional democracy," "promoting 'universal values,'" "promoting civil society," and "promoting the West's idea of journalism, challenging China's principle that the media and publishing system should be subject to Party discipline." Simultaneously, Xi "issu[ed] a call to arms about the country's unruly Internet culture, ordering the Communist Party's propaganda machine to build 'a strong army' to 'seize the ground of new media.'"[2] More concretely, media outlets were informed that all journalists would be reviewed, and would need to take a test to ascertain their political reliability before they would be re-accredited. Shortly thereafter, 250,000 journalists were ordered to attend a three-month training program that inculcates the Party's view of "socialist" journalism, and emphasizes the need to reject Western ideas about democracy and human rights. In addition, new limits were placed on the number of foreign shows that may be aired on television; a station may broadcast only one per year, and it cannot air during prime-time evening viewing hours. Further, stations may air musical talent shows only once every three months. Conversely, stations must devote at least 30 percent of their air time to "public-interest" programing, such as documentaries, educational and "morality-building" shows.[3]

It is not clear what has motivated Xi to pursue these efforts to restrict public expression. Generally speaking, popular support for the regime remains very strong, as evidenced in the survey results discussed in Chapter 1. However, there are indications that these attitudes are somewhat tenuous, and may be slipping. Indeed, in March 2013, a few months before the issuance of "Document 9," a website run by the CCP's official newspaper, the *People's Daily*, included an online survey about a new catchphrase put forth by Xi Jinping, the "Chinese Dream." The results were "quickly deleted after around 80 percent of more than 3,000 respondents replied 'no' to questions such as whether they supported one-Party rule and believed in socialism."[4] That the respondents did not express a belief in socialism is unsurprising, and is not cause for Party-state leaders' concern; the regime abandoned its ideological dogmatism decades ago. But the respondents' lack of support for one-Party rule undoubtedly worried top political authorities. At the same time, this was not a representative survey using sound statistical methods. However, even highly regarded surveys conducted by reputable international survey organizations have found a degree of slippage in public support for China's political system. As noted in Chapter 1, in the 2012 World Values Survey (WVS), nearly 85 percent of Chinese respondents expressed "quite a lot" or "a great deal" of confidence in the national government. In addition, approximately 78 percent indicated "a great deal" or "quite a lot" of confidence in the National People's Congress. Although these percentages are quite high, in the 2001 WVS, they were even higher: roughly 98 percent reported "quite a lot" or "a great deal" of confidence in the national government, and approximately 95 percent expressed "a great deal" or "quite a lot" of confidence in the National People's Congress.

Even so, it is hard to imagine how Xi's efforts to control public expression might improve the political system's standing in the eyes of the populace. To the contrary, a key contributor to the Party-state's ability to satisfactorily respond to public grievances in the late post-Mao period has been the articulation of popular complaints via the Internet, media outlets, and other informal forms of public expression. If the public is prevented from airing its complaints, the Party will have no way of knowing about those complaints, much less addressing them. In times of still very strong – but somewhat declining – public support, it seems all the more important for the regime to foster the essential mechanisms through which the political system has been able to respond to public grievances thus far. And precisely because overall regime support remains high, Party-state leaders should not fear what the public has to say.

DEMOCRACY, AUTHORITARIANISM, AND STABLE GOVERNANCE

This leads us back to some of the initial questions posed in this volume: what, exactly, do we mean by democracy, and how important is democracy for stable governance? As discussed in Chapter 1, one's answer to the first question shapes one's answer to the second. The prevailing contemporary definition of democracy in the West focuses on the existence of elections that are competitive and inclusive (in terms of voting rights), and the protection of civil liberties – the hallmarks of liberal democracy. But a more basic definition harks back to the Greek roots of the word "democracy," and has a much broader emphasis: "rule by the people." Drawing on the latter conceptualization, democracy also may be viewed as a system where the government does what the people want. Many in the West believe that it is only through liberal democratic procedures and protections that a government can attain this more general democratic ideal. But the case of China in the post-Mao period indicates that this may not necessarily be the case.

In China, one major reason why the post-Mao political system has been stable is that it has become increasingly responsive to the public. Without a doubt, the institution of electoral democracy at the local level in China has been a key contributor to the system's overall responsiveness. At the same time, the existence of local elections has made the Chinese political system much more "democratic" in both the narrow procedural sense of the word and in its broader meaning. But the responsiveness of the post-Mao political system also has come from non-electoral mechanisms, including the letters and visits system, Internet postings, and public protests. The latter two in this list can be considered "civil liberties," and to the extent that they have been allowed, they have made China's post-Mao political system more "democratic" even in the more narrow sense of the word. The letters and visits system is more difficult to categorize, but to the degree that it enables citizens to convey their grievances and demands to the government, and the government then responds, this system can be considered "democratic" in the word's more general meaning. Overall, the post-Mao Party-state has become democratic in a number of respects (particularly at the local level), and in a number of ways (procedural and general). And, these democratic features have been essential in enabling China's political system to fulfill the basic requirements of government, and remain stable.

Yet democratic changes are not the only cause of the post-Mao Party-state's ability to satisfactorily govern. The other major contributor is the pragmatism and competence of China's post-Mao leaders, particularly at high levels of the political system. And, this characteristic of the Chinese government has not been the result of the institution of democratic elements. To the contrary, the authoritarian nature of the post-Mao Party-state at the highest levels has opened the possibility for this to occur. That this possibility came to fruition was in no way inevitable; as discussed earlier, authoritarian governments are capable of horrific acts. The change in China's leadership in the

post-Mao era has been entirely the result of the will and orientation of those in positions of power – they have been uniform in their belief that in order to maintain CCP dominance of the political system (a goal that they all share), the system needs to deliver. And, they have not been constrained by ideological imperatives in their quest to do so. Rather, they have been open to local experimentation and continual adjustment, and they have sought advice from the world's experts in many areas, including the economy and the environment. They also have solicited input from lower-level political officials in the crafting of Party policy. Simultaneously, they have changed recruitment and promotion criteria and processes so as to bring into leadership positions cadres with demonstrated merit, and who are more representative of the populace.

Of course, at the same time, the authoritarian nature of the apex of China's political system also opens the possibility for serious problems. As discussed earlier, in an authoritarian system, if leaders are incompetent and/or driven by ideology, as was the case during the Maoist period, the results can be disastrous. In other words, the main shortcoming of authoritarianism is that it is difficult (short of revolution) to oust inept and/or malevolent leaders. And to the extent that China's post-Mao political system does not recruit and reward leaders based only on merit, but also based on political connections (or even outright bribery), the performance of the system as a whole is weakened. The main selling-point of liberal democratic systems is that they are much better at expelling destructive leaders.

But, as long as the top levels of China's Party-state are not occupied by malicious leaders, there is nothing to indicate that the implementation of liberal democratic elections at higher levels of the political system would make China's top leaders more pragmatic or more competent. To the contrary, doing so would mean that political elites would be chosen based on popularity. And although this can be a good thing when officials are bad, it also opens the possibility for the emergence of other kinds of problems that may inhibit effective governance. The most common are policy inconsistency (which occurs when power alternates between or among political parties with significantly different ideologies) and a short-term policy focus (as a result of the continual need to worry about the next election). In the American system, other issues also are apparent, the most serious of which is politicians' reliance on monetary support from wealthy donors. Though these problems are not the necessary result of liberal democratic procedures at the national level, they are made possible by these procedures, and they generally are not possible in authoritarian regimes.

CONCLUSION

In sum, China's post-Mao political system satisfactorily has fulfilled the basic requirements of a stable governing regime. As a result, it has enjoyed a remarkably high level of public support. At the same time, serious shortcomings persist – particularly in some areas of goods and services provision. Further, the regime's performance in terms of responding to public grievances is being threatened by the repressive measures being undertaken by the Xi administration. And, the system's management of the economy faces important challenges, most notably, shifting to domestic consumer-led growth. Moreover, according to some surveys, the Party-state's legitimacy is slipping.

Addressing these issues does not require fundamental political transformation. Within the structures and processes that comprise the existing political system, improvement in governance can occur without the institution of multi-party elections at the national level. Because the Party-state remains authoritarian at its highest levels, if China's top leaders want the political system to remain stable, they will need to remain competent, pragmatic, and open to public input – even when what the public says is not what they want to hear.

Notes

1 Sources of Stable Governance in China

1 For more on the fieldwork and sampling methods utilized by the WVS, see http://www.worldvaluessurvey.org/WVSContents.jsp.

2 World Values Survey 2012 (http://www.worldvaluessurvey.org/).

3 For more on the fieldwork and sampling methods utilized by the EAB, see http://www.asianbarometer.org/newenglish/surveys/SurveyMethods.htm

4 East Asian Barometer 2008 (http://www.jdsurvey.net/eab/AnalizeQuestion .jsp).

5 "World Public Opinion on Governance and Democracy," World Public Opinion.org and the Program on International Policy Attitudes, University of Maryland, May 13, 2008 [available online at: http://www.worldpublic opinion.org/pipa/pdf/may08/WPO_Governance_May08_packet.pdf.

6 East Asian Barometer 2008; World Values Survey 2012.

7 See Jie Chen, *Popular Political Support in Urban China* (Stanford, CA: Stanford University Press, 2004), pp. 35–6; Tianjian Shi, "Cultural Values and Political Trust: A Comparison of the People's Republic of China and Taiwan," *Comparative Politics* 33(4) (July 2001), pp. 405–7; and Wenfang Tang, *Populist Authoritarianism: Explaining Regime Sustainability in China* (New York: Oxford University Press, 2015).

8 See Xueyi Chen and Tianjian Shi, "Media Effects on Political Confidence and Trust in the People's Republic of China in the Post-Tiananmen Period," *East Asia* 19(3) (Fall 2001), pp. 84–118.

9 For an overview of scholarship on this topic, see Nina Baculinao, "Fenqing: A Study of China's 'Angry Youth' in the Era of the Internet," *Columbia East Asia Review* 5 (Spring 2012), pp. 75–97.

10 Among many examples, see Li Lianjiang, "Political Trust and Petitioning in the Chinese Countryside," *Comparative Politics* 40(2), pp. 209–26; Ching Kwan Lee, *Against the Law: Labor Protests in China's Rustbelt and Sunbelt* (Berkeley: University of California Press, 2007); Bruce Dickson and Jie Chen,

Allies of the State: Democratic Support and Regime Support among China's Private Entrepreneurs (Cambridge, MA: Harvard University Press, 2010); Chen Xi, *Social Protests and Contentious Authoritarianism in China* (NY: Cambridge University Press, 2012); Timothy Hildebrandt, *Social Organizations and the Authoritarian State in China* (NY: Cambridge University Press, 2013); and Wenfang Tang, *Populist Authoritarianism.*

11 Jie Chen and Chunlong Lu, "Social Capital in Urban China: Attitudinal and Behavioral Effects on Grassroots Self-government," *Social Science Quarterly* 88(2) (June 2007), pp. 423–4.

12 David Collier and Steven Levitsky, "Democracy with Adjectives: Conceptual Innovation in Comparative Research," *World Politics* 49(3) (1997), p. 434.

2 Party and State, or Party-State?

1 See Yongnian Zheng, *The Chinese Communist Party as Organizational Emperor* (NY: Routledge, 2010), pp. 8–16. It should be noted that the CCP was not the first political party in China to create a Chinese state; the KMT (Kuomintang) during the Republican (or Nationalist) era (1911–49) also created a state through which it governed.

2 Cheng Li, "Intra-Party Democracy in China: Should We Take It Seriously?" *China Leadership Monitor* 30 (Nov. 2009), p. 9.

3 Kenneth Lieberthal, *Governing China* (NY: W.W. Norton, 1995), p. 160.

4 Ibid.

5 Anthony Saich, "Political Representation," in Chris Ogden, ed., *Handbook of China's Governance and Domestic Politics* (NY: Routledge, 2013), p. 111.

6 Young Nam Cho, *Local People's Congresses in China* (Cambridge: Cambridge University Press, 2009), pp. 97–8.

7 The eight parties are the China Revolutionary Committee of the Kuomintang, the China Democratic League, the China Democratic National Construction Association, the China Association for the Promotion of Democracy, the Chinese Peasants' and Workers' Democratic Party, the China Zhi Gong Dang, the Jiusan Society, and the Taiwan Democratic Self-government League (http://www.china.org.cn/english/chuangye/55437.htm).

8 Xinhua, "CPPCC's new leader rejects Western political systems, champions consultative democracy," March 12, 2013 (http://news.xinhuanet.com/english/china/2013-03/12/c_132227126.htm).

9 David Shambaugh, *China's Communist Party: Atrophy and Adaptation* (Berkeley: University of California Press, 2009), pp. 137–138.

10 Anne-Marie Brady, http://www.uscc.gov/sites/default/files/4.30.09Brady .pdf, pp. 2–3.

11 Many cities are large enough that they have the same status as a county.

12 Xu Feng, "New Modes of Urban Governance: Building Community Shequ in Post-danwei China," in André Laliberte and Marc Lanteigne, eds., *The Chinese Party-State in the 21ˢᵗ Century* (NY: Routledge, 2008), pp. 22–38.

13 Lieberthal, *Governing China*, pp. 194–207.

14 Ibid., p. 194.

15 Party groups are different from Party committees, which also exist in all state entities. Party committees are elected by the people within a given state entity who are Party members, and only have authority over those Party members [Susan Shirk, *How China Opened its Door* (Washington, DC: Brookings Institution, 1994), p. 14].

3 Who Serves in the Party-State?

1 Yanjie Bian, Xiaoling Shu, and John R. Logan, "Communist Party Membership and Regime Dynamics in China," *Social Forces* 79:3 (March 2001), pp. 813–15.

2 "Party Members Increase to More Than 85 m," *Shanghai Daily*, July 1, 2013, p. A8.

3 Bruce Dickson, "Dilemmas of Party Adaptation: the CCP's Strategies for Survival," in Peter Gries and Stanley Rosen, eds., *Chinese Politics: State, Society, and the Market* (NY: Routledge, 2010), pp. 22–40.

4 Bruce Dickson, *Red Capitalists in China* (NY: Cambridge University Press, 2003), p. 38.

5 Anthony Saich, "Political Representation," in Chris Ogden, ed., *Handbook of China's Governance and Domestic Politics* (NY: Routledge, 2013), p. 110 [citing Bruce Dickson 2008, p. 70; personal communication with Bruce Dickson; and J. Lee 2011].

6 "Party Members Increase to More Than 85 m."

7 Tian Ying, "Xinhua Insight: CPC Requires 'Prudent' Recruitment of New Members," *Xinhua*, June 11, 2014.

8 Victor Shih, Wei Shan, and Mingxing Liu, "The Central Committee Past and Present: A Method of Quantifying Elite Biographies," in Mary Gallagher, Melanie Manion, and Alan Carlson, eds., *Chinese Politics: New Methods, Sources and Field Strategies* (Cambridge: Cambridge University Press, 2010), pp. 51–68.

9 Alice Miller, "The 18th Central Committee Politburo: A Quixotic, Foolhardy, Rashly Speculative, But Nonetheless Ruthlessly Reasoned Projection," *China Leadership Monitor* 33 (Spring 2010), pp. 2–3.

10 Lianjiang Li, "The Two-Ballot System in Shanxi Province: Subjecting Village Party Secretaries to a Popular Vote," *The China Journal* 42 (Jul., 1999), pp. 103–18; Xiaojun Yan, "'To Get Rich Is Not Only Glorious': Economic Reform and the New Entrepreneurial Party Secretaries," *The China Quarterly* 210 (June 2012), pp. 335–54.

11 Xu Feng, "New Modes of Urban Governance: Building Community/*shequ* in Post-*danwei* China," in André Laliberte and Marc Lanteigne, eds., *The Chinese Party-State in the 21st Century: Adaptation and the Reinvention of Legitimacy* (NY: Routledge, 2008), pp. 22–38.

12 Cheng Li, "Preparing for the 18th Party Congress: Procedures and Mechanisms," *China Leadership Monitor* 36 (Jan. 2012), pp. 1–4.

13 Ibid.

14 Ibid., p. 5.

15 Zhao Ziyang, *Prisoner of the State: The Secret Journal of Premier Zhao Ziyang* (NY: Simon and Schuster, 2010).

16 David Shambaugh, *China's Communist Party: Atrophy and Adaptation* (Berkeley, CA: University of California Press, 2008), p. 142.

17 "Quotable," *Shanghai Daily*, July 1, 2013, p. 2.

18 Gabriel Wildau, "Small Chinese Cities Steer away from GDP as Performance Metric," *Financial Times*, August 13, 2014.

19 See Kerry Brown, *The New Emperors: Power and Princelings in China* (London: I.B. Tauris, 2014).

20 Victor Shih, Wei Shan, and Mingxing Liu, "Getting Ahead in the Communist Party: Explaining the Advancement of Central Committee Members in China," *American Political Science Review* 106:1 (Feb. 2012), pp. 166–87.

21 Organic Law of the Villagers Committees of the People's Republic of China, http://www.china.org.cn/english/government/207279.htm. Recall proceedings may be initiated by a petition signed by one-fifth of all villagers. The matter then goes to a vote, and a simple majority prevails. The law also states that VCs should include "an appropriate number of women" (Article 9).

22 Josephine Ma, "Create a Uniform System for Village Polls, Says Jimmy Carter," *South China Morning Post*, Sept. 9, 2003, p. 5.

23 Kevin O'Brien and Rongbin Han, "Path to Democracy? Assessing Village Elections in China," *Journal of Contemporary China* 18(60) (June 2009), pp. 359–360; Kevin O'Brien and Lianjiang Li, *Rightful Resistance*, p. 100.

24 Jie Chen and Chunlong Lu, "Social Capital in Urban China: Attitudinal and Behavioral Effects on Grassroots Self-Government," *Social Science Quarterly* 88(2) (June 2007), pp. 423–4.
25 Richard Levy, "Village Elections, Transparency, and Anticorruption: Henan and Guangdong Provinces," in Elizabeth Perry and Merle Goldman, eds., *Grassroots Political Reform in Contemporary China* (Cambridge: Harvard University Press, 2007), pp. 20–47.
26 Evan Osnos, *Age of Ambition: Chasing Fortune, Truth, and Faith in the New China* (NY: Farrar, Straus and Giroux, 2014), p. 243.
27 "Democracy in Action: China's National People's Congress," *Economist*, Feb. 25, 2010; Ting Shi, "Book about First Independent Election Candidate is Banned," *South China Morning Post*, Dec. 10, 2006; Priscilla Jiao, "Independent Poll Candidates Harassed," *South China Morning Post*, June 23, 2011; Priscilla Jiao, "Independent Candidates Step into the Fray," *South China Morning Post*, May 28, 2011; Ying Sun, "Independent Candidates in Mainland China," *Asian Survey* 53(2) (March/April 2013), pp. 245–68.
28 Osnos, *Age of Ambition*, p. 252.
29 Nailene Chou Wiest, "Reform is Urged for CPPCC Selection," *South China Morning Post*, June 18, 2003; Huang Jingjing, "Political All-Stars," *Global Times*, Feb. 6, 2013.
30 Cheng Li, "Preparing for the 18th Party Congress," pp. 9–11; Alice Miller, "The Road to the 18th Party Congress," *China Leadership Monitor* 36 (Jan. 2012), pp. 1–7.
31 Young Nam Cho, *Local People's Congresses in China* (Cambridge: Cambridge University Press, 2009).
32 Melanie Manion, "Authoritarian Parochialism: Local Congressional Representation in China," *The China Quarterly* 218 (June 2014), p. 311.

4 Maintaining Public Relations

1 As of 2006, China had roughly one lawyer for every 10,800 people, compared with a ratio of one to 375 in England. Kelly Proctor and Tina Qiu, "Lack of Professionals Hampers China," *International Herald Tribune*, Aug. 16, 2006.
2 Lianjiang Li, "Political Trust and Petitioning in the Chinese Countryside," *Comparative Politics* 40(2) (Jan. 2008), pp. 209–26.
3 Michelle FlorCruz, "China's Illegal 'Black Jails': How A Government Incentive Created More Corruption," *International Business Times*, May 13, 2013.
4 See Xi Chen, *Social Protest and Contentious Authoritarianism in China* (Cambridge: Cambridge University Press, 2012).

5 They are able to do so through the use of proxy servers. Surveys show that roughly 25 percent of Chinese Internet users regularly use such servers, and that in times of crisis or the emergence of major events that might be censored by Chinese authorities, proxy server use jumps by 50 percent. See Patricia Thornton, "Censorship and Surveillance in Chinese Cyberspace: Beyond the Great Firewall," in Peter Gries and Stanley Rosen, eds., *Chinese Politics: State, Society, and the Market* (NY: Routledge, 2010), p. 182.

6 Thornton, "Censorship and Surveillance," p. 182.

7 See http://chinadigitaltimes.net/2013/06/grass-mud-horse-list/.

8 For an amusing account of receiving such e-mails while in China, see Osnos, *Age of Ambition*.

9 See "Digitized Parody, the Politics of Egao in Contemporary China," *China Information* 24(1) (2010), pp. 3–26.

10 Ying Yiyuan, "Private Sector Contributes over 60% to GDP," CCTV, Feb. 6, 2013. http://english.cntv.cn/program/bizasia/20130206/105751.shtml.

11 Bruce Dickson, *Red Capitalists in China: The Party, Private Entrepreneurs, and Prospects for Political Change* (Cambridge: Cambridge University Press, 2003).

12 Bjorn Alpermann, "Wrapped up in Cotton Wool: Political Integration of Private Entrepreneurs in Rural China," *The China Journal* 56 (July 2006), p. 46; Dickson, *Red Capitalists*, p. 57.

13 Dickson, *Red Capitalists*, p. 125.

14 "Siying jingji sanfen tianxia," cited in Hong, "Mapping the Evolution of New Private Entrepreneurs in China," *Journal of Chinese Political Science* 9(1) (March 2004), p. 34.

15 Because regime leaders forbade hospitals to keep track of the number of deaths and injuries inflicted on June 3–4, 1989, we have only estimates of the total count. Regardless, virtually all of those who were injured and killed were regular citizens who spontaneously had gone into the streets when they heard that the military had been sent to clear out the student protestors in Tian'anmen Square. Most of the killing occurred while the military troops were en route to the Square; when the military arrived at the Square, they peacefully escorted the remaining students out of the area. None are reported to have been harmed, although many subsequently were arrested. For a detailed account of the protests of 1989, see Teresa Wright, *The Perils of Protest: State Repression and Student Activism in China and Taiwan* (Honolulu: University of Hawaii Press, 2001).

16 Osnos, *Age of Ambition*, p. 252.

17 See Xiaobing Wang, Chengfang Liu, Linxiu Zhang, Yaojiang Shi, and Scott Rozelle, "College is a Rich, Han, Urban, Male Club: Research Notes from a

Census Survey of Four Tier One Colleges in China," *The China Quarterly* 214 (June 2013), pp. 456, 470.

18 See Human Rights Watch, "'Walking on Thin Ice;' Control, Intimidation and Harassment of Lawyers in China" (April 2008), http://www.hrw.org/reports/2008/china0408/.

19 For a detailed account of the Democracy Wall movement, see Andrew Nathan, *Chinese Democracy* (Berkeley, CA: University of California Press, 1986).

20 Teresa Wright, "The China Democracy Party and the Politics of Protest in the 1980's–1990's," *The China Quarterly* 172 (December 2002), pp. 906–26.

21 Timothy Weston, "The Iron Man Weeps: Joblessness and Political Legitimacy in the Chinese Rust Belt," in Peter Gries and Stanley Rosen, eds., *State and Society in 21st-century China: Crisis, Contention, and Legitimation* (NY: Routledge, 2012), p. 69.

22 Thomas Bernstein and Xiaobo Lu, "Taxation without Representation: Peasants, the Central and the Local States in Reform China," *The China Quarterly* 163 (September 2000), pp. 743–7.

23 Xiaolin Guo, "Land Expropriation and Rural Conflicts in China," *The China Quarterly* 166 (2001), pp. 424–7; Jean Oi and Shukai Zhao, "Fiscal Crisis in China's Townships: Causes and Consequences," in Elizabeth Perry and Merle Goldman, *Grassroots Political Reform in China* (Cambridge: Harvard University Press, 2007), p. 93.

24 The subsidy for home appliances ended in January 2013.

25 Jun Jing, "Environmental Protests in Rural China," in Elizabeth Perry and Mark Selden, eds., *Chinese Society: Change, Conflict, and Resistance* (NY: Routledge, 2010), p. 197.

5 Managing the Economy

1 The only exception was during the more chaotic early years of the Cultural Revolution (1966–1969), when urban industrial production was interrupted.

2 Martin King Whyte, "China's Post-Socialist Inequality," *Current History* (Sept. 2012), p. 234.

3 Rachel Murphy, "Introduction," in Cao Jinqing, *Huanghe biande Zhongguo* (NY: Routledge, 2005), p. 7.

4 Zhiyuan Cui, "Ruhe renshi jinri Zhongguo:'xiaokang shehui' jiedu" [How to Comprehend Today's China: An Interpretation of the 'Comparatively Well Off' Society] *Dushu* [*Reading*] 3 (March 2004), pp. 3–9.

5 Zhongguo xiangzhen qiye nianjian [Yearbook of Township and Village Enterprises] (Beijing: Nongye chubanshe, 1991), pp. 137–9.

6 "Opening to the Outside World: Special Economic Zones and Open Coastal Cities," China Internet Information Center (under the auspices of the State Council Information Office), http://www.china.org.cn/e-china/openingup/sez.htm

7 John James Kennedy, "Finance and Rural Governance: Centralization and Local Challenges," The Journal of Peasant Studies 40(6) (January 2014), pp. 1012–1014.

8 National Bureau of Statistics of China 2007a and 2007b, cited in Joachim von Braun, "The world food situation: New driving forces and required actions," Food, Agriculture and Natural Resources Policy Analysis Network, Dec. 4, 2007. http://www.fanrpan.org/documents/d00467/

9 Yiguo Zhang and Yuanheng Yang, "The Evaluation of People's Living Level of China," Shandong Province Statistical Bureau of China, http://isi.cbs.nl/iamamember/CD2/pdf/542.PDF; Chen Yang, "Rural Household Appliance Subsidy Expires," People's Daily, Jan. 31, 2013.

10 Chunping Han and Martin King Whyte, "The Social Contours of Distributive Injustice Feelings in Contemporary China," in Deborah Davis and Feng Wang, eds., Creating Wealth and Poverty in Contemporary China (Stanford: Stanford University Press, 2008), pp. 193–212.

11 Giles Guiheux, "The Political 'Participation' of Entrepreneurs: Challenge or Opportunity for the Chinese Communist Party?" Social Research 73 (Spring 2006), pp. 219–44.

12 "CPC Amends Constitution to Foster Private Sector," Xinhua, Oct. 21, 2007.

13 Zhao Xiao and Shi Guicun, "Policy Support for Private Sector," China Daily, Oct. 31, 2012.

14 Ching Kwan Lee, Against the Law: Labor Protests in China's Rustbelt and Sunbelt (Berkeley: University of California Press, 2007), p. 39.

15 Ibid., pp. 161 & 163.

16 Worker Rights Consortium, "Global Wage Trends for Apparel Workers, 2001–2011," Center for American Progress, July 11, 2013. http://www.americanprogress.org/issues/labor/report/2013/07/11/69255/global-wage-trends-for-apparel-workers-2001-2011/

17 Lee, Against the Law, p. 38.

18 Ibid.

19 Mark Frazier, "China's Pension Reform and Its Discontents," The China Journal 51 (Jan. 2004), p. 101 (fn. 11).

20 Yongshun Cai, State and Laid-off Workers in Reform China: The Silence and Collective Action of the Retrenched (NY: Routledge, 2006), pp. 28, 30.

21 Lee, *Against the Law*, pp. 130–131; Solinger, "The New Crowd of the Dispossessed," in Peter Gries and Stanley Rosen, eds., *State and Society in 21st Century China* (NY: Routledge, 2004), pp. 50–66.

22 Christopher McNally, "Sino-Capitalism: China's Reemergence and the International Political Economy," *World Politics* 64(4) (Oct. 2012), pp. 751–5.

23 Chung-min Tsai, "Guiding Business in China: Agencies and Rules in a Changing Regulatory Regime," paper presented at a conference on China Dreams: China's New Leadership and Future Impacts, National Chengchi University, Taipei, Taiwan, Dec. 2013.

24 Barry Naughton, "The Transformation of the State Sector: SASAC, the Market Economy, and the New National Champions," in Barry Naughton and Kellee Tsai, eds., *State Capitalism, Institutional Adaptation and the Chinese Miracle* (NY: Cambridge University Press, forthcoming), chapter 3, p. 8. [Cited in Kellee Tsai, "The China Dream: Tigers, Flies, and Other Challenges to Economic Reform," paper presented at a conference on China Dreams: China's New Leadership and Future Impacts, National Chengchi University, Taipei, Taiwan, Dec. 2013, p. 11].

25 "Banks in China: Too Big to Hail," *Economist*, Aug. 31, 2013.

26 "China's Big Banks: Giant Reality-Check," *Economist*, Aug. 31, 2013.

27 World Bank data on Gross Domestic Savings http://data.worldbank.org/indicator/NY.GDS.TOTL.ZS?page=2

28 Robert O. Weagley, "One Big Difference between Chinese and American Households: Debt," *Forbes*, June 24, 2010.

29 Ibid.

30 Dexter Roberts, "A Peek at China's Local Debt Mess," *Bloomberg Businessweek*, Jan. 9, 2014. http://www.businessweek.com/articles/2014-01-09/chinas-local-government-debt-is-almost-3-trillion

31 "China's Big Banks: Giant Reality-Check," *Economist*, Aug. 31, 2013.

32 Ibid.; China Merchants bank http://english.cmbchina.com/CmbIR/ProductInfo.aspx?id=intro ; China Minsheng bank http://hk.jobsdb.com/HK/en/Search/FindJobs?JSRV=1&Key=%22China+Minsheng+Banking+Corporation+Limited%22&KeyOpt=COMPLEX&SearchFields=Companies&JSSRC=SRLSC

33 Kellee Tsai, "The China Dream," p. 7.

34 "China Minsheng, Alibaba to cooperate in banking services," *Reuters*, Sept. 16, 2013 http://www.reuters.com/article/2013/09/16/minsheng-alibaba-idUSH9N0GV01F20130916?type=companyNews

35 United Nations, *Global Investment Trends Monitor* 11 (Jan. 28, 2014).

36 Wayne M. Morrison, "China's Economic Rise: History, Trends, Challenges, and Implications for the United States," *Congressional Research Service Report*, August 21, 2014.

37 IMF, 2012 *Article IV Report, People's Republic of China*, July 2012, p. 8. Cited in Morrison, "China's Economic Rise," p. 10.

38 Charles Wolf, "A Smarter Approach to the Yuan," *Policy Review* 166 (April 2011).

39 Kellee Tsai, "The China Dream," p. 8.

40 This term was coined by Christopher McNally [McNally, "Sino-Capitalism"].

41 Economist Intelligence Unit Viewswire, "How Much Worse Will It Get?" Feb. 3, 2009.

42 These predictions were made by the *Economist's* Economist Intelligence Unit and the international consulting firm, AT Kearney. The World Bank predicted a 2009 Chinese GDP growth rate of 7.5 percent. See Economist Intelligence Unit Viewswire, "How Much Worse Will It Get?" and Bao Wanxian and Xin Zhiming, "China's Growth Rate May Fall to 6%: AT Kearney," *China Daily*, Nov. 27, 2008.

43 Economist Intelligence Unit Viewswire, "How Much Worse Will It Get?"

6 Providing Goods and Services

1 See Anthony Saich, *Providing Public Goods in Transitional China* (NY: Palgrave, 2008), p. 5.

2 Ibid., pp. 23–9, 40, 73, 103–4. See also Xingyuan Gu and Shenglan Tang, "Reform of the Chinese Health Care Financing System," *Health Policy* 32 (1995), pp. 181–191.

3 Saich, *Providing Public Goods*, pp. 23, 42; Eric Li, "Debunking the Myths of Mao Zedong," *South China Morning Post*, Dec. 26, 2013.

4 In the US, Social Security payments typically amount to only 40 percent of a worker's prior salary. Internationally, the pension-to-prior-income ratio ranges from 40–60 percent. Ching Kwan Lee, *Against the State: Labor Protests in China's Rustbelt and Sunbelt* (Berkeley: University of California Press, 2007), p. 46; Tamara Trinh, "China's Pension System," *Deutsche Bank Research* Feb. 17, 2006, p. 11 http://www.dbresearch.com/PROD/DBR_INTERNET_EN-PROD/PROD0000000000196025.pdf; Andrew G. Biggs and Glenn R. Springstead, "Alternate Measures of Replacement Rates for Social Security Benefits and Retirement Income," *Social Security Bulletin* 68:2 (2008) http://www.ssa.gov/policy/docs/ssb/v68n2/v68n2p1.html

5 Andrew Walder, *Communist Neo-traditionalism: Work and Authority in Chinese Industry* (Berkeley: University of California Press, 1986), pp. 16, 42, 60, 62–6.

6 Ibid., p. 40.

7 Judith Shapiro, *Mao's War Against Nature: Politics and the Environment in Revolutionary China* (NY: Cambridge University Press, 2001).

8 Ibid.

9 Dorothy Solinger, "The State and the Poor in Northeast Asia and India: Three Models of the Wellsprings of Welfare and Lessons for China," Paper prepared for presentation at a conference on "State-Society Relations in the New Era: Lessons for and from China," Fudan Institute for Advanced Study in Social Sciences, Fudan University, Shanghai, China, June 29–30, 2013, pp. 2–4.

10 Ibid.

11 See Frances Fox Piven and Richard A. Cloward, *Poor People's Movements: Why They Succeed, How They Fail* (NY: Vintage Books, 1979).

12 Mark Frazier, *Socialist Insecurity: Pensions and the Politics of Uneven Development in China* (NY: Cornell University Press, 2010).

13 Mark Frazier, "No Country for Old Age," *New York Times*, Feb. 18, 2013.

14 Saich, *Providing Public Goods*, p. 131.

15 Robert C. Posen, "Reforming the Chinese Pension System," *Paulson Policy Memorandum*, Paulson Institute, University of Chicago, July 31, 2013; Frazier, *Socialist Insecurity*.

16 Saich, *Providing Public Goods*, pp. 154–5.

17 Posen, "Reforming the Chinese Pension System."

18 Ibid.

19 Frazier, *Socialist Insecurity*.

20 Ibid., Chapter 6.

21 *Nanfang Zhoumou*, May 29, 2003, cited in Yongshun Cai, "China's Moderate Middle Class: The Case of Homeowners' Resistance," *Asian Survey* 45(5) (Sept.–Oct. 2005), p. 779, note 10.

22 China Statistical Yearbook (2009), cited in Wendell Cox, "China's Sliver of a Housing Bubble," newgeography, Aug. 22, 2010. http://www.newgeography.com/content/001733-chinas-sliver-a-housing-bubble

23 China Labour Bulletin, "Migrant Workers and their Children," *China Labour Bulletin*, June 27, 2013. http://www.clb.org.hk/en/content/migrant-workers-and-their-children

24 Lee, *Against the Law*, p. 57.

25 *China Labour Bulletin* 11 (Feb. 1995), pp. 9, 11.

26 Hannah Beech, "How Corruption Blights China's Health Care System," *Time*, Aug. 2, 2013; Saich, *Providing Public Goods*, pp. 77, 83.

27 Saich, *Providing Public Goods*, pp. 81, 95.

28 Ibid., pp. 20, 81, 103.

29 Benjamin Shobert, "Is China's Healthcare Market Opening Too Little, Too Late?" *Forbes*, Sept. 17, 2013.

30 China Labour Bulletin, "Migrant Workers and their Children."

31 Beech, "How Corruption Blights."

32 For a recent analysis of the effects of unfunded central mandates for local social welfare provision, see Jessica Teets, "Let Many Civil Societies Bloom: The Rise of Consultative Authoritarianism in China," *China Quarterly* 213 (March 2013), pp. 19–38.

33 Stanley Rosen, "The State of Youth/Youth and the State in Early 21st-Century China: The Triumph of the Urban Rich?" in Peter Hays Gries and Stanley Rosen, eds., *State and Society in 21st Century China: Crisis, Contention and Legitimation* (NY: Routledge, 2004), p. 164.

34 "Education Finance: Pay to Play," *China Economic Quarterly* Q4 (2005), pp. 25–6.

35 Stanley Rosen, "The Victory of Materialism: Aspirations to Join China's Urban Moneyed Classes and the Commercialization of Education," *The China Journal* 51 (Jan. 2004), p. 35.

36 China Labour Bulletin, "Migrant Workers and their Children."

37 Huang Zhijian, "Qingnian xiaofei wu da qushi" (Five major trends in consumption patterns of youth), *Liaowang xinwen zhoukan* (*Outlook Weekly*) 35 (Aug. 27, 2001). For per capita income, see http://asiaecon.org/aei/index.php/inside_asia/country/china#econ_ind

38 Stanley Rosen, "The Victory of Materialism," p. 35.

39 China National Bureau of Statistics.

40 Saich, *Providing Public Goods*, p. 56.

41 Aaron Back, "Beijing Plans Infrastructure Binge," *Wall Street Journal*, Sept. 7, 2012. http://online.wsj.com/news/articles/SB10000872396390443686004577637002372028464

42 China National Bureau of Statistics.

43 Reuters, "China Plans Investment and Reform to Ease Urbanization Drive," *Reuters*, March 16, 2014. http://www.reuters.com/article/2014/03/16/us-china-urbanisation-idUSBREA2F0O420140316

44 Wuyuan Peng and Jiahua Pan, "Rural Electrification in China: History and Institution," *China & World Economy* 14(1) (2006): pp. 71–84.

45 Reuters, "China Grid Says Half of $100 bln High-Voltage Network Under Way," *Reuters*, Aug. 21, 2013.

46 Damien Ma and William Adams, "If You Think China's Air Is Bad," *New York Times*, Nov. 7, 2013; Wang Qian, "Safe Drinking Water a Top Priority for China," *China Daily*, March 21, 2014.

47 PM2.5 refers to particulate matter 2.5 micrometers or less in diameter.

48 Edward Wong, "On Scale of 0 to 500, Beijing's Air Quality Tops 'Crazy Bad' at 755," *New York Times*, Jan. 12, 2013; Elizabeth Economy, *The River Runs*

Black: The Environmental Challenge to China's Future (Ithaca: Cornell University Press, 2010).

49 Economy, *The River Runs Black*, p. 88; The World Bank and the State Environmental Protection Agency of the PRC, *Cost of Pollution in China: Economic Estimates of Physical Damages* (2007). http://siteresources.worldbank.org/INTEAPREGTOPENVIRONMENT/Resources/China_Cost_of_Pollution.pdf

50 Jun Jing, "Environmental Protests in Rural China," in Elizabeth Perry and Mark Selden, eds., *Chinese Society: Change, Conflict, and Resistance* (NY: Routledge, 2010).

51 David Shukman, "China on World's 'Biggest Push' for Wind Power," BBC, Jan. 7, 2014. http://www.bbc.com/news/science-environment-25623400

52 Ibid.

53 South China Morning Post, "China Sets World Record on Solar Power Installations," *South China Morning Post*, Feb. 9, 2014. http://www.scmp.com/lifestyle/technology/article/1424179/china-sets-world-record-solar-power-installations

54 Gilles Paris, "China Sweeps Aside Civilians in Rush for Hydropower," *Guardian*, Oct. 22, 2013. http://www.theguardian.com/world/2013/oct/22/china-hydroelectric-dam-three-gorges

55 Wencong Wu, "Beijing Gets Hard on Air Pollution," *China Daily*, Sept. 13, 2013.

56 Ibid; US Environmental Protection Agency http://www.epa.gov/otaq/standards/fuels/gas-sulfur.htm. Initially, the new standard in China will apply only to the three regions targeted for coal use reduction.

57 2015 will be the first year that China will be able to produce a sufficient amount of low-sulfur diesel fuel. Wencong Wu, "New Standard, Old Problems," *China Daily*, Sept. 13, 2013.

58 BBC, "Beijing to Restrict Private Car Use to Tackle Pollution," BBC, Oct. 17, 2013. http://www.bbc.com/news/world-asia-china-24566288

59 Paul A. Eisenstein, "China to Limit Car Sales in Fight against Air Pollution," *NBC News*, July 11, 2013. http://www.nbcnews.com/business/autos/china-limit-car-sales-fight-against-air-pollution-f6C10599665

60 "Hebei to Use Foreign Experts to Curb Air Pollution," *China Daily*, March 28, 2014.

61 Elizabeth Economy, "China's Incomparable Environmental Challenge," *The Diplomat*, Jan. 12, 2014. http://thediplomat.com/2014/01/chinas-incomparable-environmental-challenge/

62 Lei Zhao and Xin Zheng, "Tech Needed to Improve Air," *China Daily*, March 7, 2014.

63 Wu, "Beijing Gets Hard on Air Pollution."
64 Monica Martínez-Bravo, Gerard Padró i Miquel, Nancy Qian, and Yang Yao, "The Effects of Democratization on Public Goods and Redistribution: Evidence from China," April 15, 2012. http://www.irs.princeton.edu/sites/irs/files/event/uploads/Vdem_20120410_unbolded.pdf

7 Stable Authoritarianism?

1 Scholars specializing in the economic and political development of other later-industrializing countries (including post-WWII Japan, South Korea, and Taiwan) have raised similar points. See, for example, Frederic Deyo, *The Political Economy of the New Asian Industrialism* (Ithaca, NY: Cornell University Press, 1987).
2 "Chasing the Chinese Dream," *Economist*, May 2, 2013.
3 Jayadeva Ranade, "China: Document No. 9 and The New Propaganda Regime – Analysis," *Eurasia Review*, Nov. 15, 2013.
4 "Chasing the Chinese Dream."

Index _____

ABC *see* Agricultural Bank of China
Agricultural Bank of China
   (ABC) 132–3
authoritarian regime 7
  and economy 16, 85, 113, 114,
    142, 185–6
  effect on basic functions of
    government 12
  influence on infrastructure 171,
    177
  Party-state 17, 76, 109, 110, 111,
    112, 183, 188, 193–4, 195
  and political leadership 144, 147,
    183, 185
  stability of 2, 3, 180–95
  student criticisms of 89
  toleration of 3–4
  Western assumptions 3

Bank of China (BOC) 132, 133
banking system
  amount of bad debt held 134–5
  beneficial to SOEs 134
  consumer credit 133–4
  effect of one-child policy 134
  as government-owned 132
  joint-stock commercial banks 136
  largest organizations 132–3
  move from export-led to
    consumer-led 135–7

  profits through savings 133
  shadow-banking 135
Beijing Olympics 93
black jails 79
BOC *see* Bank of China
business associations 85–6

CAC *see* Central Advisory
  Commission
CC *see* Central Committee
CCB *see* China Construction Bank
CCDI *see* Central Commission for
  Discipline Inspection
CCP *see* Chinese Communist Party
CCTV *see* China Central Television
CDP *see* China Democracy Party
Central Advisory Commission
  (CAC) 51–2
Central Commission for Discipline
  Inspection (CCDI) 22,
  26
Central Committee (CC) 18, 21,
  22, 56, 127
  chooses new Politburo 56–7
  drafting group formed 69–71
  membership of 50–1
  move from provincial position
    to 60
  new rules for recruiting CCP
    members 48

organization of 23–4
power flows 181–2
Central Leading Small Groups
(CLSGs) 20, 36, 38, 39
Central Military Commission
(CMC) 18, 26, 27, 33,
52
Central Organization
Department 38, 55–6
Central Party School (CPS) 71–2,
88
Central Propaganda Department 34
Charter 08 82–3, 96
China Central Television
(CCTV) 110
China Construction Bank
(CCB) 132, 133
China Democracy Party
(CDP) 96–7
China Digital Times 81
Chinese Communist Party (CCP)
calls for greater consultation with/
input from CPPCC 33
changes in membership/ascension
within 41–9
control/authority over state 19
desire to strengthen CCP rule 42
formal structure/
composition 21–8
involvement in NPC 31–2
local branches 18
openness/responsiveness of 2
popularity/power of 2
private entrepreneurs as members
of 47, 49, 85–6, 88–9
remains political organization 61
support for economic
reform 60–1
support from rank-and-file
workers 99, 101, 111

transformation/stability 1
upward movement in 60
Chinese People's Political
Consultative Conference
(CPPCC) 18, 32–3, 67–8
citizen petitions 10
civil liberties 3, 10–11, 14
CLSGs see Central Leading Small
Groups
CMC see Central Military Commission
CMCs see community mediation
committees
college students/graduates
affluent background 94–5
dealing with grievances 184
demands made by 92–3
demonstrations 89, 90–4
expansion of 95
job prospects 94–5, 96
as key demographic group 89
marketization of system 94
party membership 44–5
quasi-dissident actions 82–3,
96–7
relationship with
Party-state 90–7
support for current
system 89–90, 93–5
Communist Youth League 43, 44
community mediation committees
(CMCs) 77–8
Company Law (1994) 47, 126
Construct a New Socialist
Countryside 155, 159
corruption 48, 72, 123, 159, 165,
176, 188–90
court system 77
CPPCC see Chinese People's Political
Consultative Conference
currency policy 139–41

Dalai Lama   107
Democracy Wall movement
      (1978–1980)   96
democracy
   American   8, 13, 20, 195
   basic requirements   3, 10–11
   Chinese system   8, 62, 63–4
   decision-making   143
   definitions   8–10
   importance of elections/civil
      liberties   3, 11
   managing the economy   3, 10–11
   problems with   13
   real-world situation   7
   satisfying key demographic groups/
      responding to public
      grievances   3, 10
   Western belief in   192
demonstrations/protests
   environmental   108–10,
      176
   ethnic minority   106–8
   student   2, 10, 26–7, 51, 66,
      79–80
Deng Xiaoping   25, 26–7, 44, 46–7,
      50–2, 60–1, 69, 90, 91, 92,
      118
   Southern Tour (1992)   46, 87,
      126, 128

EAB *see* East Asia Barometer
East Asia Barometer (EAB)
   present political situation   5–6
   trust in national government   4–5
   way democracy works   5
economy
   American system   186
   and authoritarianism   185–6
   and big business   20
   CCP support for reform   60

communist features   86–7
communist ideology as more
   important than
   growth   114–15
communist/capitalist
   system   141–4
concluding remarks   141–4
development of private
   sector   46–7
government involvement   113–14
growth rate   144
importance of growth   65, 72
international policies/
   results   137–41, 186–7
maintaining stability/
   growth   185–7
Maoist policy   114–17
move from export-led to
   consumer-led   135–7
Party-state ownership   115, 118
post-Maoist policy   117–18
pragmatic focus   118
private sector   124–9
public sector   129–37
rapid growth of   11
reform/modernization   44
rural policies/results
   post-Mao   119–23
urban conditions under Mao   115
urban policies/results
   post-Mao   124–37
education   44–5, 150, 151–2,
   165–8, 187–8
elections   3, 9, 11, 13
   democratic aspects   62, 63–4,
      182, 193
   as free, fair, competitive   29
   independent/non-Party
      members   66–7
   Party   23, 27, 42–9, 55–6

people's congresses 65–8, 86–9
role of money in 64, 65, 67
in rural areas 8, 10, 16, 53–4,
    61–3
state appointees 64–8
to CPPCC 67–8
to NPC 23, 27, 29, 65–6
urban areas 63
environment 108–10, 152, 172–8
air pollution 172–3
corrupt behavior
    concerning 176–7
dealing with grievances 184–5
encouragement of large
    families 153
foreign assistance sought 175–6
governmental policies 173–6
grim situation of 172
increase in renewable sources 174
local authority level 177
NGO input 176
Party-state commitment
    to 177–8
pollution across territorial
    boundaries 177
reduction in heavily polluting
    vehicles 175
shortsightedness/haste in dealing
    with 176
ethnic minorities 106–8, 185
European Union 172, 174

farmers
acceptance of political status
    quo 106
conditions under Mao 115–16
dealing with grievances 184
economic freedom of 102–3
effect of land requisitions
    on 104–5

general situation of 102
household responsibility
    system 119–20
as key demographic group 101–2
living conditions 103–4
New Socialist Countryside
    initiative 105–6
rural policies/results in post-Mao
    era 119–23
foreign direct investment
    (FDI) 138–9
Fujian province 59
functional systems (xitong) 36, 37,
    64–5

Gang of Four 77
General Secretary 18, 25, 27, 32,
    51, 52, 56, 59, 66, 70, 181
geographic units 27–8
goods and services 11
access to 145
child care 151
concluding remarks 178–9
deterioration in 179
education 150, 151–2,
    165–8
ensuring provision of 187–8
food shortage/starvation of
    millions 147
government control over 145–6
health care 147, 148–9, 154,
    162–5
housing/land 149, 151, 160–2
hybrid approach to 146–7
infrastructure 149–50,
    168–72
in Maoist era 147–53
natural environment 152, 172–8
pension provision 150–1, 157–9
in post-Maoist era 153–4

goods and services (cont.)
  poverty alleviation   154–6
  rural/urban differences   148,
    150–1
  SOEs as providers in cities   146
Great Leap Forward (1958–1960)
    32, 39, 100, 122, 147–8
Great Proletarian Cultural Revolution
    (1966–1976)   39, 43, 44, 49,
    116, 152

Han Chinese   93, 106–8, 185
health care   147, 148–9, 154,
    162–5, 187
Health and Family Planning
    Commission   34
Hebei province   59
household responsibility
    system   119–20, 157
housing/land provision   149, 151,
    160–2
Hu Jintao   25, 27, 32, 33, 51–2, 56,
    60, 69
Hu Yaobang   51, 66, 91

ICBC *see* Industrial and Commercial
    Bank of China
Industrial and Commercial Bank of
    China (ICBC)   132, 133,
    135
Industrial and Commercial
    Federation   85
infrastructure   11
  electricity provision   170
  government control/direction as
    key   171
  investment/improvements
    in   168–70
  results of cutting corners   171–2
  safe drinking water   170–1

safety concerns   172
international economic policies
  availability of low-cost
    workers   139
  effect of entry into WTO   138
  encouragement of foreign direct
    investment   138–9
  move from export-led to
    consumer-led   135–7
  currency policy   139–41
  state intervention/free market
    mix   137–8
Internet   81–3
iron rice bowl system   98, 129, 134
IST *see* University of Science and
    Technology

Japan   93
Jiang Zemin   25, 27, 47, 51–2, 56,
    60, 69, 71–2, 88

KMT *see* Kuomintang
Kuomintang (KMT)   43

labor unions   20, 32
letters and visits (*xinfang*)   78–9,
    184
Li Keqiang   32
Li Peng   92
Lin Bao   49
Liu Shaoqi   49
Liu Xiaobo   82–3, 96
Long March (1934/5)   116

manual laborers *see* rank-and-file
    workers
Mao Zedong   1, 2, 26, 49–50, 51,
    152, 185
Martial Law   30, 31
media   190–1

Minimum Livelihood Guarantee
  (*dibao*) 154–5, 156
Minister of Health 33
Minister of Science and
  Technology 33
Ministry of Civil Affairs
  (MOCA) 35, 61, 158–9
Ministry of Education 33
Ministry of Foreign Affairs 33
MOCA *see* Ministry of Civil Affairs
Mongolians 106, 107

National Development and Reform
  Commission (NDRC) 132
National Party Congress (NPC) 18
  call for economic
    liberalization 46–7
  choosing delegates for 54–7
  consultation process in 69–70
  draft/submit bills for
    consideration 69–71
  functions/powers 22, 23
  as highest leading body 29
  organization of 21–2
  ratifies decisions 23
  retirement age 52, 53
  selection/election of
    candidates 23, 27
  Three Represents 47
National People's Congress 4,
  confidence in 191
  draft/submit bills for
    consideration 31
  functions/powers 22
  as highest leading body 29
  informal functions 29–30
  interaction with citizens 30–1
  non-Party members 66–7
  selection/election of
    candidates 29, 65–6

wealth of members 67
  see also National People's
    Congress
New Socialist Countryside
  initiative 105–6, 122
NGOs *see* non-governmental
  organizations
Nine Black Categories 43
Ningxia Hui Autonomous
  Region 59
non-governmental organizations
  (NGOs) 176
NPC *see* National Party Congress

OD *see* Organization Department
Organization Department
  (OD) 25–6, 55, 71, 177
Osnos, Evan 67

Party Congresses 18, 27–8, 126,
  127
  see also National Party Congress
Party Constitution 19, 29,
  181
Party groups (*dangzu*) 36, 38
Party leadership
  ability to ensure economic growth/
    political stability 59
  background checks 55
  changes under Deng
    Xiaoping 50–2
  choice as highly politicized 54–5
  college-educated 51, 60
  dominance of Mao 49–50
  election process 55–6, 65, 182–3
  loyalty less important than
    economic growth/political
    stability 65
  mechanism for choosing
    leaders 53–8

Party leadership (cont.)
  modicum of competition
    introduced   56–8
  more open from input from
    below   54, 55, 194
  new/younger leaders
    encouraged   50–1
  non-reliance on monetary
    donations   142–3
  pragmatism as guiding
    principle   58–9, 193
  public assessment of   74–5
  regularized succession at the
    top   51–3
  removal of   194
  retirement age enforced   53
  selection criteria   58–61
  selection process   49–58
  stabilization of process   52
  support for economic reform   60
  top-level decision-making   56–7
  upward movements   60
Party membership
  annual review/appraisals   59
  application/probationary
    period   43–4
  business owners/capitalists   46–7
  as exclusive   42–3
  female members   48
  loyalty pre-eminent
    requirement   49
  new rules for recruitment   48
  percentage of population   48
  selection processes/criteria   42–9
  small-scale family farmers/
    blue-collar workers   47–8
  university/college students   44–5
Party-state
  as authoritarian   183, 188, 193–4,
    195
  capitalist connections   46
  changes in goals   41–2
  concluding remarks   38–40, 74–5
  Constitution   19, 28, 46, 125
  democracy, authoritarianism, stable
    governance   192–5
  dismantled communist controls
    over labor   87–8
  eight legal parties apart from
    CCP   32
  formal structure/composition of
    CCP   21–8
  formal/official institutions   19
  formulating preferences/perceiving
    tasks   68–74
  hybrid policies   180
  informal/unofficial groups   19–20
  informal/unofficial political
    entities   36–8
  key bodies   18
  leadership selection
    criteria   58–61
  leadership selection
    processes   49–58,
    182
  membership selection
    processes/criteria   42–9, 182
  new developments under Xi
    Jinping   188–92
  political systems differences   20–1
  popular legitimacy of   180
  powers/responsibilities   19
  provincial offices   34–6
  relationship   19
  sanctions small-scale private
    businesses   124–5
  stasis/change in   181–3
  state institution selection
    processes/demographic
    composition   61–8

structure/composition of
state   28–36
success/failure in governmental
functions   183–8
support for   191
pension provision   150–1,
157–9
People's Armed Police   55
people's congresses
county/township   65–6
elections to   65–8
formulation of preferences/
perception of tasks   73–4
independent candidates   66–7
tasked with bridge-building   73
wealthy individuals   67
see also National People's Congress
People's Daily   191
People's Liberation Army (PLA)   26,
55
People's Republic of China
(PRC)   26
PIPA see Program on International
Policy Attitudes
policy formulation
appraisal system   72
by people's congresses   73–4
as consultative   69–71
importance of economic growth/
political stability   72
influence of training system   71–2
input from below/directives from
above   69
Politburo   18, 24, 27, 51, 52, 56, 57,
70
surveys of public opinion   4–7, 191
criticisms of   6
political system
American   186
basic functions   3, 10–11, 12–14

concluding remarks   195
continuous change under Mao   1
corruption in   13–14
democratic aspects   8, 9, 75, 181,
193
fear of civil liberties   14
informal groups   20
local elites/central government
differences   7
move towards free-wheeling,
convoluted, contradictory
blend   1–2
policy inconsistencies   195
pragmatic/competent   13
as stable/adaptable   2
surveys   4–7
Western-Chinese
differences   20–1
workings of   2–3
poverty   154–6
PRC see People's Republic of China
Premier   18, 32, 39
President   18, 32, 33, 142, 181
Private Enterprises' Association   85
private entrepreneurs
agreements with state/Party
officials   72
availability of labor   87–8
comparison with Industrial
Revolution in England   89
connection with Three Represents
theory   71–2
dealing with grievances   184
development of   46–7, 86–7
elevated status of   47, 87, 88–9
as key demographic group   84
as members of CCP   47, 49,
85–6
as members of CPPCC   68
as people's congress delegates   73

private entrepreneurs (cont.)
   relationship with ruling Party-
     state 84, 85–6
   Western expectations 84–5, 86
private sector
   difficulties encountered 125
   economic liberalization
     embraced 126
   emergence of small-scale
     enterprises 124
   establishment of socialist market
     economy 126
   growth of 126
   labor supply/mobility 127–8
   non-existence under Mao 124
   promotion/support for free
     markets 125–7
   SEZs created 125–6, 128
   as suspect 124–5
   wages/working conditions 128–9
Program on International Policy
   Attitudes (PIPA) 4
Provincial Party Congresses 18
Provincial People's Congresses 18
public expression, control of 190–2
public grievances
   collective actions 79–80
   college students/graduates 89–97
   community mediation
     committees 77–8
   concluding remarks 110–12
   court system 77
   environmental protests 108–10
   ethnic minorities 106–8
   farmers 101–6
   Internet communication 81–3
   letters and visits (*xinfang*) 78–9
   private business people 84–9
   rank-and-file workers 97–101
   repression/sympathy 72, 79–80

   responding to 76–83, 192
   satisfying key demographic
     groups 83–4, 183–5
public sector
   banking system 132–7
   dealing with SOEs 129–31, 132,
     133, 134, 137
   interventionist/communist
     measures 131, 132
   introduction of capitalism 130–1
   iron rice bowl benefits 129
   large enterprises
     privatized 131–2
   lifetime job security 129
   medium/small enterprises
     privatized 131

Railway Ministry 65
rank-and-file workers
   dealing with grievances 184
   dissatisfaction/protests 98–9,
     100–1
   effect of SOE privatization
     on 98–9
   iron rice bowl benefits 98
   as key demographic group 97
   labor mobility 127–8
   pension system 98, 99
   private sector
     circumstances 99–101
   public sector circumstances 98–9
   public/private sector
     difference 97
   support for CCP 99, 101
RCs *see* residents' committees
redness notion 48–9
residential registration system
     (*hukou*) 122–3, 127–8, 138,
     139, 151, 154, 156, 158,
     160–1, 165, 166, 187

residents' committees (RCs)   36
rights protection movement (*weiquan
    yundong*)   96
rural conditions
    collectivization under
        Mao   115–16
    combination of free market/
        interventionist
        mechanisms   119, 123
    development of TVEs   102–4,
        120–1, 123
    health care   148–9
    household responsibility
        system   119–20, 123
    improvement in living
        conditions   122–3
    New Socialist Countryside
        initiative   105–6,
        122
    Party-state ownership of
        land   120
    post-Mao era   119–23
    poverty alleviation in   155
    relaxation of residential registration
        (*hukou*)   122–3, 127–8, 138,
        139
    tax collection   121–2

SASAC *see* State-owned Assets
    Supervision and
    Administration Commission
school system   71–2
Secretariat   18, 25
Self-Employed Laborers'
    Association   85
SEZs *see* Special Economic/
    Enterprise Zones
Shanghai Pilot Free Trade
    Zone   140
SIAs *see* social insurance agencies

Sino-Capitalism   142
social insurance agencies
    (SIAs)   158
SOE *see* state-owned enterprise
Special Economic/Enterprise Zones
    (SEZs)   103, 118, 121,
        125–6, 128, 138–9
special interest groups   20
Standing Committee of CPPCC   68
Standing Committee of the
    National People's
    Congress   30, 31
Standing Committee of the
    Politburo   18, 24–6, 27, 39,
        49, 60, 181–2
Standing Committee of the State
    Council   18
State *see* Party-state
State Administration for Religious
    Affairs   35
State Central Military
    Commission   18
State Constitution   19, 46
State Council   39, 131
    autonomy of   32
    oversees official Chinese news
        agency   34
    selection/election to   31–2, 33
State Council Information
    Office   82
State Environmental Protection
    Agency   173
state institutions
    importance of economic/political
        performance   65
    people's congresses   65–8
    province-level guidelines   61–2
    role of money in   64, 65, 67
    selection/election processes   61–8
    villages/rural areas   62–4

State-owned Assets Supervision and
    Administration Commission
    (SASAC)   131–2
state-owned enterprise
    (SOE)   35–6, 98–9
banking sector   132–7
dealing with   129–34, 137
as drag on economy   129
effect of banking system on   134
effect of downsizing on workforce
    130–1, 154–5, 157, 163
forced to become profitable   130
interventionist/communist
    interventions   131–2
lifetime employment   129
as providers of goods/services in
    cities   146
Stinking Old Ninth   43, 44
surveys of public opinion   6

Temporary Office for Rural Social
    Insurance Pensions   158–9
Three Gorges Dam   30
Three Represents   72, 88
advanced culture   47
advanced productive forces   47
interests of the majority of
    citizens   47
Tian'anmen Square (1989)   26–7,
    30, 44–5, 51, 92, 107
Tibet, Tibetans   27, 93, 106, 107,
    108, 185
Township and Village Enterprises
    (TVEs)   102–4, 120–1,
    123, 157
Township/County People's
    Congresses   18
TVEs see Township and Village
    Enterprises
Two Meetings (Liang Hui)   32

Uighurs   106, 107, 185
universities   44–5
University of Maryland   4
University of Science and Technology
    (UST)   91
urban administration   35–6, 53, 182
urban policies
    private sector   124–9
    public sector   129–37
    under Mao   115

VCs see village councils/committees
village councils/committees
    (VCs)   18, 35, 184
democratic aspects   9, 62, 63, 104
influence on urban elections   63
nominations/elections   8, 10, 16,
    53–4, 61–3, 104, 182
private entrepreneurs as candidates
    for   86
Village Party Secretary   54

Weber, Max   7
Weibo   82
WHO see World Health
    Organization
World Bank   163, 173
World Health Organization
    (WHO)   172, 173
World Public Opinion (WPO)
    democratic responsiveness   5
    supportive of political system   4
World Trade Organization
    (WTO)   138
World Values Survey Association   4
World Values Survey (WVS)   191
    confidence in national government/
        legislative body   4
    democracy in China   5
    respect for individual rights   5

WPO *see* World Public Opinion
WTO *see* World Trade Organization
WVS *see* World Values Survey
(WVS)

Xi Jinping   27, 32, 52, 59, 60, 108,
126, 181, 184, 188–92, 195
Xinhua (official news agency)   34,
45, 59
Xinjiang Uighur Autonomous
region   107

Yao Lifa   67
Young Pioneers   43, 44
Yu Zhengsheng   33

Zhao Ziyang   26, 27, 51, 57, 91, 92